D1558333

GRADUATE TEXTS IN COMPUTER SCIENCE

Editors
David Gries
Fred B. Schneider

Springer

New York
Berlin
Heidelberg
Barcelona
Budapest
Hong Kong
London
Milan
Paris
Santa Clara
Singapore
Tokyo

GRADUATE TEXTS IN COMPUTER SCIENCE

Rolf Socher-Ambrosius   Patricia Johann

DEDUCTION SYSTEMS

With 34 illustrations

Springer

Rolf Socher-Ambrosius
Fachhochschule Ostfriesland
FB Elektrotechnik und Informatik
26723 Emden Germany

Patricia Johann
Pacific Software Research Center
Oregon Graduate Institute
Beaverton, OR 97006-1999 USA

Series Editors

David Gries
Fred B. Schneider

Department of Computer Science
Cornell University
Upson Hall
Ithaca, NY 14853-7501 USA

Library of Congress Cataloging-in-Publication Data
Socher-Ambrosius, Rolf.
    Deduction systems / Rolf Socher-Ambrosius. Patricia Johann.
      p.   cm. — (Graduate texts in computer science)
    Includes bibliographical references and index.
    ISBN 0-387-94847-3
    1. Automatic theorem proving. I. Johann, Patricia. II. Title.
  III. Series: Graduate texts in computer science (Springer-Verlag
  New York Inc.)
    QA76.9.A96S 63   1996
    511.3′0285′51—dc20   96–32221

Printed on acid-free paper.

Originally published in German as *Deduktionssysteme* by Spektrum Akademischer Verlag, Heidelberg, Germany.

Production managed by Robert Wexler; manufacturing supervised by Jacqui Ashri.
Photocomposed copy prepared from the author's LaTeX files using Springer's svwidecm style file.
Printed and bound by R.R Donnelley and Sons, Harrisonburg, VA.
Printed in the United States of America.

9 8 7 6 5 4 3 2 1

ISBN 0-387-94847-3 Springer-Verlag New York Berlin Heidelberg SPIN 10524187

Preface

The idea of mechanizing deductive reasoning can be traced all the way back to Leibniz, who proposed the development of a *rational calculus* for this purpose. But it was not until the appearance of Frege's 1879 *Begriffsschrift*—"not only the direct ancestor of contemporary systems of mathematical logic, but also the ancestor of all formal languages, including computer programming languages" ([Dav83])—that the fundamental concepts of modern mathematical logic were developed. Whitehead and Russell showed in their *Principia Mathematica* that the entirety of classical mathematics can be developed within the framework of a formal calculus, and in 1930, Skolem, Herbrand, and Gödel demonstrated that the *first-order predicate calculus* (which is such a calculus) is *complete*, i.e., that every valid formula in the language of the predicate calculus is derivable from its axioms. Skolem, Herbrand, and Gödel further proved that in order to mechanize reasoning within the predicate calculus, it suffices to consider only interpretations of formulae over their associated *Herbrand universes*. We will see that the upshot of this discovery is that the validity of a formula in the predicate calculus can be deduced from the structure of its constituents, so that a machine might perform the logical inferences required to determine its validity.

With the advent of computers in the 1950s there developed an interest in *automatic theorem proving*. The observation that attention can be restricted to interpretations over the Herbrand universe for a formula when considering its validity has served as the basis for most computer-implemented theorem provers. Early implementations of theorem provers, including some for the predicate calculus, did not perform especially well, but soon computational inroads were being made. The effort to incorporate efficiency improvements into a theorem prover for predicate logic ultimately led to a "mating" procedure for literals requiring the fundamental computation, which is now called *unification*.

J. A. Robinson began his work on mechanizing logical deduction in the early 1960s, and like those before him, sought a formalization of first-order logic that could serve as the basis of an automatic theorem proving program. In 1963, he introduced to the computer science community a revolutionary unification-based computation, called *resolution*, which would provide its effective mechanization. Unlike the intentionally simple inference principles that had previously been used in automating deduction, resolution is machine-oriented rather than human-oriented in the sense that it allows as single inferences deductions, which often require of a human many separate inferences. This, together with the fact that resolution alone was proved complete for first-order logic, has made it very powerful and especially well-suited to automation.

This book explores the central ideas of resolution theorem proving in the first-order predicate calculus by tracing a main thread—essentially mirroring the historical evolution outlined above—through its development. The book is intended to provide an introduction to the theory of formal first-order logic, as well as a solid basis in the fundamentals of resolution theorem proving. Its main emphasis is therefore on formal concepts and methods rather than on the practical realization of theorem proving procedures.

For several reasons we have chosen, in the early parts of the book, to describe the proof theory of first-order logics in terms of Gentzen calculi. First, Gentzen calculi offer a very natural means of developing proof systems and also reflect the semantics of the logical connectives. Second, our experience accords with that of the many other authors who have spoken so well to their pedagogical advantages, especially as compared with Hilbert-style calculi or resolution calculi. In particular, Gentzen calculi do not require clausal form as do resolution calculi, and their completeness can be proved in a very direct and elegant manner. Finally, Gentzen calculi lead naturally to a proof of Herbrand's Theorem, which is fundamental in establishing the completeness of resolution.

The treatment of first-order resolution theorem proving presented here should in no way be regarded as comprehensive. Since the 1960s, formal logic and automated deduction have become increasingly important in many areas of computer science and artificial intelligence, and this has in turn led to rapid development in both theory and methods in the field. Many new and important concepts and techniques have been developed to accommodate automated deduction in extensions of classical first-order logic such as equational, order-sorted, and higher-order logics, and a treatment of all these topics would be far beyond the scope of this book; indeed each could easily be the subject of a treatise on its own. In an effort to maintain accessibility of the book to those with no specialized knowledge of automatic theorem proving, we do not include discussions of such contemporary issues as equational theorem proving, deduction in higher-order logics, or proof procedures like tableau-based and graph-based methods. Instead, the first seven chapters of this book are devoted to the basics of first-order predicate logic and first-order resolution theorem proving, and Chapter 8 considers some of the very important and recent developments in automated theorem proving concerning restrictions of resolution, strategies to prune deduction search spaces, the problem of redundancy of solutions, and constraint calculi. We do, however, include a chapter discussing deduction in order-sorted logics; this development in automated deduction dates only from the late 1980s, and has not been treated in any other textbook at this level (even though unordered many-sorted logic is treated in several standard textbooks). While we restrict our attention here to the development of efficient unsorted and order-sorted first-order resolution theorem proving based on Gentzen calculi, it is nevertheless our hope that this book will prepare and inspire the reader to investigate automated deduction in considerably more depth and scope.

This book is a revised and expanded version of Rolf Socher-Ambrosius' German language book *Deduktionssysteme*, which grew out of class notes written for a two-semester course for beginning graduate students in computer science at the Universität Kaiserslautern. In this version, more expository material and more robust discussions have been added throughout, and, in an effort to make the book more self-contained than its precursor, an introductory chapter expressly treating the mathematical prerequisites for reading the book has also been included. The book is appropriate for use by graduate students, computer scientists, and other persons interested in a firm grounding in the fundamentals of first-order resolution theorem proving.

A detailed outline of this book follows. Chapter 1 provides a brief overview of the material to be discussed throughout the text, and Chapter 2 covers the mathematical prerequisites necessary for reading the remaining chapters. Chapter 3 introduces the syntax of first-order logic, and its semantics is studied in Chapter 4. Interpretations are considered there as mathematical structures, and the concepts of satisfiability and validity for first-order formulae are introduced.

The notion of a proof as a syntactic counterpart to the semantic notion of validity is central to Chapter 5. The first part of this chapter presents Gentzen's sequent calculus and provides a proof of its soundness. In the second part, Herbrand structures are discussed and the completeness of the sequent calculus is proved.

Chapter 6 is devoted to Gentzen's Sharpened Hauptsatz and Herbrand's Theorem. In the first part of the chapter, the notions of prenex normal form and clausal normal form for formulae are introduced, the latter being of particular importance for resolution theorem proving. In addition, a transformation of open formulae into clausal form is given. In preparation for the statement and proof of Herbrand's Theorem, the second part of this chapter is devoted to Gentzen's Sharpened Hauptsatz for formulae in prenex normal form. The proof of this theorem uses proof transformation methods to show that every Gentzen proof tree can be transformed into a tree in a certain normal form in which the quantifier rules of the Gentzen calculus are all applied at the root of the tree. The final part of this chapter discusses skolemization and Herbrand's Theorem, which are the foundations of the resolution method.

Chapter 7 introduces unification as equation solving and presents an inference system that transforms equational systems into solved form. A more elaborate version of the unification algorithm which improves on computational complexity is presented in Section 7.3, and Section 7.4 presents the concepts of resolution, factorization, subsumption, and tautology on which our first-order resolution calculus is based. The completeness of the resolution calculus is shown in two steps: first completeness is proved for ground clauses by constructing a model for saturated and consistent clause sets, and then general completeness is shown via a "lifting lemma." This section also introduces the concept of fairness for resolution derivations, and shows that every fair resolution derivation out of an unsatisfiable clause set eventually results in the empty clause. Finally, fairness of some particularly useful derivation strategies is demonstrated.

Practical experience with resolution-based automatic theorem provers has shown that in general they require far too much time to find proofs or theorems. It is thus necessary to restrict deduction search spaces, which grow unreasonably fast even for small problems. In Chapter 8 a "lazy" resolution calculus, in which unification is separated from resolution, is introduced, and this revised calculus is seen to serve as the basis of several strategies for doing restricting deduction search spaces. Linear resolution, hyperresolution, the set-of-support strategy, as well as selection and ordering concepts are discussed, and the completeness of each is considered. Finally, a notion of redundancy based on well-founded orderings on terms is presented.

Besides the development of methods for restricting resolution search spaces—some of which are discussed in Chapter 8—there exist other approaches to achieving efficiency in automated reasoning. One such is the introduction of sort mechanisms into deduction calculi. The basic idea is to use sort information to reduce the number of well-formed formulae of a calculus, and so to shift as much as possible of the deduction to be performed from the nondeterministic resolution inference system to the deterministic unification algorithm. Chapter 9 presents the syntax and semantics of an order-sorted logic with linear term declarations, as well as a calculus for order-sorted unification. A resolution calculus suitable for this order-sorted setting is obtained as a modification of the "lazy" resolution calculus from Chapter 8. Incorporating sorts into resolution calculi as described there has—both in theory and practice—been shown to reduce search spaces in first-order resolution theorem proving quite dramatically.

Contents

1

Introduction

The use of logic in the formalization of human reasoning can be traced back to the Greek philosophers, most notably Aristotle, whose primary concern was the investigation of the laws of human thought. With a collection of well-chosen axioms of logical deduction as a point of departure, Aristotle erected a theory of reasoning that endured nearly two thousand years before being developed further by such eminent logicians as Gottlob Frege (1848-1925), George Boole (1815-1864), and Bertrand Russell (1872-1970).

A typical Aristotelean rule of inference was *modus ponens*, a rule allowing deductions of the form

> If all men are mortal
> and if Socrates is a man
> then Socrates is mortal.

While *modus ponens* was regarded by Aristotle as a fundamental rule of nature, as well as of logic, it is currently considered just one among many possible inference rules employed in the construction of proofs. Indeed, toward the end of the nineteenth century, as the study of philosophical logic experienced a stormy renaissance, the Aristotelean view of logic reluctantly conceded the importance of such other logics as modal, temporal, and intuitionistic logics; as a result, each of these "alternative" logics is today regarded as occupying a position of status comparable to that of classical logic. Formal logic has become increasingly widespread as a deduction tool, and, in problem solving, logic engineers now choose from their toolboxes logics appropriate to the task at hand. If the temporal behavior of systems plays a role, then a logic engineer will require a temporal logic, and if the matter at hand concerns itself with statements that can only be known with a certain probability, then a probabilistic logic will be most suitable. But it makes little sense to formalize mathematical statements in a temporal logic—that is, in a manner such as "2 + 2 has always equaled 4 in the past, and will also equal 4 in the future"—or in a probabilistic logic—as in "2 + 2 = 4 with 100% probability"—and so classical logic, in which every statement is either true or false in a given model, is still regarded as the chief deduction tool for pure mathematics. It is therefore on classical logic that we will focus in this book, and from the area of mathematics that we will draw our examples. In fact, we will restrict ourselves even further, namely, to first-order classical logics, in contrast to those of second, third, and higher orders. This is not a grave restriction, however, since first-order logic is in fact very expressive: some logicians even maintain that if mathematicians were to completely formalize the properties of the structures in which they are interested, then the axiom systems they would construct would always be expressible in first-order logic. Many-sorted first-order logic, for example, which is sufficient for expressing much of the reasoning of working mathematicians, is both more efficient for deduction and arguably more natural than first-order logic without sorts, but it can nevertheless be represented fully in its unsorted counterpart. Of course there are other logics, such as higher-order logics, which truly are more expressive than first-order classical logic. Indeed, second-order classical logic is so much more expressive than first-order classical logic that, regardless of how much time and effort is put into the enterprise, it will never be possible to construct a mechanizable deduction system for it.

Classical logic makes use of notions like "not," "and," "or," "if-then," "for all," and "there exists"—which already have fixed meanings in everyday language—and certain formal symbols are set aside to syntactically capture these notions. Symbols representing them are collectively referred to as *connectives*, with symbols representing "for all" and "there exists" singled out as *quantifiers*. In addition to connectives, other symbols—such as predicate and function symbols—are used to construct permissible expressions. These permissible expressions form a *language* over the symbols. At the level of languages, we differentiate between *terms*, i.e., expressions of the form $x * y$ and $f(x, f(y, z))$ built from function symbols and variables, and *(logical) formulae*, i.e., expressions such as $\forall x \, (P(x, f(x)) \Rightarrow Q(x, x))$, built out of terms, predicate symbols, connectives, and quantifiers. An exact specification of the intended meanings of the expressions in first-order languages is given in Chapter 4, where the manner in which first-order languages and their interpretations can be used to make precise statements about certain classes of mathematical objects is also discussed.

To illustrate the relation between semantic notions and syntactic constructs, consider briefly an axiomatization of partially ordered sets. A *partially ordered set*, or *poset*, is a mathematical structure comprising a set S and a transitive and irreflexive binary relation R on S (see Section 2.3). The

$$\forall x \, \neg R(x,x)$$
$$\forall x \forall y \forall z \, ((R(x,y) \wedge R(y,z)) \Rightarrow R(x,z)).$$

FIGURE 1.1.

properties of posets can be formalized as in Figure 1.1. The logical symbols $\neg$, $\Rightarrow$, and $\wedge$ denote negation, implication, and conjunction, respectively, and the quantifier $\forall$ is used to denote universal quantification.

In giving semantics to a formula like those of Figure 1.1, its variables are interpreted as objects in a concrete mathematical structure and its predicate and function symbols are interpreted as functions and relations on objects in that structure. In general, n-ary predicate symbols are interpreted as n-ary relations over the structure and n-ary function symbols are interpreted as n-ary functions over it. (It is important here not to confuse symbols, like f and P, with actual mathematical objects such as functions and predicates.) The formulae themselves are then interpreted, according to the rules of classical first-order logic, as expressions which can take on either the value *true* or the value *false*.

Roughly speaking, an *interpretation* $\mathcal{I}$ is a mathematical structure M together with a mapping of variables, function symbols, and predicate symbols to objects over M. We say that $\mathcal{I}$ *satisfies* a formula φ, or that $\mathcal{I}$ is a *model* for φ, if φ is true under the mapping of $\mathcal{I}$. For example, if $\mathcal{I}$ comprises the set N of natural numbers together with any mapping which sends y to 1, $>$ to the usual greater-than relation on N, and $+$ to the usual addition function on N, then $\mathcal{I}$ satisfies $\forall x \, x + y > x$; if $\mathcal{I}'$ comprises the set N of natural numbers together with any mapping which sends R to the usual greater-than relation on N, then $\mathcal{I}'$ satisfies the formulae of Figure 1.1. We say that an interpretation $\mathcal{I}$ satisfies a set Φ of formulae if it satisfies every formula in Φ. If Φ is any set of formulae, we write $\Phi \models \varphi$ in case the formula φ is satisfied by every model of Φ, and we say that φ is a *semantic consequence* of Φ. The formula

$$\forall x \forall y \, (\neg R(x,y) \vee \neg R(y,x)),$$

for instance, is not only satisfied by $\mathcal{I}'$, but is in fact satisfied by every model of the formulae in Figure 1.1 and is therefore a semantic consequence of them. The formula

$$\forall x \exists y \, R(y,x),$$

on the other hand, is certainly true in the interpretation $\mathcal{I}'$, but there are other interpretations satisfying the axioms for posets—such as any interpretation comprising N and a mapping sending R to the usual less-than ordering on N—in which this formula is not satisfied. This formula is therefore *not* a semantic consequence of the axioms of Figure 1.1.

It is the function of automatic theorem provers to mechanize the deduction of semantic consequences of sets of formulae. But we immediately see that a mechanical deduction of semantic consequence which is based solely on its definition is not possible: given a set of formulae, the validity of each of its purported semantic consequences, however obtained, would have to be tested in every model of the given formulation, and there are uncountably many such models in general for a given formulation. Instead, the notion of *formal proof* is employed to establish that a formula is a semantic consequence of a given set of other formulae; that is, the notion of semantic consequence is captured by means of a purely syntactic calculus of formal reasoning. The notion of proof therefore emerges as fundamental to our investigations and will occupy our attention in Chapter 5. In this book we will formalize the process of proof development in such a way that the proofs can be found, and therefore semantic consequence can be established, via automated deduction.

A *derivation* in a calculus $\mathcal{C}$ is a sequence $\varphi_0, \varphi_1, \varphi_2, \ldots$, of formulae over the language of $\mathcal{C}$, each of which is either an axiom of $\mathcal{C}$ or is derived by means of the inference rules of $\mathcal{C}$ from previous formulae in the sequence; a proof is a finite such sequence. A calculus therefore comprises a set of axioms and a set of inference rules (the latter sometimes referred to as an *inference system*) which permit the construction, by some finite sequence of applications of rules to axioms, of new logical formulae from old ones. In constructing derivations, no use is made of the intended meanings of formulae, but rather formulae are manipulated according only to their syntactic structure and the inference rules of the calculus. The formalization of *modus ponens*, our example of a typical inference rule, is

$$\frac{P,\ P \Rightarrow Q}{Q}$$

and it is to be read in the following way: if in the course of a derivation the formulae P and $P \Rightarrow Q$ have been derived, then—regardless of the intended meanings of the formulae P and Q—it is permissible to conclude the formula Q.

The development of any mathematical theory proceeds from its axiomatization, i.e., from the set of formulae which are assumed to describe the theory. A theory is in fact understood to be the set of all formulae which can be deduced in some specified calculus from the axiomatization of the theory. Generally speaking, we require of any useful calculus that its syntactic constructs adequately reflect the semantic properties of the mathematical theories it is being used to investigate, and in particular we require that the notions of proof and semantic consequence correspond in the following way:

every formula of a theory should be a semantic consequence of the axioms of that theory. For example, since we can logically deduce from the axioms for posets given in Figure 1.1 that $\neg R(x, y) \vee \neg R(y, x)$, this statement must hold in every concrete poset, i.e., it must be satisfied by all models of the axioms for posets. A clear understanding of the interplay between syntactic and semantic notions is essential to our study of automated deduction in mathematical and other theories.

In this book we will become acquainted with two types of calculi, namely, *Gentzen calculi* and *resolution calculi*. While the latter are considerably less "natural" than the former, they are especially well-suited to automation. We will always make use of mechanical calculi as proof procedures, and so expect that such procedures derive from a set of axioms no "false theorems," i.e., we expect, as above, that if we have derived in our calculus a proof of the formula φ from a given set of formulae, then φ must be a semantic consequence of those formulae. Equivalently, we require that a formula which is not a semantic consequence of a set of formulae should not be provable from them. This property of calculi is known as *soundness*. Unfortunately, only a weaker result regarding the converse result can be established, since one result of Church's Theorem is that semantic consequence for formulae is in general undecidable. This means that there can be no algorithm which, given an arbitrary set of formulae Φ and a formula φ, terminates with answer "yes" if φ is a semantic consequence of Φ and terminates with "no" otherwise. We can, however, insist that a calculus always be able to find a proof of a formula φ from a set Φ of formulae *if φ is a semantic consequence of Φ* (although we cannot require that it be able to determine that φ is not a semantic consequence of Φ). That is, we can require of a calculus that it be *complete*. Soundness and completeness are the minimal requirements for a calculus to be most suitable for deduction purposes: in a calculus which is not sound the ability to derive from a set Φ of formulae the formula φ does not guarantee that φ is necessarily a semantic consequence of Φ, and in a calculus which is not complete the fact that φ is a semantic consequence of Φ would not guarantee the existence of some proof of φ from Φ. The Gentzen and resolution calculi presented in this book are both sound and complete.

Although the completeness of a calculus guarantees that φ can be derived from Φ whenever φ is a semantic consequence of Φ, it need not provide any indication of how such a proof is to be realized. That is, the fact that a calculus is complete does not in and of itself provide any information indicating the manner in which the application of the inference rules of the calculus might be controlled in proof derivation. It turns out that the choice of a control strategy for the application of the inference rules essentially amounts to the choice of a strategy for searching the space of all possible derivations out of Φ. This is because the problem of generating a proof of φ from Φ can be viewed as the problem of searching the space of derivations from Φ. The inference rules of a calculus are therefore not by themselves sufficient to determine a concrete algorithm for automatically proving theorems—a specific search strategy must be given as well. It is, of course, essential to the utility of a search strategy that it examine enough of the search space to reflect the completeness of a complete calculus. A strategy which guarantees that every element of the search space be examined at some point in the search obviously reflects the completeness of a complete calculus, and such strategies are said to be *fair*. Breadth-first search and—under certain conditions for the heuristic function—best-first search are well-known general purpose search strategies which are fair.

The selection of a complete calculus and a fair search strategy guarantees that if φ is a semantic consequence of Φ, then a proof of φ from Φ will eventually be found using the calculus. Such a selection in no way guarantees, however, that a proof will be found within a reasonable amount of time. Indeed, resolution calculi together with even cleverly chosen fair search strategies may waste far too much time with useless derivations to be truly useful. Even solutions to simple deduction problems cannot always be found within acceptable amounts of time. This phenomenon is merely a reflection of the fact that the search spaces spanned by resolution calculi are, in general, quite large.

There are two principal approaches to circumventing the difficulties of large resolution search spaces without sacrificing completeness. The first approach is to reduce search spaces by restricting applications of the inference rules underlying the resolution calculus being considered. Of course, the reduced search spaces must still reflect the completeness of the calculus, i.e., the search space originating from each set of formulae Φ must contain at least one proof of φ whenever the latter is a semantic consequence of the former. The second approach is to remove redundant elements from search spaces. Roughly speaking, redundant elements are those that can be replaced by "better" elements in any proof.

In this book we examine techniques for restricting resolution search spaces based on both of these approaches. We discuss some important resolution calculi such as those for hyperresolution, linear resolution, and ordered resolution based on noetherian orderings. The use of noetherian orderings also allows us to define an abstract notion of redundancy which realizes the aforementioned concept of a "better" element in a resolution search space. Specific instances of this abstract concept of redundancy are the notions of tautology and subsumption (see Definitions 7.4.1 and 7.4.2).

Another important technique for improving the poor behavior of resolution theorem proving methods is to transfer as much as possible of deduction otherwise performed by the nondeterministic inference system into the (deterministic) unification, or pattern matching, procedure. This is often possible, for example, when the function or predicate symbols satisfy special axioms—such as those for associativity and commutativity—since customized unification algorithms have been developed to perform the required unification in many of these cases. Moving the bulk of the computation from the inference mechanism into the unification computation is an approach which is also used to automate deduction in order-sorted logics, which can be viewed as logics with unary predicate symbols possessing certain properties. Order-sorted logic makes possible a very natural formulation of deduction problems for which an order hierarchy on classes of objects—like the taxonomic hierarchy in the animal kingdom—can be given. The prototypical example of a problem of this kind is "Schubert's Steamroller" (see Example 9.1.1). The main advantage of posing a deduction problem in terms of an order-sorted logic when possible is an increase in deduction efficiency—fewer permissible terms can actually be built in a sorted logic than in a corresponding unsorted one, unification involving terms with incompatible sorts can be broken off immediately, and therefore shorter resolution derivations result than would likely be obtained using unsorted formulations of problems. In this book we will give the syntax and semantics of an order-sorted logic with term declarations, a calculus for unifying terms in this logic, and a description of a resolution calculus for it.

2

Mathematical Preliminaries

In this chapter we discuss the basic mathematical notions that we will need in the rest of this book. We expect that the concepts mentioned here are familiar to the reader, and so we do not provide a comprehensive treatment of them. Instead, our intent is to indicate briefly those ideas which will be used in later chapters, and to set the notation and terminology we will use in discussing them. For a more complete treatment of propositional and first-order logics, we recommend [Fit90], [Gal86], and [Men79]. Halmos' treatment of introductory set theory ([Hal60]) is both elegant and accessible. Pure and algorithmic graph theory are the topics of [BM76] and [Gib85], respectively.

2.1 Sets and Relations

A *set* is a collection of objects, called the *elements* of the set. If the object s is an element of the set S, then we say that s is *in* S, or that s is a *member* of S. We write $s \in S$ to indicate that s is an element of S, and write $s \notin S$ to indicate that s is not an element of S. The (unique) set which has no elements is denoted by $\emptyset$ and is called the *empty set*.

A set T is a *subset* of the set S provided every element of T is also an element of S. In this case we write $T \subseteq S$ or $S \supseteq T$. We write $S = T$ to indicate that $S \subseteq T$ and $T \subseteq S$, i.e., to indicate that S and T contain precisely the same elements. If $S = \emptyset$, then S is *empty*, and S is *nonempty* otherwise. We write $T \nsubseteq S$ in case T is not a subset of S; in this case there must be some element of T which is not an element of S. We use the notation $S \neq T$ to indicate that $S = T$ does not hold. Finally, we write $T \subset S$ or $S \supset T$ to indicate that $T \subseteq S$, but $T \neq S$ also holds; in this case we say that T is a *proper subset* of S.

There are many ways of constructing new sets from a given collection of sets, among them:

- If S and T are sets, then their *union*, denoted $S \cup T$, is the set comprising all objects which are either elements of S or elements of T;

- If S and T are sets, then their *intersection*, denoted $S \cap T$, is the set comprising all objects which are elements of S and are also elements of T;

- If S and T are sets, then their *difference*, denoted $S - T$, is the set comprising all objects which are elements of S but are not elements of T;

- If S is a set, then the *power set* of S, denoted 2^S, is the set comprising all subsets of S.

By convention, any object can occur at most once in a given set, and so sets contain no duplicate elements.

It is well-known that set union and intersection are *associative*, i.e., that for any sets S, T, and U, $(S \cup T) \cup U = S \cup (T \cup U)$ and $(S \cap T) \cap U = S \cap (T \cap U)$. Set union and intersection are also *commutative*, so that $S \cup T = T \cup S$ and $S \cap T = T \cap S$ hold for all sets S and T, as well. Moreover, for all sets S, T, and U, we have $S \cap (T \cup U) = (S \cap T) \cup (S \cap T)$ and $S \cup (T \cap U) = (S \cup T) \cap (S \cup U)$, i.e., set union and intersection are *mutually distributive*. If $S \cap T = \emptyset$, then S and T are said to be *disjoint*. Note that $T \subseteq S$ iff $T \in 2^S$, and that $\emptyset \in 2^S$ for every set S.

There is another way of constructing new sets from old ones which will be of interest to us. If $S_1, \ldots, S_n$ are sets, then the *product* of $S_1, \ldots, S_n$, denoted $S_1 \times \ldots \times S_n$, is defined to be the set of all ordered n-tuples $\langle s_1, \ldots, s_n \rangle$ with $s_i \in S_i$ for $i = 1, \ldots, n$. For example, if S_1 is the set N of natural numbers and S_2 is the set Z of integers, then $S_1 \times S_2$ is the set of all ordered pairs whose first components are natural numbers and whose second components are integers. Thus, $\langle 3, -4 \rangle$ is an element of $S_1 \times S_2$, for instance, whereas $\langle -4, 3 \rangle$ is not.

An *n-ary relation*, or simply a *relation*, on the sets $S_1, \ldots, S_n$ is a subset of the product $S_1 \times \ldots \times S_n$. If R is a relation on $S_1, \ldots, S_n$, we usually write $R(s_1, \ldots, s_n)$ provided $\langle s_1, \ldots, s_n \rangle \in R$, and in this case we say that $R(s_1, \ldots, s_n)$ *holds*.

A 1-ary relation R is called a *property*, and if $R(s)$ holds, then we may say that s *possesses* property R. If R is a property, then $\{s \mid R(s)\}$ denotes the set comprising all objects s such that s possesses property R. A 2-ary relation is called a *binary relation* or a *mapping*. Following custom, we use the infix notation sRt to indicate that $R(s,t)$ holds; in this case we sometimes say that R *maps* s *to* t. The *inverse* of a binary relation R is the relation $R^{-1} = \{\langle s,t \rangle \mid R(t,s)\}$. It is immediate that $(R^{-1})^{-1} = R$.

Special terminology is associated with binary relations, which play an especially important role in this book, as well as in mathematics and in computer science more generally. If R is a binary relation on sets S and T, then S is the *domain* of R and T is its *range*; we sometimes say that R is a *relation from S to T*. If R is a binary relation with domain S and if $U \subseteq S$, then the *restriction* of R to U, denoted $R \mid_U$, is the relation on U and T given by: $R \mid_U (s,t)$ holds iff $R(s,t)$ holds and $s \in U$.

A binary relation R whose domain and range are both S is called a binary relation *on S*. A binary relation R on S is *reflexive* if, for all $s \in S$, sRs holds; R is *symmetric* if, for all $s, t \in S$, sRt implies tRs; and R is *transitive* if, for all $s, t, u \in S$, sRt and tRu imply sRu. A binary relation R on S is *irreflexive* if sRs does not hold for any $s \in S$.

The *reflexive closure* of a binary relation R on S is defined to be $R \cup \{\langle s,s \rangle \mid s \in S\}$. The *symmetric closure* of R is $R \cup \{\langle t,s \rangle \mid \langle s,t \rangle \in R\}$. The *transitive closure* of R, denoted R^+, is the set of all ordered pairs $\langle s,t \rangle \in S \times S$ such that there exist a natural number $n \geq 1$ and elements $s_0, \ldots, s_n$ of S with $s_0 = s$, $s_n = t$, and $s_i R s_{i+1}$ for $i = 0, \ldots, n-1$. The *reflexive, transitive closure* of R, denoted R^*, is the set of all ordered pairs $\langle s,t \rangle \in S \times S$ such that there exist a natural number $n \geq 0$ and elements $s_0, \ldots, s_n$ of S with $s_0 = s$, $s_n = t$, and $s_i R s_{i+1}$ for $i = 0, \ldots, n-1$. The *reflexive, symmetric, and transitive closure* of R is the set of all ordered pairs $\langle s,t \rangle \in S \times S$ such that there exist a natural number $n \geq 0$ and elements $s_0, \ldots, s_n$ of S with $s_0 = s$, $s_n = t$, and $\langle s_i, s_{i+1} \rangle$ in the symmetric closure of R. That is, the reflexive, symmetric, and transitive closure of R is the reflexive, transitive closure of the symmetric closure of R.

A binary relation on a set S which is reflexive, symmetric, and transitive is called an *equivalence relation* on S, and the reflexive, symmetric, and transitive closure of an arbitrary relation R is called the *equivalence relation determined by R*. For any equivalence relation R on a set S, and for any $s \in S$, the *R-equivalence class* of s is the set of all $t \in S$ such that sRt. It is not hard to see that any two distinct equivalence classes are disjoint, so that an equivalence relation R partitions its underlying set into disjoint subsets of objects that are indistinguishable by R.

A *partial order*, or *ordering*, on a set S is an irreflexive and transitive relation on S. If R is a partial order on S and s and t are elements of S

such that neither sRt nor tRs holds, then s and t are said to be *incomparable* with respect to R. A partial order R on S is a *total order*, or is *total*, if either sRt or tRs holds for every pair of distinct elements s and t of S. For any set S, the proper containment relation $\supset$ is an example of a partial order on 2^S; this ordering is total iff $S = \emptyset$ or S contains exactly one element. It is easily seen that R is a partial order if R^{-1} is.

A collection $R_1, \ldots, R_n$ of partial orders on sets $S_1, \ldots, S_n$, respectively, can be used to define a new partial order on the set $S_1 \times \ldots \times S_n$. We define the *lexicographic combination* of $R_1, \ldots, R_n$ to be the relation R on $S_1 \times \ldots \times S_n$ defined by $\langle s_1, \ldots, s_n \rangle R \langle t_1, \ldots, t_n \rangle$ provided there exists an $i \in \{1, \ldots, n\}$ such that $s_j = t_j$ for all $j < i$ and $s_i R_i t_i$ holds. If $S_i = S_j$ for $i, j \in \{1, \ldots, n\}$ and $R_i = R_j$ for $i, j \in \{1, \ldots, n\}$, then we call the lexicographic combination of $R_1, \ldots, R_n$ the *lexicographic extension* of R (to $S_1 \times \ldots \times S_n$). We abuse notation and denote all lexicographic extensions of a relation R in exactly the same way, namely, by R_{lex}. If, for example, N is the set of natural numbers, $>$ is the usual greater-than relation on N, Z is the set of integers, and $>_Z$ is the usual greater-than relation on Z, then the lexicographic combination of the (total) orderings $>$ and $>_Z$ is the (total) ordering R given by $\langle n, z \rangle R \langle n', z' \rangle$ iff either $n > n'$, or $n = n'$ and $z >_Z z'$. The lexicographic extension $>_{lex}$ of $>$ to triples of natural numbers, on the other hand, is given by $\langle n, m, k \rangle >_{lex} \langle n', m', k' \rangle$ iff $n > n'$, or $n = n'$ and $m > m'$, or $n = n'$, $m = m'$, and $k > k'$. That is, $>_{lex}$ is the "dictionary order" on triples of natural numbers.

It will be useful to have at our disposal another extension of binary relations as well. As noted above, sets do not contain multiple occurrences of the same element. Nevertheless, it will sometimes be convenient to talk about collections of objects which *do* contain more than one occurrence of certain elements. A *multiset over S* is a collection of objects from S in which each object may occur any number of times (in discussing multisets we do not explicitly mention the underlying set S unless it is necessary to do so). The collection $M = \{1, 2, 2, 5, 7, 7, 7, 7, 10\}$, for example, is not a set, although it is indeed a multiset. As for sets, we call the objects occurring in a multiset the *elements* of the multiset, and we call the number of occurrences of elements in a multiset the *size* of the multiset. The multiset M has size 9 and elements 1, 2, 5, 7, and 10.

If R is a partial order on a set S, then the *multiset extension of R* is the ordering R_{mul} on multisets over S defined by: $M R_{mul} M'$ iff M' can be obtained from M by replacing some element $m \in M$ by zero or more elements m' of S, each of which satisfies mRm', and leaving all other elements of M unchanged. If N is the set of natural numbers, $>$ is the usual greater-than relation on N, and M is the multiset from the preceding paragraph, then $M >_{mul} M'$ where $M' = \{1, 2, 2, 2, 3, 3, 4, 5, 5, 5, 5, 7, 7, 7, 10\}$. This is because M' can be obtained from M by replacing one occurrence of 7 in M with one occurrence of 2, two occurrences of 3, one occurrence of 4, and three occurrences of 5.

2.2   Functions and Countability

A *function from S to T* is a relation f from S to T such that for each $s \in S$ there is exactly one $t \in T$ such that sft. We write $f : S \rightarrow T$ to indicate that f is a function from S to T, and for each $s \in S$ we write $f(s)$ or fs for the unique t such that sft holds. The *identity function id_S* on a set S is the (unique) function $f : S \rightarrow S$ such that $f(s) = s$ for all $s \in S$.

Two functions f and g are considered equal provided they have the same domain and $sf = sg$ for each s in that common domain; note that this is precisely the notion of equality for functions obtained by considering them as (special kinds of) relations. If $f : S \rightarrow T$ and $U \subseteq S$, then the *restriction* of f to U can be realized as the function $f \mid_U : U \rightarrow T$, where $f \mid_U (s) = sf$ if $s \in U$ and $f \mid_U (s)$ is undefined otherwise.

Note that although every element in the domain S of $f : S \rightarrow T$ must map to some element of T, not every element of T is $f(s)$ for some element $s \in S$. The set of elements t in T such that $t = f(s)$ for some $s \in S$ is called the *codomain* of f. A function $f : S \rightarrow T$ with the property that every $t \in T$ is $f(s)$ for some $s \in S$ is *onto T*, or *surjective*. Of course, every function maps onto its codomain. A function f is *one-to-one*, or *injective*, if for all $s, s' \in S$, $f(s) = f(s')$ implies $s = s'$, i.e., if distinct elements in the domain of f are mapped to distinct elements of the codomain of f. A one-to-one and onto function from S to T is said to be *bijective*, or is called a *bijection* between S and T. The existence of a bijection between sets S and T implies that sets S and T are really "renamed versions" of the same set, since there is a one-to-one correspondence between the elements of S and those of T.

If $f : S \rightarrow T$ and $g : T \rightarrow U$ are functions, then their *composition*, denoted gf, is defined by $(gf)(s) = g(f(s))$ for all $s \in S$. Function composition is easily seen to be associative, i.e., $(hg)f = h(gf)$ holds for all $f : S \rightarrow T$, $g : T \rightarrow U$, and $h : U \rightarrow V$. If f is a bijection between S and T, then there exists a function $g : T \rightarrow S$ such that $gf = id_S$ and $fg = id_T$. In fact, g must itself be a bijection in this case.

A set S is said to be *finite* if there is a bijection between S and some initial segment $\{1, \ldots, n\}$ of the set N of natural numbers; S is *countably infinite* if there is a bijection between S and N itself. If S is neither finite nor countably infinite, then S is said to be *uncountable*. We will be concerned exclusively with finite and countably infinite sets in this book, and so "infinite" will mean "countably infinite" unless otherwise specified.

A *finite sequence* is a function whose domain is $\{1, \ldots, n\}$ for some natural number n, and an *infinite sequence* is a function whose domain is N. We use the neutral terminology "sequence" for a sequence which may be either finite or infinite. If s is a sequence, we usually write s_i in place of $s(i)$, so that finite sequences are of the form $s_1, \ldots, s_n$ and infinite sequences are of the form $s_1, s_2, \ldots$.

2.3 Posets and Zorn's Lemma

Zorn's Lemma will emerge as a key tool in establishing the completeness of resolution in Chapter 7 (see Lemma 7.4.5). In order to state and understand Zorn's Lemma, we require a bit more terminology concerning sets endowed with partial orders; whereas the focus in Section 2.1 was on partial orders themselves, in this section we are concerned with properties of partially ordered sets and their elements.

A *partially ordered set*, or *poset* for short, is a set S together with a partial order on S, i.e., a partially ordered set is an ordered pair $\langle S, R \rangle$ where S is a set and R is a partial order on S. In the sequel we will use suggestive notation, writing $\succ$ for the partial order on S. Note carefully, however, that $\succ$ is not necessarily the usual greater-than ordering on natural numbers (after all, S will not be the set of natural numbers in general), and in fact need not be any familiar ordering on the set S.

If $\langle S, \succ \rangle$ is a poset and if there is no $t \in S$ such that $t \succ s$, then s is said to be a $\succ$-*maximal element* of S; if there is no $t \in S$ such that $s \succ t$, then s a $\succ$-*minimal element*, or $\succ$-*smallest element*, of S. If s is a $\succ$-minimal element of S, we sometimes also say that s is $\succ$-*irreducible* or in $\succ$-*normal form*. Note that a $\succ$-maximal element s of S does not necessarily satisfy $s \succ t$ for all $t \in S$, and that a $\succ$-minimal element of S does not necessarily satisfy $t \succ s$ for all $t \in S$. Indeed, if S is any set with at least two elements, then the set of all nonempty subsets of S, together with the proper containment relation $\supset$ on $2^S - \emptyset$, is a poset with one $\supset$-minimal element corresponding to each of its elements; none of these $\supset$-minimal elements satisfies $t \supset s$ for all $t \in 2^S$. It is also worth noting that a given partially ordered set need not have any maximal or minimal elements. For instance, the partially ordered set $\langle N, > \rangle$, where N is the set of natural numbers and $>$ is the usual greater-than ordering on N, has no $>$-maximal element, and the partially ordered set $\langle Z, >_Z \rangle$, where Z is the set of integers and $>_Z$ is the usual greater-than ordering on Z, has neither $>_Z$-maximal nor $>_Z$-minimal elements.

An element s of a poset $\langle S, \succ \rangle$ is a $\succ$-*maximum element* of S if $s \succ t$ for all $t \in S$ such that $t \neq s$; s is a $\succ$-*minimum element* of S, if $t \succ s$

for all $t \in S$ such that $t \neq s$. Although every $\succ$-maximum element is a $\succ$-maximal element and every $\succ$-minimum element is a $\succ$-minimal element, it is important that $\succ$-maximal elements are not confused with $\succ$-maximum elements, and that $\succ$-minimal elements are not confused with $\succ$-minimum elements. In the example of the preceding paragraph, for instance, $2^S - \emptyset$ has $\supset$-minimal elements but no $\supset$-minimum element. On the other hand, for any set S, the empty set is the $\supset$-minimum element of 2^S.

A *decreasing sequence in* $\langle S, \succ \rangle$ is a sequence $s_0, s_1, s_2, \ldots$ of elements of S such that $s_i \succ s_{i+1}$ holds for all natural numbers i. Such sequences can, of course, be either finite or infinite. A partial order $\succ$ on a set S is said to be *noetherian*[1] if there is no infinite decreasing sequence in $\langle S, \succ \rangle$. If $\succ$ is a noetherian ordering on S, then for every element of S there is at least one element t of S such that $s \succ^* t$ and t is $\succ$-minimal; in this case we say that t is a $\succ$-*normal form* of s.

If T is a partially ordered subset of a poset $\langle S, \succ \rangle$, then an element s of S with the property that $s \succ t$ for all $t \in T$ distinct from s is called a $\succ$-*upper bound (in S)* for T. Similarly, if s is such that $t \succ s$ for all $t \in T$ distinct from s, then s is a $\succ$-*lower bound (in S)* for T. Note that in neither case is s itself required to be in T.

In discussing a poset $\langle S, \succ \rangle$ we omit explicit reference to the partial order R on S if the particular partial order is unimportant, or if doing so will not lead to confusion. We may therefore speak of a "poset S," or a "minimal element in S." Using this simplified terminology, we have

Theorem 2.3.1   *(Zorn's Lemma) If S is a nonempty poset such that every decreasing sequence in S has a lower bound in S, then S contains a minimal element.*

Proof Sketch. This proof sketch is adapted from [Hal60].

Let R be the partial order in question on S. Since S is nonempty, it must contain some element, say, s_0. If s_0 is minimal, then we are done. Otherwise there must exist an element s_1 of S such that $s_0 R s_1$. If s_1 is minimal, then we are done. Otherwise there must exist an element s_2 of S such that $s_1 R s_2$. We can continue producing elements of S in this manner until we arrive at a minimal element.

The question now is: must this process always stop? If so, when? It may very well be that "continuing in this manner" never produces a minimal element, instead producing an infinite decreasing sequence of nonminimal elements. By hypothesis, this decreasing sequence in S must have a lower bound s'. We now start the entire process over again, this time starting with s' instead of with s_0. And so on. Seeing that this whole procedure

---

[1] Named after the mathematician Emmy Noether (1882-1935).

must come to an end is the crux of the formal proof, for which the reader is referred to [Hal60]. □

Zorn's Lemma describes sufficient conditions under which the *existence* of a minimal element of S can be deduced. Neither the proof sketch above nor the formal proof of Zorn's Lemma provides a method for actually *constructing* such a minimal element. Indeed, the existence of a general method for constructing minimal elements in arbitrary posets with minimal elements is not possible.

2.4 Trees

Trees will appear in this book in many settings. We will speak, for example, about "tree representations of terms," "proof trees," "derivation trees," etc.

A *tree* T is a set M together with an irreflexive relation $>$ on M such that M has a $>^+$-maximum element[2] Λ, $(>^+)^{-1}$ is noetherian, and for all elements m of M other than Λ, $|\{x \mid x > m\}| = 1$. Note that since M has a $>$-maximum element, it must be nonempty. Of course, $|\{x \mid x > \Lambda\}| = 0$ by the maximality of Λ. The elements of M are called the *nodes* of T. The maximum element Λ of M is called the *root* of T, and the minimal nodes of T are called its *leaves*. A tree $T = \langle M, > \rangle$ is said to be *finite* or *infinite* accordingly as M is finite or infinite.

Let $T = \langle M, > \rangle$ be any tree. If $k > k'$, then the ordered pair $\langle k, k' \rangle$ is called an *arc* in T. In this case, k' is said to be a *child* of k, and k is said to be a *parent* of k'. The node k' is *adjacent* to k if k is the parent of k'. The relation $>^*$ is called the *descendant relation* and the relation $(>^{-1})^*$ is called the *ancestor relation*.

A *path from k to k'* is a sequence $k_0, k_1, \ldots, k_n$ of nodes such that $k_0 = k$, $k_n = k'$, and $k_i > k_{i+1}$ for $i = 0, \ldots, n - 1$; such a path is said to have *length n*. A *maximal path from k to k'* in T is a path from k to k' such that there exists no path from k to k' in T which has greater length; a path is *maximal (in T)* if there is no path in T which has greater length. A *branch* of T is a sequence $k_0, k_1, k_2, \ldots$ of nodes such that $k_0 = \Lambda$ and $k_i > k_{i+1}$ for all natural numbers i. Branches may, of course, be either finite or infinite.

Note that because, for each tree $T = \langle M, > \rangle$, the relation $>^{-1}$ is noetherian, trees are *acyclic*; i.e., they contain no *cycles* or paths $k_0, k_1, \ldots, k_n$ of length at least one such that $k_0 = k_n$. Moreover, there is at most one path from any node k to any other node k' of T. We can interpret the fact that two

[2]Observe that $>^+$ is indeed a partial order since $>$ is irreflexive.

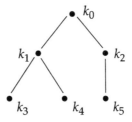

FIGURE 2.1.

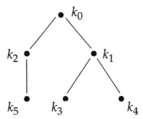

FIGURE 2.2.

nodes k and k' are related by the reflexive, transitive closure $>^*$ of $>$, i.e., that $k >^* k'$, as indicating that there is a path from k to k'. Trees satisfy the additional property that if $k >^+ m$ and $k' >^+ m$, then k and k' are comparable with respect to $>^*$.

Trees get their name from their natural graphical representation. The tree

$$T = \langle \{k_0, k_1, k_2, k_3, k_4, k_5, k_6\}, \{\langle k_0, k_1 \rangle, \langle k_0, k_2 \rangle, \langle k_1, k_3 \rangle, \langle k_1, k_4 \rangle, \langle k_2, k_5 \rangle\} \rangle,$$

for example, is represented graphically by Figure 2.1. As is customary, we label the nodes of a tree with their names and draw the arcs of the tree as undirected lines, even though arcs are *ordered* pairs of nodes. The arcs in a tree are understood to be directed away from the root. Of course, this tree could just as "naturally" be represented by either the drawing in Figure 2.2 or that in Figure 2.3, and so graphical representations of trees are not at all unique. This difficulty can be remedied by providing a left-to-right sequencing for the parents of each node to arrive at an *orientation* for the tree. In practice, however, this is rarely done, and two graphical representations of a tree are instead considered the same if they differ only in their orientations.

In discussing tree representations of terms, proof trees, derivation trees, and the like, we will often want to be able to label the nodes of trees. We may therefore postulate the existence of a set L of *labels*, as well as a function λ assigning a label to each node of a tree, to arrive at the notion of a *labeled tree*. If $L = \{+, s, 0\}$ and $\lambda = \{\langle k_0, + \rangle, \langle k_1, + \rangle, \langle k_2, s \rangle, \langle k_3, 0 \rangle, \langle k_4, 0 \rangle, \langle k_5, 0 \rangle\}$, for example, then a labeled

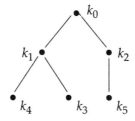

FIGURE 2.3.

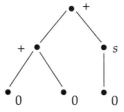

FIGURE 2.4.

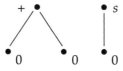

FIGURE 2.5.

version of the tree in Figure 2.1 is depicted in Figure 2.4. Note that we replace the node names by their labels in the graphical representation of a labeled tree.

If k is a node in a tree T, then the *subtree of T with root k* is the tree $T' = \langle M', >' \rangle$, where

- $k' \in M'$ iff $k >^* k'$, and

- $>'$ is precisely $>|_{M'}$.

It is easy to check that a subtree of a (labeled) tree is itself a (labeled) tree, and that the (labeled) subtree of T with root k is unique. If T is labeled by λ, then T' is labeled by $\lambda |_{M'}$. If T is the tree of Figure 2.4, then graphical representations of the subtrees of T with roots k_1 and k_2 are the labeled trees of Figure 2.5.

We may graphically represent infinite trees in a similar manner.

2.5 Mathematical Induction

One of the most useful techniques we have at our disposal for defining mathematical objects and proving theorems about them is the *Principle of Mathematical Induction*. The Principle of Mathematical Induction can be used to define mathematical objects in terms of the natural numbers, as well as to prove theorems about the natural numbers and objects that have been defined in terms of them. Although a remarkably rich collection of mathematical notions can be defined using the Principle of Mathematical Induction, in this book we will also find it useful to have other notions of induction at our disposal. The Principle of Mathematical Induction is reviewed in this section; other principles of induction are briefly mentioned at the end of this section, and are described in detail in Chapter 3. When a definition or proof proceeds by appeal to a principle of induction and it is clear which such principle is being used, we may say that the definition or proof is "by induction" without naming the precise principle of induction to which we are appealing.

The basic idea underlying the Principle of Mathematical Induction is quite a simple one. The crucial observation is that the entire (countably infinite) set of natural numbers can be obtained by starting with 0 and repeatedly adding 1. This observation implies that in order to prove that a statement S holds for all natural numbers n, we need only establish that $S(0)$ holds, and that $S(n + 1)$ holds whenever $S(n)$ does. Then $S(0)$ holds by direct demonstration, $S(1)$ holds because $S(0)$ does and because $1 = 0 + 1$, $S(2)$ holds because $S(1)$ does and because $2 = 1 + 1$, and so on. More formally we have

Definition 2.5.1 The *Principle of Mathematical Induction* is the following proof scheme. To show that $S(n)$ holds for all $n \in N$ it suffices to show that

- $S(0)$ holds, and

- if $S(n)$ holds then $S(n + 1)$ holds.

In the second clause of Definition 2.5.1, the assumption that $S(n)$ holds is called the *induction hypothesis*. We give an example illustrating the use of the Principle of Mathematical Induction to prove a simple statement about the set of natural numbers.

Example 2.5.1 The Principle of Mathematical Induction can be used to show that

$$\sum_{i=0}^{n} i = \frac{n(n + 1)}{2}$$

holds for all natural numbers n.

Let $\mathcal{S}(n)$ be the statement that $\sum_{i=0}^{n} i = \frac{n(n+1)}{2}$. According to the Principle of Mathematical Induction, in order to establish that $\mathcal{S}(n)$ holds for every natural number n we need only see that

- $\mathcal{S}(0)$ holds, i.e., $0 = \frac{0 \cdot 1}{2}$, and

- if $\mathcal{S}(n)$ holds then $\mathcal{S}(n+1)$ holds, i.e., if $\sum_{i=0}^{n} i = \frac{n(n+1)}{2}$ then $\sum_{i=0}^{n+1} i = \frac{(n+1)(n+2)}{2}$.

That $\mathcal{S}(0)$ holds is easily seen by inspection. Verifying the second assertion requires a little more work.

Suppose that $\mathcal{S}(n)$ holds, i.e., suppose that $\sum_{i=0}^{n} i = \frac{n(n+1)}{2}$. Then

$$
\begin{aligned}
\sum_{i=0}^{n+1} i &= \sum_{i=0}^{n} i + (n+1) \\
&= \frac{n(n+1)}{2} + (n+1) \\
&= \frac{n(n+1)}{2} + \frac{2(n+1)}{2} \\
&= \frac{n^2+3n+2}{2} \\
&= \frac{(n+1)(n+2)}{2},
\end{aligned}
$$

as desired. The induction hypothesis is used to obtain the third expression above from the second.

We can also use the Principle of Mathematical Induction to define mathematical objects in terms of the natural numbers and then to prove theorems about them. To illustrate, we use the Principle of Mathematical Induction to give an alternative definition of the reflexive, transitive closure of a binary relation.

Example 2.5.2

1. For any binary relation R on a set S, define the relation R^n on S inductively as follows:

   - $R^0 = \{\langle s, s \rangle \mid s \in S\}$, and
   - $R^{n+1} = \{\langle s, t \rangle \in S \times S \mid \text{there is a } u \in S \text{ with } sR^n u \text{ and } uRt\}$.

2. Using the Principle of Mathematical Induction, we can see that

$$
R^* = \bigcup_{n \geq 0} R^n
$$

holds. We do this by first using the Principle of Mathematical Induction to establish that for all natural numbers n, $sR^n t$ iff there exists a sequence $s_0, \ldots, s_n$ of elements of S such that $s_0 = s$, $s_n = t$, and $s_i R s_{i+1}$ holds for $i = 1, \ldots, n$. Let $\mathcal{S}(n)$ be the statement that this assertion is true for n.

If $n = 0$, then $\mathcal{S}(0)$ holds by inspection, so suppose that $\mathcal{S}(n)$ holds, i.e, suppose that $sR^n t$ iff there exists a sequence $s_0, \ldots, s_n$ of elements of S such that $s_0 = s$, $s_n = t$, and $s_i R s_{i+1}$ holds for $i = 1, \ldots, n-1$. Consider the relation R^{n+1}. By definition, $sR^{n+1}t$ holds iff there exists some $u \in S$ such that $sR^n u$ and uRt hold. By the induction hypothesis, $sR^n u$ holds iff there exists a sequence $s_0, \ldots, s_n$ of elements of S such that $s_0 = s$, $s_n = u$, and $s_i R s_{i+1}$ for all $i = 0, \ldots, n-1$. If we define s_{n+1} to be t, then we have a sequence $s_0, \ldots, s_n, s_{n+1}$ of elements of S such that $s_0 = s$, $s_{n+1} = t$, and $s_i R s_{i+1}$ holds for $i = 0, \ldots, n$. Thus $\mathcal{S}(n+1)$ holds provided $\mathcal{S}(n)$ does. By the Principle of Mathematical Induction, then, $\mathcal{S}(n)$ holds for all natural numbers n.

It is now easy to see that

$$R^* \subseteq \bigcup_{n \geq 0} R^n \quad \text{and} \quad \bigcup_{n \geq 0} R^n \subseteq R^*,$$

and so we may conclude that $R^* = \bigcup_{n \geq 0} R^n$, as desired.

There is, of course, no reason that inductive definitions or proofs must start at 0. Indeed, by virtue of the fact that we can build up the set of all natural numbers greater-than or equal to a specified number k by starting at k and repeatedly adding 1, we can prove that a statement holds for all natural numbers greater-than or equal to k by establishing that it holds for k, and that it holds for $n + 1$ whenever it holds for $n \geq k$. Then the statement holds for k, it holds for $k + 1$ because it holds for k, it holds for $k + 2$ because it holds for $k + 1$, and so on.

Example 2.5.3 Let $\mathcal{S}(n)$ be the statement that $2^n > n^2$. Although $\mathcal{S}(n)$ does not hold for all natural numbers n, it does hold for $n \geq 5$. We can prove this using the (revised) Principle of Mathematical Induction by showing that

- $\mathcal{S}(5)$ holds, i.e., $2^5 > 5^2$, and

- if $\mathcal{S}(n)$ holds and if $n \geq 5$, then $\mathcal{S}(n+1)$ also holds, i.e., if $2^n > n^2$ and if $n \geq 5$, then $2^{n+1} > (n+1)^2$.

That $\mathcal{S}(5)$ holds is true by inspection. To see that $\mathcal{S}(n+1)$ holds whenever $\mathcal{S}(n)$ holds and $n \geq 5$, assume that $\mathcal{S}(n)$ holds and that $n \geq 5$. Then

$$
\begin{aligned}
2^{n+1} &= 2 \cdot 2^n \\
&> 2n^2 \\
&= n^2 + n^2 \\
&\geq n^2 + 5n \\
&= n^2 + 2n + 3n \\
&> n^2 + 2n + 1 \\
&= (n+1)^2.
\end{aligned}
$$

The third expression is obtained from the second by the induction hypothesis. That $n^2 \geq 5n$ follows from the assumption that $n \geq 5$, together with the fact that $3n > 1$ holds trivially for all natural numbers n such that $n \geq 1$.

In the following, we will refrain from explicitly identifying the statement $S(n)$ to be proved by the Principle of Mathematical Induction when this is clear from context.

Sometimes statements that appear to be good candidates for proof by induction do not immediately yield to that proof technique. The following example illustrates this phenomenon.

Example 2.5.4   We try to prove by induction that, for all natural numbers n, the sum of the first n odd numbers is a perfect square, i.e., that for every natural number n there exists a natural number k such that

$$\sum_{i=0}^{n-1}(2i+1) = k^2.$$

We first observe that $S(0)$ holds trivially with $k = 1$. Now suppose that there exists a k such that

$$\sum_{i=0}^{n-1}(2i+1) = k^2.$$

Then

$$\begin{aligned}
\sum_{i=0}^{n}(2i+1) &= \sum_{i=0}^{n-1}(2i+1) + (2n+1) \\
&= k^2 + 2n + 1.
\end{aligned}$$

Unfortunately, there is no assurance that $k^2 + 2n + 1$ is a perfect square, and so the proof by induction cannot proceed.

At this point we might be tempted to conclude that the Principle of Mathematical Induction will not be useful in proving this statement about the natural numbers, but this is a bit too hasty. The problem here is that our induction hypothesis is too weak to push the induction through. By appropriately strengthening the statement of the theorem we are proving— so that the theorem we really want to prove is a corollary of the new, stronger theorem—we also strengthen the induction hypothesis enough to unblock the proof.

In Example 2.5.4, the induction cannot go through because $k^2 + 2n + 1$ cannot necessarily be recognized as a perfect square. But if k were n, then $k^2 + 2n + 1 = n^2 + 2n + 1 = (n+1)^2$ would hold. This observation suggests trying to prove the stronger statement that the sum of the first n odd numbers equals n^2, from which the assertion to be proved in Example 2.5.4 would follow immediately.

Example 2.5.5   We prove by induction that, for all natural numbers n, the sum of the first n odd numbers equals n^2, i.e., that for every natural number n,

$$\sum_{i=0}^{n-1}(2i+1) = n^2.$$

As before, we observe that $\mathcal{S}(0)$ holds trivially. Now, suppose that

$$\sum_{i=0}^{n-1}(2i+1) = n^2.$$

Then

$$
\begin{aligned}
\textstyle\sum_{i=0}^{n}(2i+1) &= \textstyle\sum_{i=0}^{n-1}(2i+1) \ + \ (2n+1) \\
&= n^2 + 2n + 1 \\
&= (n+1)^2,
\end{aligned}
$$

as desired.

There is another way in which the "obvious" induction hypothesis can fail to be strong enough to prove the desired result.

Example 2.5.6   Suppose we want to show that every natural number greater-than or equal to 2 can be written as a product of primes. Observe that 2 itself can be so written, since it is trivially a product of primes (it is the product of the single prime 2).

Now, suppose that n is greater-than or equal to 2, and that n can be written as a product of primes. Consider $n + 1$. If $n + 1$ is prime, then there is nothing to prove, since $n + 1$ is then trivially a product of primes. Otherwise, $n+1$ can be written as pq for some p and q such that $2 \le p \le n$ and $2 \le q \le n$. But since both p and q cannot be n, and since in fact neither need be equal to n, the induction hypothesis cannot apply, and the proof attempt is thwarted.

In order to complete the above proof, a stronger induction hypothesis is needed. An alternative, but completely equivalent, formalization of the Principle of Mathematical Induction is appropriate in such situations. This alternative formulation is given by

Definition 2.5.2   The *Strong Form of the Principle of Mathematical Induction* is the following proof scheme: to show that $\mathcal{S}(n)$ holds for all $n \in N$ it suffices to show that

- $\mathcal{S}(0)$ holds, and

- $S(n+1)$ holds whenever $S(k)$ holds for $0 \leq k \leq n$.

According to the Strong Form of the Principle of Mathematical Induction, $S(n)$ holds for all natural numbers n provided that $S(0)$ holds, and that $S(n+1)$ holds whenever $S(k)$ holds for $0 \leq k \leq n$. Then $S(0)$ holds by direct demonstration, $S(1)$ holds since $S(0)$ does, $S(2)$ holds since $S(1)$ and $S(0)$ do, $S(3)$ holds since $S(2)$, $S(1)$, and $S(0)$ do, and so on. We illustrate by completing the proof in Example 2.5.6.

Example 2.5.7   Suppose we want to show that every natural number greater-than or equal to 2 can be written as a product of primes. Observe that 2 itself can be so written, since it is trivially the product of primes.

Now, suppose that n is greater-than or equal to 2, and that n can be written as a product of primes. Consider $n+1$. If $n+1$ is prime, then there is nothing to prove, since $n+1$ is then a trivial product of primes. Otherwise, $n+1$ can be written as pq for some p and q such that $2 \leq p \leq n$ and $2 \leq q \leq n$. By the induction hypothesis, both p and q can be written as products of primes. Multiplying these representations of p and q as products of primes yields a representation of $n+1$ as a product of primes.

In this example we apply the induction hypothesis to only two numbers which are smaller than $n+1$, but in general the induction hypothesis can be applied to arbitrarily many such numbers. To further illustrate, we prove that every finite tree has one fewer arc than nodes.

Example 2.5.8   Let T be a (finite) tree with n nodes. We want to show that T contains $n-1$ arcs. We use the Strong Form of the Principle of Mathematical Induction, inducting on n.

If T is a tree with one node, then T necessarily contains no arcs, and so T clearly contains one fewer arc than nodes.

Suppose that every tree with n or fewer nodes contains one fewer arc than nodes, and let T be a tree with $n+1$ nodes. It can be checked that removing the root Λ of T and all k edges of the form $\langle s, \Lambda \rangle$ yields a collection of subtrees $T_1, \ldots, T_k$ of T with $n_1, \ldots, n_k$ nodes, respectively, where $n-1 = n_1 + \ldots + n_k$. Then $n_i < n$ for $i = 1, \ldots, k$, and so by the induction hypothesis, each tree T_i contains $n_i - 1$ arcs. But then T must have $(n_1 - 1) + (n_2 - 1) + \ldots + (n_k - 1) + k = n_1 + \ldots + n_k = n-1$ arcs.

The Strong Form of the Principle of Mathematical Induction corresponds most closely to the kinds of induction that we will use later in this text. We will typically prove statements about classes of objects by inducting over certain kinds of structures that the objects exhibit, and in order to conclude that these statements hold for a given object, we will need to know that they hold for *all* smaller such objects.

3

Syntax of First-order Languages

3.1 First-order Languages

In this section the formal syntax of first-order logic is defined. As for any natural or artificial language, we require on the one hand an alphabet on which the language is based, and on the other a grammar according to which sentences in the language are constructed.

Definition 3.1.1   An *alphabet for a first-order language* comprises the following symbols:

- the *connectives* $\neg$, $\wedge$, $\vee$, $\Rightarrow$, $\Leftrightarrow$, $\forall$, $\exists$, and $\approx$,

- a countably infinite set $\mathcal{V}$ of *variables*,

- the *auxiliary symbols* "(" and ")",

- a countably infinite set $\mathcal{F}_n$ of *function symbols of arity n* for each natural number n, and

- a countably infinite set $\mathcal{P}_n$ of *predicate symbols of arity n* for each natural number n.

The symbols $\neg$, $\wedge$, $\vee$, $\Rightarrow$, $\Leftrightarrow$, $\forall$, $\exists$, and $\approx$ are read as "not," "and," "or," "implies," "if and only if," "for all," "there exists," and "equals," and they stand for negation, conjunction, disjunction, implication, equivalence, universal quantification, existential quantification, and equality, respectively. The connectives $\forall$ and $\exists$ are called *quantifiers*.

Variables will typically be denoted by (possibly indexed) letters like v, x, y, and z; function symbols are denoted by f, g, $+$, etc., and predicate symbols are denoted by P, Q, R, $>$, etc. The sets $\mathcal{F} = \bigcup_{n \geq 0} \mathcal{F}_n$ and $\mathcal{P} = \bigcup_{n \geq 0} \mathcal{P}_n$ are the sets of *function symbols* and *predicate symbols* of the alphabet, respectively. We assume that the sets $\mathcal{V}$, $\mathcal{F}_n$, and $\mathcal{P}_n$, as well as the sets of connectives and auxiliary symbols, are pairwise disjoint.

Every function symbol and every predicate symbol is assumed to have a specified arity telling how many arguments the symbol takes. Function symbols of arity zero are called *constant symbols*, and predicate symbols of arity zero are, by analogy, called *predicate constant symbols* or *propositions*. Since all countably infinite sets of variables are the same up to renaming of the variables, we assume a fixed set $\mathcal{V}$ of variables for inclusion in all alphabets for first-order languages. Since, moreover, the connectives and auxiliary symbols are likewise uniquely determined for an alphabet, we may indicate an alphabet for a first-order language simply by specifying an ordered pair $\langle \mathcal{F}, \mathcal{P} \rangle$. Such a pair is called a *signature* for first-order logic.

Informally speaking, then, an alphabet is just a nonempty set of symbols. A *word* over an alphabet A is a finite string of symbols from A. The set of all words over the alphabet A is denoted by A^*. For each word $w \in A^*$, $|w|$ is defined to be the number of symbols occurring in w. The empty string of symbols is always considered a word, and is denoted by ϵ. A word w is a *(proper) prefix* of the word v if there exists a (nonempty) word u such that $v = wu$, where wu denotes the *concatenation* of the word w with the word u. We will always denote the concatenation of two words u and v by the juxtaposition uv, and we assume that concatenation associates to the left.

We single out for special consideration certain words over alphabets for first-order languages—*terms* are the elementary building blocks of first-order languages. Terms such as $3+4$, $\sin(x+y)$, or $f(x, y, g(z))$ are familiar from mathematics, where they are built from constants (like 3 and 4), variables (like x, y, and z), and function symbols (like $+$, $\sin$, and f) according to a certain set of rules. In the context of first-order logic we have

Definition 3.1.2 Let $\Sigma = \langle \mathcal{F}, \mathcal{P} \rangle$ be a signature, and suppose $\mathcal{G} \subseteq \mathcal{F}$ and $\mathcal{W} \subseteq \mathcal{V}$. Then the set $\mathcal{T}(\mathcal{G}, \mathcal{W})$ of words over $\mathcal{G} \cup \mathcal{W}$ is built inductively using the following rules:

- every variable in $\mathcal{W}$ is in $\mathcal{T}(\mathcal{G}, \mathcal{W})$, and

- if $f \in \mathcal{G}$, f has arity n, and $t_1, \ldots, t_n$ are in $\mathcal{T}(\mathcal{G}, \mathcal{W})$ then $ft_1 \ldots t_n$ is also in $\mathcal{T}(\mathcal{G}, \mathcal{W})$.

If $\mathcal{G} = \mathcal{F}$ and $\mathcal{W} = \mathcal{V}$, then $\mathcal{T}(\mathcal{F}, \mathcal{V})$ is called the set of *terms (over Σ)*.

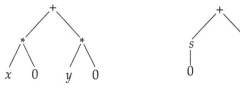

FIGURE 3.1.

We will be concerned with terms over various signatures. But when the sets $\mathcal{F}$ and $\mathcal{V}$ are clear from context, we may suppress reference to them and simply write $\mathcal{T}$ in place of $\mathcal{T}(\mathcal{F}, \mathcal{V})$. In light of Definition 3.1.2, we sometimes call function symbols *term constructors*.

Terms, which are really just words over an alphabet formed according to the rules of Definition 3.1.2, can be represented as ordered, labeled trees whose leaves are labeled with variables and constants, and whose inner nodes with n children are labeled with function symbols of arity n. We often blur the distinction between a term and its tree representation, and so refer to the nodes or leaves of a term, or the variables in a tree, without hesitation.

Example 3.1.1   Let Σ be the signature of arithmetic comprising the constant symbol 0, the one-place function symbol s, the two-place function symbols $+$ and $*$, and the two-place predicate symbol $>$. The tree representations of the terms $+ * x0 * y0$ and $+s0ss0$ over Σ are shown in Figure 3.1.

Although in the second clause of Definition 3.1.2 we have used *prefix notation* (corresponding to a top-down parse of the tree representation of a term) we could just as easily have used another well-known linear representation of terms, namely, *infix notation*. In infix notation, the two terms in Figure 3.1 read $(x * 0) + (y * 0)$ and $s(0) + s(s(0))$. Unlike prefix notation, infix notation requires the use of parentheses to avoid ambiguity, but it is usually more easily understood by humans. Thus while prefix notation is, strictly speaking, required by Definition 3.1.2, in the interest of legibility we will use infix notation when convenient.

Other words over signatures for first-order languages are also objects of special attention.

Definition 3.1.3   Let $\Sigma = \langle \mathcal{F}, \mathcal{P} \rangle$ be a signature.

1. An *atomic formula* or *atom (over Σ)* is a word over $\mathcal{F} \cup \mathcal{P} \cup \mathcal{V}$ of the form $Pt_1 \ldots t_n$ for $P \in \mathcal{P}_n$ and $t_1, \ldots, t_n \in \mathcal{T}(\mathcal{F}, \mathcal{V})$, or a word of the form $s \approx t$ where $s, t \in \mathcal{T}(\mathcal{F}, \mathcal{V})$.

2. The set of *formulae (over Σ)* is the set of words over $\mathcal{F} \cup \mathcal{P} \cup \mathcal{V}$ built inductively using the following rules:

- every atom is a formula over Σ,

- if φ and ψ are formulae over Σ, then $\neg\varphi$, $(\varphi \wedge \psi)$, $(\varphi \vee \psi)$, $(\varphi \Rightarrow \psi)$ and $(\varphi \Leftrightarrow \psi)$ are also formulae over Σ, and

- if φ is a formula over Σ and $x \in \mathcal{V}$, then $\exists x\, \varphi$ and $\forall x\, \varphi$ are also formulae over Σ.

We denote by $\mathcal{A}(\mathcal{F}, \mathcal{P})$ the set of all atoms over $\Sigma = \langle \mathcal{F}, \mathcal{P} \rangle$ and by $\mathcal{L}(\mathcal{F}, \mathcal{P})$ the set of formulae over Σ. We write simply $\mathcal{A}$ and $\mathcal{L}$ when this practice will not lead to confusion. $\mathcal{L}$ is said to be a *first-order language over the signature* Σ.

Example 3.1.2   Let $\mathcal{F}$ be any set of function symbols, and let $\mathcal{P}$ consist of the two-place predicate symbol R. The expressions

$\forall x\, Rxx,$
$\forall x \forall y\, (Rxy \Rightarrow Ryx),$ and
$\forall x \forall y \forall z\, ((Rxy \wedge Ryz) \Rightarrow Rxz),$

which are axioms for the theory of equivalence relations, are formulae over $\Sigma = \langle \mathcal{F}, \mathcal{P} \rangle$.

Predicate symbols, like function symbols, can be written in either prefix or infix notation. As explained in Chapter 2, in examples we will often write terms involving two-place predicate symbols using infix notation, so that we would write $x R y$, rather than Rxy, in Example 3.1.2. In addition, we assume left-associativity of iterated connectives. And although we may omit unneccessary parentheses in terms and formulae—and so write $(\varphi \wedge \psi) \wedge \chi$ rather than $((\varphi \wedge \psi) \wedge \chi)$—we sometimes make use of extraneous parentheses for clarity. Thus we write $f(g(x, y), g(y, z))$ in place of $fgxygyz$, and $(x+y) \approx (y+z)$ in place of $\approx +xy+yz$, even though—to be completely precise—the latter linear representations of the terms and formulae are the ones called for by Definitions 3.1.2 and 3.1.3. Finally, we adopt standard conventions for binding, so that quantifiers always bind more tightly than do the other connectives.

In this book we will denote terms by (possibly indexed) letters such as s, t, u, and w, and we denote formulae by the (possibly indexed) Greek letters φ, ψ, etc.

For the remainder of the text, let $\Sigma = \langle \mathcal{F}, \mathcal{P} \rangle$ be a fixed but arbitrary signature unless otherwise noted.

3.2   Induction over Terms and Formulae

"Structural induction" is one of the most useful techniques at our disposal for proving statements about terms and formulae. The principle underlying this proof technique is similar to that underlying induction over the natural numbers, and gives rise to the *Principle of Structural Induction for terms* and the *Principle of Structural Induction for formulae*. The former states that because terms are defined inductively, in order to show that a statement S holds for all terms, one need only show first that $S(x)$ holds for all variables, and then that $S(ft_1 \ldots t_n)$ holds for every composite term $ft_1 \ldots t_n$ provided $S(t_1), \ldots, S(t_n)$ hold. The latter makes a similar observation for formulae.

Definition 3.2.1

1. The *Principle of Structural Induction for terms (over Σ)* is the following proof scheme: to show that $S(t)$ holds for all $t \in \mathcal{T}(\mathcal{F}, \mathcal{V})$ it suffices to show that

   - $S(x)$ holds for every $x \in \mathcal{V}$, and

   - if $S(t_1), \ldots, S(t_n)$ hold and $f \in \mathcal{F}_n$, then $S(ft_1 \ldots t_n)$ holds as well.

2. The *Principle of Structural Induction for formulae (over Σ)* is the following proof scheme: to show that $S(\varphi)$ holds for every $\varphi \in \mathcal{L}(\mathcal{F}, \mathcal{P})$ it suffices to show that

   - $S(A)$ holds for every atom A,

   - if $S(\varphi)$ and $S(\psi)$ hold, then $S(\neg\varphi)$, $S(\varphi \wedge \psi)$, $S(\varphi \vee \psi)$, $S(\varphi \Rightarrow \psi)$, and $S(\varphi \Leftrightarrow \psi)$ hold as well, and

   - if φ is a formula such that $S(\varphi)$ holds and $x \in \mathcal{V}$, then $S(\exists x\, \varphi)$ and $S(\forall x\, \varphi)$ hold.

In the second clause of the first part of Definition 3.2.1, the assumption that $S(t_1), \ldots, S(t_n)$ hold is called the *induction hypothesis*; in the second and third clauses of the second part, the assumption that $S(\varphi)$ and $S(\psi)$ hold is the induction hypothesis. This terminology is in accordance with that used for induction over the natural numbers. As discussed in Chapter 2, in that familiar setting, one proves that a statement holds for all natural numbers by proving that it holds for a smallest natural number, and then showing that it holds for an arbitrary natural number n assuming it holds for all natural numbers smaller than n. In first-order logic, one proves that a statement holds for all terms by showing that it holds for the simplest terms, namely, the variables, and then showing that it holds for an arbitrary term assuming it holds for all "smaller" terms. Similarly, one proves that a statement holds for all formulae by showing that it holds for the simplest formulae, namely, the atoms, and then showing that it holds for an arbitrary formula assuming it holds for all "smaller" formulae. Here "smaller" is a synonym for "syntactically simpler"; by any reckoning, $t_1, \ldots, t_n$ are syntactically simpler than $ft_1 \ldots t_n$, and φ and ψ are syntactically simpler than $(\varphi \wedge \psi)$, and so on.

We give an example of an application of the Principle of Structural Induction.

Example 3.2.1   The Principle of Structural Induction for formulae can be used to prove that every $\varphi \in \mathcal{L}$ contains exactly as many left parentheses as right parentheses.

First we can use the Principle of Structural Induction for terms to show that terms contain neither left nor right parentheses (note that here we are using the strict notation of Definition 3.1.2), and so contain equal numbers of these. Variables are not themselves parentheses and so no variable contains parentheses. Moreover, each composite term $ft_1 \ldots t_n$ contains no parentheses since by the induction hypothesis $t_1, \ldots, t_n$ do not. Thus each term contains precisely the same number of left and right parentheses, namely, zero. We will use this fact about terms in proving—by the Principle of Structural Induction for formulae—that atomic formulae are parenthesis-balanced.

Since each $P \in \mathcal{P}_n$ contains no parentheses, and no terms $t_1, \ldots, t_n$ contain parentheses, each atomic formula of the form $Pt_1 \ldots t_n$ is free of parentheses. If s and t are terms, then $s \approx t$ also contains no parentheses. Each atomic formula thus has zero left parentheses and zero right parentheses.

Now, if γ is a formula of the form $(\varphi \wedge \psi)$, $(\varphi \vee \psi)$, $(\varphi \Rightarrow \psi)$, or $(\varphi \Leftrightarrow \psi)$, then by the induction hypothesis we may assume that φ and ψ have equal numbers of left and right parentheses. In forming such terms from φ and ψ, one left and one right parenthesis are added to the parentheses of φ and ψ, and so we may conclude that terms of these forms contain equal numbers of left and right parentheses. In forming $\neg\varphi$, $\forall x\, \varphi$, and $\exists x\, \varphi$ from φ, by the induction hypothesis we may again assume that φ has equal numbers of left and right parentheses. Since no parentheses are added, the desired conclusion necessarily follows.

Interestingly, we have proven a stronger statement for terms and atoms, namely, that they contain no parentheses at all. This stronger result is not needed in proving that all formulae are parenthesis-balanced, but is worth noting. As an exercise, the reader should try to prove, using the Principle of Structural Induction for terms together with that for formulae, that the empty word is neither a term nor a formula. (Hint: show that if t is a term or φ is a formula, then t (resp., φ) is not the empty word.)

We now show that terms and formulae can be uniquely decomposed into parts.

Lemma 3.2.1   *1. Let s and t be any terms. If $t = sw$ for some word $w \in (\mathcal{F} \cup \mathcal{V})^*$ then $w = \epsilon$, i.e., no term is a proper prefix of another term.*

2. Let φ and ψ be formulae. Then φ is not a proper prefix of ψ.

Proof. 1. The proof is by the Principle of Structural Induction for terms. We induct on t, showing that no term is a proper prefix of t. If t is a variable, then t has no proper prefix at all. Now, without loss of generality, we may suppose that $t = ft_1 \ldots t_n$ and $t = sw$ for some word w. Then s must be a term of the form $fs_1 \ldots s_n$, and we must therefore have that $t_1 \ldots t_n = s_1 \ldots s_n w$. Since for $i = 1, \ldots, n$, t_i and s_i are terms smaller than t, the induction hypothesis guarantees that neither t_i nor s_i are proper prefixes of one another. Thus, for $i = 1, \ldots, n$, $t_i = s_i$ follows. This leaves the equality $w = \epsilon$, from which we conclude that $t = s$, as desired.

2. Exercise, using the Principle of Structural Induction for formulae. □

Using Lemma 3.2.1 we can easily prove the Unique Parsing Theorem:

Theorem 3.2.1   *1. Every term is either a variable or a constant symbol, or is a composite term of the form $ft_1 \ldots t_n$ for a unique function symbol f and unique terms $t_1, \ldots, t_n$.*

2. Every formula is uniquely of one of the following forms:

- *$s \approx t$,*
- *$Pt_1 \ldots t_n$,*
- *$\neg\varphi$,*
- *$(\varphi * \psi)$, with $* \in \{\wedge, \vee, \Rightarrow, \Leftrightarrow\}$, or*
- *$Qx\,\varphi$, with $Q \in \{\forall, \exists\}$.*

Theorem 3.2.1 says that terms and formulae have unique decompositions in terms of their constituents. This allows us to define functions over $\mathcal{T}$ and $\mathcal{L}$ inductively, using the *Principle of Structural Induction for terms* and the *Principle of Structural Induction for formulae*. The Unique Parsing Theorem says that in order to define a function σ on $\mathcal{T}$ it suffices to define σ on $\mathcal{V}$ and to define the action of σ on $ft_1 \ldots t_n$ under the hypothesis that $\sigma(t_1), \ldots, \sigma(t_n)$ are known, and that in order to define σ on $\mathcal{L}$ it suffices to define σ on atomic formulae, on formulae of the form $\neg\varphi$ and $Qx\,\varphi$ for $Q \in \{\forall, \exists\}$ under the assumption that $\sigma(\varphi)$ is known, and on formulae of the form $(\varphi * \psi)$ for $* \in \{\wedge, \vee, \Rightarrow, \Leftrightarrow\}$ under the assumption that $\sigma(\varphi)$ and $\sigma(\psi)$ are known. That such inductive definitions assign unique values to each term in $\mathcal{T}$ and to each formula in $\mathcal{L}$ is left to the reader to verify.

We give definitions for two important inductively defined functions on $\mathcal{T}$.

Definition 3.2.2 The function $Var : \mathcal{T} \longrightarrow 2^{\mathcal{V}}$ assigning to each term the set of variables *occurring* in that term is defined by

- $Var(x) = \{x\}$, and
- $Var(ft_1 \ldots t_n) = Var(t_1) \cup \ldots \cup Var(t_n)$.

If Σ is a signature, then any term t over Σ for which $Var(t) = \emptyset$ is said to be a *ground term over* Σ. The set of all ground terms over $\Sigma = \langle \mathcal{F}, \mathcal{P} \rangle$ is denoted $\mathcal{T}(\mathcal{F})$.

Definition 3.2.3 The function $| \cdot | : \mathcal{T} \longrightarrow N$ assigning to each term the *length* of the term is given by

- $|x| = 1$, and
- $|ft_1 \ldots t_n| = 1 + |t_1| + \ldots + |t_n|$.

3.3 Free and Bound Variables

Variables which occur in formulae are distinguished according to whether or not they are *bound*, i.e., according to whether or not they are in the scope of a quantifier. For example, the variable x is bound in the formula $\forall x \, (Px \wedge Qy)$, while the variable y is not, and all occurrences of variables in terms are clearly free. Definitions 3.3.1 and 3.3.2 rely on the Unique Parsing Theorem and on the Principle of Structural Induction for formulae.

Definition 3.3.1 The function $FV : \mathcal{L} \longrightarrow 2^{\mathcal{V}}$ assigning to each formula the set of *free variables* occurring in it is defined by

- $FV(s \approx t) = Var(s) \cup Var(t)$,
- $FV(Pt_1 \ldots t_n) = Var(t_1) \cup \ldots \cup Var(t_n)$,
- $FV(\neg\varphi) = FV(\varphi)$,
- $FV(\varphi * \psi) = FV(\varphi) \cup FV(\psi)$ for $* \in \{\wedge, \vee, \Rightarrow, \Leftrightarrow\}$, and
- $FV(Qx \, \varphi) = FV(\varphi) - \{x\}$ for $Q \in \{\forall, \exists\}$.

Definition 3.3.2 The function $BV : \mathcal{L} \longrightarrow 2^{\mathcal{V}}$ assigning to each formula the set of *bound variables* occurring in it is defined by

- $BV(s \approx t) = \emptyset$,

- $BV(Pt_1 \ldots t_n) = \emptyset,$

- $BV(\neg \varphi) = BV(\varphi),$

- $BV(\varphi * \psi) = BV(\varphi) \cup BV(\psi)$ for $* \in \{\wedge, \vee, \Rightarrow, \Leftrightarrow\}$, and

- $BV(Qx\,\varphi) = BV(\varphi) \cup \{x\}$ for $Q \in \{\forall, \exists\}$.

Note that the same variable can occur both free and bound in a given formula, and so we must refer to free and bound *occurrences* of variables, rather than simply to free and bound variables. Furthermore, for a given formula φ, it is not necessarily the case that $BV(\varphi) = Var(\varphi) - FV(\varphi)$. For example, if

$$\varphi = Pxy \Rightarrow \forall x \forall z\, (Qx \wedge Pxz),$$

then

$$
\begin{aligned}
FV(\varphi) &= FV(Pxy) \cup FV(\forall x \forall z\,(Qx \wedge Pxy)) \\
&= \{x,y\} \cup (FV(Qx \wedge Pxz) - \{x,z\}) \\
&= \{x,y\} \cup \emptyset \\
&= \{x,y\}
\end{aligned}
$$

and

$$
\begin{aligned}
BV(\varphi) &= BV(Pxy) \cup BV(\forall x \forall z\,(Qx \wedge Pxy)) \\
&= \emptyset \cup \{x,z\} \cup BV(Qx \wedge Pxz) \\
&= \{x,z\}.
\end{aligned}
$$

A formula in which no variable occurs free is said to be *closed*, or is called a *sentence*; a formula containing at least one free occurrence of a variable is *open*. A formula containing no quantifiers is said to be *quantifier-free*.

3.4 Substitutions

Formulae of first-order logic which are not closed contain free variables eligible for replacement by other terms. Such replacement, which gives rise to new and more complicated formulae, plays a fundamental role in deduction systems. We therefore consider it in detail.

Definition 3.4.1   A *substitution* is a function $\sigma : \mathcal{V} \longrightarrow \mathcal{T}$ such that the set

$$Dom(\sigma) = \{x \in \mathcal{V} \mid \sigma(x) \neq x\}$$

is finite.

We denote substitutions with lower case Greek letters like σ, τ, and θ. The *identity substitution*, denoted by ε, is the (unique) substitution σ such that $Dom(\sigma)$ is empty. We call the set $Dom(\sigma)$ the *domain* of σ and the set $Cod(\sigma) = \{\sigma(x) \mid x \in Dom(\sigma)\}$ the *codomain* of σ. A substitution is said to be a *ground substitution* if $Cod(\sigma)$ consists only of ground terms. If $Dom(\sigma) = \{x_1, \ldots, x_n\}$ and $\sigma(x_i) = t_i$ for $i = 1, \ldots, n$, then σ is often represented as

$$\sigma = \{x_1 \leftarrow t_1, \ldots, x_n \leftarrow t_n\},$$

where $\leftarrow$ is read as "is replaced by."

According to Section 2.2 the restriction of a substitution σ to a subset $\mathcal{W}$ of $\mathcal{V}$ is the function $\sigma \mid_{\mathcal{W}}: \mathcal{W} \to \mathcal{T}$ given by: $\sigma \mid_{\mathcal{W}} (x) = \sigma(x)$ if $x \in \mathcal{W}$ and $\sigma \mid_{\mathcal{W}} (x)$ is undefined otherwise. It is useful, however, to consider the restriction of a substitution again to be a substitution, i.e., to be a mapping from all of $\mathcal{V}$ to $\mathcal{T}$. For this reason we extend $\sigma \mid_{\mathcal{W}}$ to be the identity on variables not in $\mathcal{W}$, which gives

Definition 3.4.2 If $\mathcal{W} \subseteq \mathcal{V}$, then the *restriction* of the substitution σ to the set $\mathcal{W}$ of variables is defined by

$$\sigma \mid_{\mathcal{W}} (x) = \begin{cases} x & \text{if } x \notin \mathcal{W} \\ \sigma(x) & \text{otherwise} \end{cases}$$

Each substitution has (unique) inductively defined extensions to functions on terms and on formulae as in the next definition.

Definition 3.4.3 Let σ be a substitution. The *extension* σ' of σ is a function on $\mathcal{T}$ defined inductively by

- $\sigma'(x) = \sigma(x)$ if $x \in \mathcal{V}$, and

- $\sigma'(ft_1 \ldots t_n) = f(\sigma't_1) \ldots (\sigma't_n)$.

The *extension* σ^* of σ is a function on $\mathcal{L}$ defined inductively by

- $\sigma^*(Pt_1 \ldots t_n) = P(\sigma't_1) \ldots (\sigma't_n)$,

- $\sigma^*(s \approx t) = \sigma'(s) \approx \sigma'(t)$,

- $\sigma^*(\neg\varphi) = \neg(\sigma^*\varphi)$,

- $\sigma^*(\varphi * \psi) = (\sigma^*\varphi) * (\sigma^*\psi)$ for $* \in \{\wedge, \vee, \Rightarrow, \Leftrightarrow\}$,

- $\sigma^*(Qx\,\varphi) = Qx\,(\sigma^*\,|_{FV(Qx\varphi)}\,(\varphi))$ for $Q \in \{\forall, \exists\}$.

We see that by definition all variable occurrences in formulae except those which are bound are replaced. We will abuse both terminology and notation, referring to extensions σ' and σ^* of a substitution σ as substitutions, and denoting them both simply by σ. Since they are defined inductively, substitutions are uniquely determined by their behavior on variables. Indeed, we will see that if σ and τ are two substitutions agreeing on a term t (on the free variables of a formula φ), then $\sigma(t) = \tau(t)$ (resp., $\sigma(\varphi) = \tau(\varphi)$).

If t is a term and σ is a substitution, then the term $\sigma(t)$ is called an *instance* of t (and is called a *ground instance* of t) provided $Var(\sigma(t)) = \emptyset$. Similarly, if φ is a formula and σ is a substitution, then the formula $\sigma(\varphi)$ is called an *instance* of φ (and is called a *ground instance* of φ) provided $FV(\sigma(\varphi)) = \emptyset$.

Example 3.4.1   Let $t = f(x, g(x, y))$, $\varphi = Px \Rightarrow \exists x\, Qx$, and $\sigma = \{x \leftarrow f(a, y)\}$. Then

$$\sigma(t) = f(f(a, y), g(f(a, y), y))$$

is an instance of t and

$$\sigma(\varphi) = P(f(a, y)) \Rightarrow \exists x\, Qx$$

is an instance of φ.

Since substitutions are special kinds of functions, we have

Definition 3.4.4   Let σ and τ be substitutions. The *composition* of σ and τ is the substitution $\tau\sigma$ defined by $(\tau\sigma)x = \tau(\sigma(x))$ for all $x \in \mathcal{V}$.

Example 3.4.2   Let $\sigma = \{x \leftarrow fz, y \leftarrow a\}$, and $\tau = \{z \leftarrow b, y \leftarrow c\}$. Then $\tau\sigma = \{x \leftarrow fb, y \leftarrow a, z \leftarrow b\}$ and $\sigma\tau = \{x \leftarrow fz, y \leftarrow c, z \leftarrow b\}$.

It is easily verified that the set of substitutions forms a semigroup with identity under composition, i.e., that associativity—$(\theta\tau)\sigma = \theta(\tau\sigma)$ for all substitutions σ, τ, and θ—and the identity property—$\sigma\varepsilon = \sigma = \varepsilon\varphi$ for all substitutions σ—hold.

Although for all terms t and substitutions σ and τ we have $(\tau\sigma)(t) = \tau(\sigma(t))$, for an arbitrary formula φ, the relationship $(\tau\sigma)(\varphi) = \tau(\sigma(\varphi))$ need not hold. For example, if $\varphi = \forall z\, P(x, z)$ and if σ and τ are as in Example 3.4.2, then $(\tau\sigma)(\varphi) = \forall z\, P(fb, z)$ but $\tau(\sigma(\varphi)) = \forall z\, P(fz, z)$. The difficulty here is that in applying σ to φ, the variable z introduced by replacing x by $f(z)$ becomes bound and cannot be further instantiated, while in applying $\tau\sigma$ to φ, x is replaced directly by fb. To avoid such technicalities, we introduce a restriction on the application of substitutions.

Definition 3.4.5   A term t is *free for the variable x in φ* if either

- φ is atomic,

- $\varphi = \neg\psi$ and t is free for x in ψ,

- $\varphi = \varphi_1 * \varphi_2$ for $* \in \{\wedge, \vee, \Rightarrow, \Leftrightarrow\}$, and t is free for x in φ_1 and φ_2,

- $\varphi = Qx\,\psi$, or

- $\varphi = Qy\,\psi$, $x \neq y$, $Q \in \{\forall, \exists\}$, $y \notin Var(t)$, and t is free for x in ψ.

In other words, a term t is free for a variable x in the formula φ in case t can be substituted for x in φ without free variable capture.

Example 3.4.3   Let $\varphi = \forall x\,(Px \Rightarrow Q(x, fy))$. Then the term gy is free for y in φ, but gx is not because substitution would render bound the occurrence of x in gx.

When applying a substitution σ to a formula φ we will always require that, for every $x \in Dom(\sigma)$, the term $\sigma(x)$ is free for x in φ. Under this assumption, $(\tau\sigma)(\varphi) = \tau(\sigma(\varphi))$ indeed holds for all formulae φ.

Two final notions will be useful in the chapters to come. A substitution σ is *idempotent* if $Dom(\sigma) \cap Var(Cod(\sigma)) = \emptyset$, or equivalently, if $\sigma(\sigma(x)) = \sigma(x)$ for all $x \in \mathcal{V}$. If $\sigma = \{x_1 \leftarrow t_1, \ldots, x_n \leftarrow t_n\}$, then σ is idempotent iff none of the variables x_i appear in the terms t_j, for $i, j = 1, \ldots, n$. The substitutions σ and τ of Example 3.4.2 are both idempotent. The substitution $\theta = \{x \leftarrow fx\}$, on the other hand, is not.

Definition 3.4.6   1. A substitution ρ is a *renaming substitution* if there exists a substitution ρ^- such that $\rho\rho^- = \rho^-\rho = \varepsilon$ holds.

2. The term t is said to be a *variant* of the term s if there is a renaming substitution ρ such that $s = \rho(t)$ holds.

Formulated slightly differently, a renaming substitution is a bijection on $\mathcal{V}$. It follows immediately from the definition that the variant relation is an equivalence relation on terms. In addition, if s is an instance of t and t is also an instance of s, then s and t must be variants of one another.

4

Semantics of First-order Languages

4.1 Structures and Interpretations

Formulae, it must be remembered, are nothing more than words over an alphabet. But logical formulae were originally developed as a means of describing properties of mathematical structures, and so a reasonable semantics of a first-order language would be one which interprets its formulae in a concrete mathematical structure.

In assigning meaning to first-order formulae it is necessary to specify in which mathematical structure formulae are to be interpreted, as well as to indicate which functions over the structure the function symbols are intended to denote, and for which predicates over the structure the predicate symbols are intended to stand. In general, there are many such structures and many such ways of assigning functions and predicates over these structures to function and predicate symbols.

Consider, for instance, the signature of arithmetic introduced in Example 3.1.1 and let

$$\varphi = \forall x \forall y \left((x + y > x) \vee (y \approx 0) \right).$$

If we take the set N of natural numbers as the set in which our formulae are interpreted, and if we interpret the symbol 0 as the natural number zero, interpret $+$, $*$, and s as addition, multiplication, and the successor function on N, respectively, and interpret the predicate symbol $>$ as the greater-than relation on N, then φ yields a true statement in the structure $\mathcal{N}$ comprising the set N with the (standard) interpretation just specified. We say that $\mathcal{N}$ is a *model* for φ. If, on the other hand, we choose the set Z

of integers as our underlying set and choose the analogous interpretations for the function and predicate symbols, then the statement φ is false in the resulting structure $\mathcal{Z}$. That is, $\mathcal{Z}$ is *not* a model for φ.

Below we make precise the idea of a Σ-structure for any given signature Σ. Such a structure is determined by specifying an underlying set M, the assignment of an n-ary relation to each n-ary predicate symbol of Σ, and the assignment of an n-ary function to every n-ary function symbol of Σ. As suggested by the above example, it is in Σ-structures that first-order languages over the signature Σ are interpreted, and from Σ-structures that models for formulae are built.

Definition 4.1.1 Let $\Sigma = \langle \mathcal{F}, \mathcal{P} \rangle$ be a signature. A Σ-*structure* $\mathcal{M}$ is an ordered pair $\langle M, I \rangle$ such that

1. M is a nonempty set, called the *underlying set* or *carrier* of $\mathcal{M}$.

2. I is a function on $\mathcal{F} \cup \mathcal{P}$ such that

   - if $f \in \mathcal{F}_n$ then $I(f) : M^n \to M$ is an n-ary function, and
   - if $P \in \mathcal{P}_n$ then $I(P) \subseteq M^n$ is an n-ary relation on M.

We see that $\mathcal{N}$ and $\mathcal{Z}$ described above are Σ-structures when Σ is as in Example 3.1.1.

For a Σ-structure $\mathcal{M} = \langle M, I \rangle$ we will often write f^M and P^M instead of $I(f)$ and $I(P)$. When discussing a structure $\mathcal{M}$ in the following, we will always denote its carrier by M. We will often specify a structure $\mathcal{M}$ over a signature $\Sigma = \{f_1, ..., f_n, P_1, ..., P_m\}$ by $\langle M, f_1^M, ..., f_n^M, P_1^M, ..., P_m^M \rangle$.

In general, the meanings of terms and formulae will depend on the meanings of their free variables, predicate symbols, and function symbols. The meaning of a term or formula may vary as interpretations of its free variables vary. To describe the interpretations of variables on which the meanings of terms and formulae depend, we introduce the notion of a *valuation*.

Definition 4.1.2   1. A *valuation* in a Σ-structure $\mathcal{M}$ is a function $\beta : \mathcal{V} \to M$.

2. An *interpretation* $\mathcal{I}$ (over Σ) is an ordered pair $\langle \mathcal{M}, \beta \rangle$ comprising a Σ-structure $\mathcal{M}$ and a valuation β in $\mathcal{M}$.

Once we have an interpretation assigning meaning to the variables, function symbols, and predicate symbols of a first-order language, we can determine the meanings of arbitrary terms and formulae.

Definition 4.1.3   Let $\mathcal{I} = \langle \mathcal{M}, \beta \rangle$ be an interpretation. The function $\mathcal{I}_\beta : \mathcal{T} \to \mathcal{M}$ is defined by

- $\mathcal{I}_\beta(x) = \beta(x)$ for $x \in \mathcal{V}$, and

- $\mathcal{I}_\beta(ft_1...t_n) = f^M(\mathcal{I}_\beta(t_1), ..., \mathcal{I}_\beta(t_n))$ for $f \in \mathcal{F}_n$ and $t_1, ..., t_n \in \mathcal{T}$.

We identify the interpretation $\mathcal{I}$ and the mapping $\mathcal{I}_\beta$, denoting them both simply by $\mathcal{I}$ when this will not lead to confusion.

Example 4.1.1   Let Σ be the signature of arithmetic given in Example 3.1.1 and let β be any valuation such that $\beta(x) = 2$ and $\beta(y) = 4$. The term $y * (x + y)$ is then interpreted in the Σ-structure $\mathcal{N}$ as $4 *^N (2 +^N 4) = 24$.

The following shift operators on valuations and interpretations will also be useful as we assign meanings to formulae.

Definition 4.1.4   Let β be a valuation in $\mathcal{M}$, let x be a variable, and let $a \in M$. The valuation $\beta[x \to a]$ is defined by

$$\beta[x \to a](y) = \begin{cases} a & \text{if } y = x \\ \beta(y) & \text{otherwise} \end{cases}$$

If $\mathcal{I} = \langle \mathcal{M}, \beta \rangle$, then $\mathcal{I}[x \to a]$ is defined to be $\langle \mathcal{M}, \beta[x \to a] \rangle$.

In defining the model relation on formulae we use the colloquial notions of "and," "or," "not," "if-then," and "if-and-only-if." The use of these words is not entirely standardized—"or," for example, is frequently used in the sense of *exclusive or*, i.e., in the sense of either-or. But we will always use "or" in the inclusive sense: when we use an expression of the form "*A* or *B*," we will mean that *at least* one of *A* and *B* holds.

Definition 4.1.5   Let $\mathcal{I} = \langle \mathcal{M}, \beta \rangle$ be an interpretation. We define the *model relation* $\mathcal{I} \models \varphi$ inductively on the structure of formulae by:

$$
\begin{array}{lll}
\mathcal{I} \models s \approx t & \text{iff} & \mathcal{I}(s) = \mathcal{I}(t) \\
\mathcal{I} \models Pt_1...t_n & \text{iff} & (\mathcal{I}(t_1),...,\mathcal{I}(t_n)) \in P^M \\
\mathcal{I} \models \neg\varphi & \text{iff} & \mathcal{I} \models \varphi \text{ does not hold} \\
\mathcal{I} \models \varphi \wedge \psi & \text{iff} & \mathcal{I} \models \varphi \text{ and } \mathcal{I} \models \psi \\
\mathcal{I} \models \varphi \vee \psi & \text{iff} & \mathcal{I} \models \varphi \text{ or } \mathcal{I} \models \psi \\
\mathcal{I} \models \varphi \Rightarrow \psi & \text{iff} & \mathcal{I} \models \psi \text{ whenever } \mathcal{I} \models \varphi \\
\mathcal{I} \models \varphi \Leftrightarrow \psi & \text{iff} & \mathcal{I} \models \psi \text{ whenever } \mathcal{I} \models \varphi \\
& & \text{and } \mathcal{I} \models \varphi \text{ whenever } \mathcal{I} \models \psi \\
\mathcal{I} \models \forall x\,\varphi & \text{iff} & \text{for all } a \in M,\ \mathcal{I}[x \to a] \models \varphi \text{ holds} \\
\mathcal{I} \models \exists x\,\varphi & \text{iff} & \text{for some } a \in M,\ \mathcal{I}[x \to a] \models \varphi \text{ holds}
\end{array}
$$

Since we have chosen classical logic as our underlying logic, every statement of the form $\mathcal{I} \models \varphi$ is either true or false. If Φ is a set of formulae we write $\mathcal{I} \models \Phi$ in case $\mathcal{I} \models \varphi$ for each $\varphi \in \Phi$. If $\mathcal{I} \models \Phi$ we say that $\mathcal{I}$ *satisfies* Φ, or that $\mathcal{I}$ is a *model* for Φ. We say that $\mathcal{I}$ *falsifies* Φ if $\mathcal{I} \not\models \Phi$. A set of formulae is said to be *satisfiable* if it possesses a model.

If $\mathcal{I} = \langle \mathcal{M}, \beta \rangle$ satisfies Φ for each valuation β in $\mathcal{M}$, then we say that Φ is *valid in* $\mathcal{M}$ and write $\mathcal{M} \models \Phi$. The set of formulae Φ is *universally valid*, or simply *valid*, if it is true in every interpretation, i.e., if $\mathcal{I}$ satisfies Φ for every interpretation $\mathcal{I}$.

Example 4.1.2   Let Σ be the signature of Example 3.1.1. Then the formula $\varphi = \forall x \forall y\,((x < x + y) \vee (y \approx 0))$ is valid in $\mathcal{N}$ but is not valid in $\mathcal{Z}$ because it is falsified by any interpretation $\langle \mathcal{Z}, \beta \rangle$ such that $\beta(y) < 0$.

Example 4.1.3   Consider the signature Σ comprising binary function symbol $*$ and the constant symbol 1. Let Φ be the set of the following three formulae:

$$\forall x \forall y \forall z\,((x * y) * z \approx x * (y * z))$$
$$\forall x\,(x * 1 \approx x)$$
$$\forall x \exists y\,(x * y \approx 1).$$

The set Φ describes an axiom system for group theory. Let $G = \{a, b, c, d\}$ and let $f : G \times G \to G$ be defined by the following table:

f	a	b	c	d
a	a	b	c	d
b	b	a	d	c
c	c	d	a	b
d	d	c	b	a

Then under any interpretation of the variables, the structure $\mathcal{G} = \langle G, f, a \rangle$, where $*$ is interpreted as the function f on G and 1 is interpreted as the element a of G, is a model for Φ. That is, Φ is valid in $\mathcal{G}$.

By way of illustration we will verify the validity in $\mathcal{G}$ of the second axiom (the property of having an identity element). Let β be an arbitrary assignment in G and let $\mathcal{I} = \langle \mathcal{G}, \beta \rangle$. Then

$$\mathcal{I} \models \forall x\, (x * 1 \approx x)$$
$$\text{iff} \quad \mathcal{I}[x \to g] \models x * 1 \approx x \text{ for all } g \in G$$
$$\text{iff} \quad \mathcal{I}[x \to g](x * 1) = \mathcal{I}[x \to g](x) \text{ for all } g \in G$$
$$\text{iff} \quad f(g, a) = g \text{ for all } g \in G.$$

That the last line actually holds can be verified by referring directly to the table for f. We can similarly verify the validity in $\mathcal{G}$ of the other two axioms.

A further fundamental idea of logic is the notion of *semantic consequence*. Mathematical theorems are typically of the form: "Let the theory Φ be given. Then the following theorem holds... ." What is meant is that the theorem (actually just some formula φ) must be true in every model of the theory Φ. More precisely, φ must be true in every model of every axiom system Φ representing the theory Φ. We express this relation between Φ and φ by writing $\Phi \models \varphi$.

Definition 4.1.6 Let Φ be a set of formulae and let φ be a formula. We write $\Phi \models \varphi$ (φ *semantically follows* from Φ, or φ is a *semantic consequence* of Φ) if every model of Φ is also a model of φ. We write $\varphi \models \psi$ instead of $\{\varphi\} \models \psi$, and $\models \varphi$ in place of $\{\} \models \varphi$. We say that φ and ψ are *semantically equivalent*, denoted $\varphi \simeq \psi$, if $\varphi \models \psi$ and $\psi \models \varphi$.

Example 4.1.4 Let Φ be the axiom system for groups in Example 4.1.3, and let $\varphi = \forall x \exists y\, (y * x \approx 1)$. Then $\Phi \models \varphi$ holds since in every group the right inverse of an element is also a left inverse of that element, i.e., every group satisfies φ.

Observe that in none of its usages is $\models$ a symbol in the *object language*, i.e., a symbol in the language of first-order formulae; it belongs rather to the *metalanguage*, i.e., to the language in which we speak about the language of first-order logic. Although both $\Rightarrow$ and $\models$ are often read as "implies"— whether because of Theorem 4.1.1 below or out of sheer inaccuracy—it is extremely important that $\models$ and $\Rightarrow$ not be confused.

The next lemma further reflects our decision to work in classical logic.

Lemma 4.1.1   *Let Φ be a set of formulae and φ be a formula. Then*

$$\Phi \models \varphi \text{ iff } \Phi \cup \{\neg\varphi\} \text{ is unsatisfiable.}$$

Proof. We have that $\Phi \models \varphi$ holds iff every model of Φ is also a model of φ, and this holds iff there is no interpretation which is a model of Φ but not of φ. But this is the case precisely when there exists no interpretation which is a model of $\Phi \cup \{\neg\varphi\}$, i.e., iff $\Phi \cup \{\neg\varphi\}$ is unsatisfiable. □

The Deduction Theorem (Theorem 4.1.1) allows us to derive from a proof of the validity of the implication $\varphi_1 \wedge ... \wedge \varphi_n \Rightarrow \varphi$ the validity of a formula φ in all models of the axiom system $\Phi = \{\varphi_1, ..., \varphi_n\}$, and conversely. As a useful consequence we have $\Phi \cup \{\varphi_1\} \models \varphi$ iff $\Phi \models \varphi_1 \Rightarrow \varphi$, but note that, as discussed above, this fact does not in any way imply that $\Rightarrow$ and $\models$ are identical. A similar observation governs the relationship between the symbols $\Leftrightarrow$ of the object language and $\simeq$ of the metalanguage: although we see from Definition 4.1.6 that for any two formulae φ and ψ we have $\varphi \simeq \psi$ iff $\varphi \Leftrightarrow \psi$ is valid, the two symbols $\simeq$ and $\Leftrightarrow$ are in no way interchangeable.

Theorem 4.1.1   *(Deduction Theorem) Let $\Phi = \{\varphi_1, ..., \varphi_n\}$ be a set of formulae and let φ be a formula. Then*

$$\Phi \models \varphi \text{ iff } \models \varphi_1 \wedge ... \wedge \varphi_n \Rightarrow \varphi.$$

Proof. We have that $\Phi \models \varphi$ iff every interpretation satisfying φ_i, for $i = 1, ..., n$, also satisfies φ. This happens precisely when every interpretation which satisfies $\varphi_1 \wedge ... \wedge \varphi_n$ also satisfies φ, which in turn holds iff $\models \varphi_1 \wedge ... \wedge \varphi_n \Rightarrow \varphi$. □

As indicated above, the proof of a mathematical theorem is nothing more than a proof of a statement of the form $\Phi \models \varphi$. Under normal circumstances it is not practical to verify directly that such a satisfiability relation holds, since this requires considering all models of Φ, and in general there will be infinitely many. To verify, for instance, that the formula φ in Example 4.1.4 is a semantic consequence of Φ, one would have to verify that, in every group, the right inverse of an element is also a left inverse of that element. In the next chapter we will see ways to express semantic consequence as a syntactic relation, and, therefore, to prove that this relationship holds for a set of formulae Φ and a formula φ using a purely syntactic calculus of formal reasoning. This is the basic insight underlying the automation of mathematical deduction.

Suppose conversely that the formula φ does *not* follow from the axiom system Φ. At first glance, this appears to be an easier fact to establish: only one interpretation satisfying Φ but not φ must be exhibited. That is, only a single counterexample for $\Phi \models \varphi$ must be found. But although the semantic consequence relation does permit automatization, the search for a counterexample does not. The deep explanation for this is the *Undecidability Theorem* for first-order logic. A more superficial, but perhaps equally compelling, explanation is the widely observed mathematical phenomenon that the search for a counterexample to a conjecture is often at least as difficult as the search for a proof.

4.2   The Substitution Lemma

The next lemma formalizes our earlier observation that the interpretation of terms in a structure depends only on the accompanying valuation.

Lemma 4.2.1 *Let t be a term over Σ and let $\mathcal{I}_1 = \langle \mathcal{M}, \beta_1 \rangle$ and $\mathcal{I}_2 = \langle \mathcal{M}, \beta_2 \rangle$ be two interpretations over Σ. If $\beta_1(x) = \beta_2(x)$ holds for all $x \in Var(t)$, then $\mathcal{I}_1(t) = \mathcal{I}_2(t)$.*

Proof. By the Principle of Structural Induction for terms. If $t = y$ is a variable, then $\mathcal{I}_1(t) = \beta_1(y) = \beta_2(y) = \mathcal{I}_2(t)$. If $t = ft_1...t_n$ then $\mathcal{I}_1 = f^M(\mathcal{I}_1(t_1))...(\mathcal{I}_1(t_n))$. By the induction hypothesis, $\mathcal{I}_1(t_i) = \mathcal{I}_2(t_i)$ holds for all $i = 1, ..., n$, and so

$$
\begin{aligned}
\mathcal{I}_1(ft_1...t_n) &= f^M(\mathcal{I}_1(t_1))...(\mathcal{I}_1(t_n)) \\
&= f^M(\mathcal{I}_2(t_1))...(\mathcal{I}_2(t_n)) \\
&= \mathcal{I}_2(ft_1...t_n).
\end{aligned}
$$

$\square$

That substitution and interpretation are in some sense commutative is the content of

Lemma 4.2.2 *(Substitution Lemma) Let Σ be a signature, $\mathcal{M}$ be a Σ-structure, $\mathcal{I} = \langle \mathcal{M}, \beta \rangle$ be an interpretation, and t be a term. Then for every term s and every formula φ the following hold:*

1. *$\mathcal{I}[x \to \mathcal{I}(t)](s) = \mathcal{I}(s\{x \leftarrow t\})$.*

2. *$\mathcal{I}[x \to \mathcal{I}(t)] \models \varphi$ iff $\mathcal{I} \models \varphi\{x \leftarrow t\}$ provided t is free for x in φ.*

Proof. Let $\mathcal{I}' = \mathcal{I}[x \to \mathcal{I}(t)]$.

1. We prove the assertion by the Principle of Structural Induction for terms. First let s be a variable y distinct from x. Then

$$
\mathcal{I}'(y) = \beta[x \to \mathcal{I}(t)](y) = \beta(y) = \beta(y\{x \leftarrow t\}) = \mathcal{I}(y\{x \leftarrow t\}).
$$

For $s = x$ we have

$$\mathcal{I}'(x) = \beta[x \to \mathcal{I}(t)](x) = \mathcal{I}(t) = \mathcal{I}(x\{x \leftarrow t\}).$$

Finally, if $s = ft_1...t_n$ then by the induction hypothesis we have

$$
\begin{aligned}
\mathcal{I}'(ft_1...t_n) &= f^M(\mathcal{I}'(t_1), ..., \mathcal{I}'(t_n)) \\
&= f^M(\mathcal{I}(t_1\{x \leftarrow t\}), ..., \mathcal{I}(t_n\{x \leftarrow t\})) \\
&= \mathcal{I}((ft_1...t_n)\{x \leftarrow t\}).
\end{aligned}
$$

2. The proof is similar to that above, and is by the Principle of Structural Induction for formulae. We prove the theorem only for the formula $\varphi = \forall y \, \psi$ and leave the other cases as an exercise. Let t be free for x in φ.

   - Case 1: If $x \neq y$ then

     $$
     \begin{aligned}
     \mathcal{I}' \models \forall y \, \psi \quad &\text{iff} \quad \mathcal{I}'[y \to a] \models \psi \text{ for all } a \in M \\
     &\text{iff} \quad \mathcal{I}[y \to a][x \to \mathcal{I}(t)] \models \psi \text{ for all } a \in M.
     \end{aligned}
     $$

     By Lemma 4.2.1, $\mathcal{I}(t) = \mathcal{I}[y \to a](t)$ since $y \notin Var(t)$. This observation and the induction hypothesis result in

     $$
     \begin{aligned}
     \mathcal{I}' \models \forall y \, \psi \quad &\text{iff} \quad \mathcal{I}[y \to a][x \to \mathcal{I}(t)] \models \psi \text{ for all } a \in M \\
     &\text{iff} \quad \mathcal{I}[y \to a][x \to \mathcal{I}[y \to a](t)] \models \psi \text{ for all } a \in M \\
     &\text{iff} \quad \mathcal{I}[y \to a] \models \psi\{x \leftarrow t\} \text{ for all } a \in M \\
     &\text{iff} \quad \mathcal{I} \models \forall y \, (\psi\{x \leftarrow t\}) \\
     &\text{iff} \quad \mathcal{I} \models (\forall y \, \psi)\{x \leftarrow t\}.
     \end{aligned}
     $$

   - Case 2: If $x = y$ then

     $$\mathcal{I}' \models \forall x \, \psi \text{ iff } \mathcal{I}'[x \to a] \models \psi \text{ for all } a \in M.$$

     From $\mathcal{I}'[x \to a] = \mathcal{I}[x \to a]$ and $\forall x \, \psi = (\forall x \, \psi)\{x \leftarrow t\}$ follows

     $$
     \begin{aligned}
     \mathcal{I}' \models \forall x \, \psi \quad &\text{iff} \quad \mathcal{I}[x \to a] \models \psi \text{ for all } a \in M \\
     &\text{iff} \quad \mathcal{I} \models \forall x \, \psi \\
     &\text{iff} \quad \mathcal{I} \models (\forall x \, \psi)\{x \leftarrow t\}.
     \end{aligned}
     $$

This proves the assertion of the lemma. □

Example 4.2.1 Let Σ be a signature with unary function symbols s and p and the constant symbol 0. Let $\mathcal{Z}$ be the Σ-structure comprising the set Z of integers together with any function which assigns to the constant symbol 0 the integer zero (also denoted 0), to the symbol s the successor function on Z (so that $s^Z(n) = n + 1$), and to the symbol p the predecessor function on Z (so that $p^Z(n) = n - 1$). Let φ be the formula $p(p(z)) \approx 0$. Then for any interpretation $\mathcal{I} = \langle \mathcal{Z}, \beta \rangle$, $\mathcal{I}[z \to 2] \models \varphi$, and so by the Substitution Lemma $\mathcal{I} \models \varphi\{z \leftarrow s(s(0))\} \approx 0$ also holds, i.e. $I \models p(p(s(s(0)))) \approx 0$, holds as well.

Corollary 4.2.1 *Let φ be a formula and let t be free for x in φ. Then*

1. *$\forall x \, \varphi \models \varphi\{x \leftarrow t\}$.*

2. *$\varphi\{x \leftarrow t\} \models \exists x \, \varphi$.*

The second part of this corollary can be expressed as follows: every interpretation which falsifies $\exists x \, \varphi$ also falsifies $\varphi\{x \leftarrow t\}$.

The next result is a counterpart for formulae to Lemma 4.2.1, and says that the interpretation of an arbitrary formula in a given structure $\mathcal{M}$ is completely determined by the interpretations of its free variables. In particular, the interpretation of a *closed* formula—i.e., of a formula with no free variables—is independent of any valuation on variables. Note, however, that because the model relation for quantified formulae is defined in terms of their instances, which are not in general subformulae of them, an induction principle other than the Principle of Structural Induction for formulae is sometimes needed to prove satisfaction properties of models. We define the *rank* of a formula φ by

- $rank(\varphi) = 0$ if φ is atomic,

- $rank(\neg\varphi) = rank(\varphi) + 1$,

- $rank(\varphi * \psi) = max(rank(\varphi), rank(\psi)) + 1$ if $* \in \{\wedge, \vee, \Rightarrow, \Leftrightarrow\}$, and

- $rank(Qx \, \varphi) = rank(\varphi) + 1$ if $Q \in \{\forall, \exists\}$.

It is not hard to see that the rank function is well-defined and well-founded. Induction on the rank of formulae is a standard proof technique, of which we will make repeated use in proving semantic properties of formulae. We now use it to prove

Lemma 4.2.3 *Let φ be a formula over Σ and let $\mathcal{I}_1 = \langle \mathcal{M}, \beta_1 \rangle$ and $\mathcal{I}_2 = \langle \mathcal{M}, \beta_2 \rangle$ be two interpretations over Σ. If $\beta_1(x) = \beta_2(x)$ holds for all $x \in FV(\varphi)$, then $\mathcal{I}_1 \models \varphi$ iff $\mathcal{I}_2 \models \varphi$.*

Proof. By induction on the rank of φ. We show the assertion of the lemma in the case $\varphi = \forall x \, \psi$. The other cases are left as exercises.

First note that $\mathcal{I}_1 \models \forall x \, \psi$ iff $\mathcal{I}_1[x \to a] \models \psi$ for all $a \in M$, and that $\mathcal{I}_2 \models \forall x \, \psi$ iff $\mathcal{I}_2[x \to a] \models \psi$ for all $a \in M$. Let $a \in M$ be arbitrary. Then $\mathcal{I}_1[x \to a] = \langle \mathcal{M}, \beta_1[x \to a] \rangle$ and similarly $\mathcal{I}_2[x \to a] = \langle \mathcal{M}, \beta_2[x \to a] \rangle$. Since $\beta_1(y) = \beta_2(y)$ for all $y \in FV(\psi)$ by assumption, we have $\beta_1[x \to a](y) = \beta_2[x \to a](y)$ for all $y \in FV(\varphi) = FV(\psi) - \{x\}$. In addition, $\beta_1[x \to a](x) = a = \beta_2[x \to a]$, so that $\beta_1[x \to a](y) = \beta_2[x \to a](y)$ holds for all $y \in FV(\psi)$. By the induction hypothesis, $\mathcal{I}_1[x \to a] \models \psi$ iff $\mathcal{I}_2[x \to a] \models \psi$. But since a is arbitrary, we may therefore conclude that $\mathcal{I}_1 \models \forall x \, \psi$ iff $\mathcal{I}_2 \models \forall x \, \psi$. □

A formula φ is *rectified* if $FV(\varphi) \cap BV(\varphi) = \emptyset$ and if different quantifiers bind different variables. It is easy to see that the bound variables in a formula can be renamed without changing the meaning of the formula. For every formula φ, we can construct through renaming a rectified formula φ' which is semantically equivalent to φ. We illustrate with an example.

Example 4.2.2   Let

$$\varphi = \forall x\,(Rxy \Rightarrow Px) \wedge \forall y\,(\neg Rxy \wedge \forall x\,Px).$$

Then

$$\varphi' = \forall z\,(Rzy \Rightarrow Pz) \wedge \forall v\,(\neg Rxv \wedge \forall w\,Pw)$$

is a rectified formula which is semantically equivalent to φ.

Without loss of generality, then, we may assume that all formulae appearing in the remainder of this text are rectified, and we may rename bound variables whenever we find it convenient to do so.

5

The Gentzen Calculus G

5.1 The Calculus G

One of the central concepts introduced in the previous chapter is the notion of semantic consequence and, as indicated, mathematical theorem development is based on this notion. Unfortunately, semantic consequence as defined there is not mechanizable, since it is not possible in general to investigate all of the—potentially infinitely many—models of a given set of formulae. In this chapter we introduce a notion of *syntactic consequence* and prove that it is equivalent to that of semantic consequence. The notion of syntactic consequence we will discuss corresponds to an efficiently mechanizable calculus, namely, the *Gentzen calculus G* of Gerhard Gentzen.

A calculus comprises a set Ψ of logical axioms and a set of syntactic inference rules for deriving new formulae from already derived formulae. To prove in a calculus that a formula φ follows from a set Φ of formulae, the inference rules are used to derive new formulae from $\Phi \cup \Psi$, and then to derive new formulae from $\Phi \cup \Psi$ and the new formulae, and so on, until the desired formula φ is produced. The resulting proof is a "positive" proof of φ from Φ, and can be used to show that $\Phi \models \varphi$ holds in every model of the axioms of the calculus, provided the inference rules of the calculus preserve satisfiability. But it is also possible to prove $\Phi \models \varphi$ using a *proof by contradiction*. In such a "negative" proof one derives in the calculus a contradiction from the assumption that $\Phi \cup \{\neg\varphi\}$ is satisfiable, i.e., from the assumption that φ is falsifiable by some model of Φ. In classical calculi, such a contradiction establishes that $\Phi \cup \{\neg\varphi\}$ is unsatisfiable and so by Lemma 4.1.1, φ must be a semantic consequence of Φ. It follows that positive and negative classical calculi are equivalent.

Although we will not otherwise discuss them in this book, we note that Hilbert-style calculi—which typically consist of a number of logical axioms and a few rules of inference, and are taken in most logic texts to be the basic characterization of proof systems—are positive calculi. Gentzen calculi, on the other hand, more accurately capture the way that mathematicians reason in practice, comprising as they do few logical axioms and many (at least two for each logical symbol) easily understandable rules of inference. As we will see, Gentzen calculi can be regarded both as positive calculi and as negative calculi: proofs in Gentzen calculi are typically *constructed* as negative proofs but are most often *read* as positive proofs. The Gentzen calculus G presented in this book is a negative calculus. In fact, most implemented calculi are negative calculi. In Chapter 7 we will become acquainted with one of the most important classes of negative calculi, namely, resolution calculi.

In the context of automated deduction, two properties of a calculus are especially important. First, a calculus must be such that no false conclusions can be drawn from it. For a negative calculus, this means that if a contradiction is derivable from $\Phi \cup \{\neg\varphi\}$ then $\Phi \models \varphi$ must hold, and for a positive calculus, this means that if φ is derivable from Φ then $\Phi \models \varphi$ must hold. These properties are referred to as *soundness*. Secondly, a negative calculus must be such that a refutation of $\Phi \cup \{\neg\varphi\}$ can always be found if φ is a semantic consequence of Φ. That is, a negative calculus must be such that a contradiction can always be derived from $\Phi \cup \{\neg\varphi\}$ if φ is a semantic consequence of Φ. A positive calculus, on the other hand, must be such that if φ is a semantic consequence of Φ then there exists a derivation of φ from Φ and the axioms of the calculus. These properties are called *refutation completeness* of negative calculi and *completeness* of positive calculi, respectively. Of course, the undecidability of predicate logic guarantees that we cannot, in general, expect a calculus actually to *determine* whether or not φ semantically follows from Φ; generally speaking, neither a positive nor a negative calculus will be able to determine (syntactically) that a formula φ is *not* a semantic consequence of Φ.

In this book we consider only first-order languages not containing the symbol $\approx$. The reason for this restriction is that the equality symbol requires rather special handling, and a detailed treatment of the theory of equational proofs would take us too far from the main topics of this book. The interested reader is referred to [Gal86].

By the Deduction Theorem (Theorem 4.1.1), φ is a semantic consequence of $\Phi = \{\varphi_1, \ldots, \varphi_n\}$ iff $\varphi_1 \wedge \ldots \wedge \varphi_n \Rightarrow \varphi$ is universally valid. We may therefore view all questions of semantic consequence as questions about the validity of single (perhaps complicated) formulae, and we need only require of a calculus intended to capture semantic consequence that it be capable of capturing universal validity. The essential motivation behind negative Gentzen calculi is thus the search for a counterexample for a (perhaps complicated) formula φ to be proved, i.e., an interpretation falsifying φ is sought.

Before giving its formal definition, consider the following example illustrating the fundamental notions of the Gentzen calculus G.

Example 5.1.1   1. Let P and Q be propositions, and suppose we must show that the formula

$$\varphi = (P \Rightarrow Q) \Rightarrow (\neg Q \Rightarrow \neg P)$$

is universally valid. Our strategy is to suppose that there is some interpretation $\mathcal{I}$ which falsifies φ and to derive a contradiction based on this assumption. Then from the fact that no interpretation falsifies φ, i.e., that every interpretation satisfies φ, it will follow that φ is valid.

To specify an interpretation falsifying φ, we build a table with two columns. In the left column we write formulae that $\mathcal{I}$ must satisfy, and in the right column we write formulae that $\mathcal{I}$ must falsify (see Table 5.1 below). Since $\mathcal{I}$ must falsify φ, we write φ in the right column.

In order to falsify φ, by Definition 4.1.5, $\mathcal{I}$ must satisfy the formula $P \Rightarrow Q$ and falsify $\neg Q \Rightarrow \neg P$. Accordingly, we write the former in the left column and the latter in the right.

Next we turn our attention to the right column. In order to falsify $\neg Q \Rightarrow \neg P$, $\mathcal{I}$ must satisfy $\neg Q$ and falsify $\neg P$. We therefore write $\neg Q$ in the left column and $\neg P$ in the right column.

If $\neg Q$ is to be satisfied, then Q must be falsified, so we write Q in the right column. Similarly, P is written in the left column.

Now it remains to ensure that $\mathcal{I}$ satisfies $P \Rightarrow Q$ in the right column. For this, $\mathcal{I}$ must either falsify P or satisfy Q. If $\mathcal{I}$ is to falsify P, we must write P in the right column. But this creates a situation in which

TABLE 5.1.

TRUE	FALSE
	$(P \Rightarrow Q) \Rightarrow (\neg Q \Rightarrow \neg P)$
$P \Rightarrow Q$	$\neg Q \Rightarrow \neg P$
$P \Rightarrow Q,\ \neg Q$	$\neg P$
$P \Rightarrow Q,\ P$	Q
CASE 1: P	Q, P
CASE 2: Q, P	Q

the interpretation $\mathcal{I}$ must both satisfy and falsify P, since P appears in both columns, and this is obviously impossible. If, on the other hand, $\mathcal{I}$ is to satisfy Q, we find ourselves in a similar situation: we must find an interpretation which both satisfies and falsifies Q. The only possible conclusion is that there exists no interpretation $\mathcal{I}$ which falsifies φ. In other words, every interpretation satisfies φ, and so φ is universally valid.

2. Let Σ be a signature comprising a constant symbol a and a unary predicate symbol P, and suppose we want to prove the formula

$$\varphi = \forall x\, P(x) \Rightarrow \exists y\, P(y).$$

Again, we seek an interpretation which falsifies φ, and so we write the formula in the right column of a table. Proceeding as in the first part of this example, we write $\forall x\, P(x)$ in the left column and $\exists y\, P(y)$ in the right. If $\mathcal{I}$ satisfies $\forall x\, P(x)$, then, by Corollary 4.2.1, $\mathcal{I}$ satisfies $P(a)$ since a is free for x in $P(x)$. We may therefore write $P(a)$ in the left column. Similarly, if $\mathcal{I}$ falsifies $\exists x\, P(x)$, then, again by Corollary 4.2.1, $\mathcal{I}$ falsifies $P(a)$ in particular, and so we may write $P(a)$ in the right column. Therefore $\mathcal{I}$ must both satisfy and falsify $P(a)$. Since this is impossible, the proof is complete (see Table 5.2).

There is a duality between proofs in the Gentzen calculus G and tables of the kind generated above to falsify formulae. Gentzen calculi operate on ordered pairs $\langle \Phi, \Psi \rangle$ of sets of formulae, called *sequents* and are normally written in the form $\Phi \to \Psi$. For this reason, Gentzen calculi are often called *sequent calculi*. In Φ are formulae which must be satisfied, and in Ψ are formulae which must be falsified, in order to falsify a given formula φ.

To represent a proof of a formula φ in G, we may consider the rows of Tables 5.1 and 5.2 as sequents of the form $\Phi \to \Psi$, with the set Φ of formulae on the left of an arrow representing the formulae in the row which appear in the left column of the table, and the set Ψ of formulae on the right of an arrow representing the formulae in the row which appear in the right column of the table. We then think of such a table as being turned upside down, so that it may be regarded as an ordered labeled tree whose

TABLE 5.2.

TRUE	FALSE
	$\forall x\, P(x) \Rightarrow \exists y\, P(y)$
$\forall x\, P(x)$	$\exists y\, P(y)$
$P(a)$	$\exists y\, P(y)$
$P(a)$	$P(a)$

root is labeled with the sequent $\to \varphi$. In this manner Table 5.1 gives rise to the following proof tree for the formula $P \Rightarrow Q \Rightarrow \neg Q \Rightarrow \neg P$:

$$\frac{\dfrac{P \to Q, P \qquad\qquad\qquad\qquad Q, P \to Q}{P \Rightarrow Q, P \to Q}}{\dfrac{\dfrac{}{P \Rightarrow Q, \neg Q \to \neg P}}{\dfrac{P \Rightarrow Q \to \neg Q \Rightarrow \neg P}{\to (P \Rightarrow Q) \Rightarrow (\neg Q \Rightarrow \neg P)}}}$$

The proof of the formula $(P \Rightarrow Q) \Rightarrow (\neg Q \Rightarrow \neg P)$ now consists in the fact that all leaves of the tree are labeled with sequents of the form $\Phi \to \Psi$ for which $\Phi \cap \Psi \neq \emptyset$. Such sequents will serve as the axioms of G (see Definition 5.1.1 below).

There are two different ways in which to read such a proof tree (equivalently, to prove a formula). The *analytical* method is that which is used in the construction of the above tables and hence—practically speaking—of proof trees. With this "negative" method, the formula φ to be proved is repeatedly dissected into its constituents as we try to find an interpretation which falsifies it; the proof tree is read from the root to the leaves. The *synthetic* method, on the other hand, begins with the leaves of the tree, and thus from the axioms of the calculus. Proceeding from the axioms, new consequences are derived and new formulae *synthesized*. The synthetic method reflects both the "positive" proof style and the way in which we most commonly read proofs, if not the manner in which we actually construct them. Of course, it is not surprising that, for the construction of proof trees, the analytic method is more amenable than the synthetic: it is certainly easier to stepwise decompose a complex formula into its constituents than to construct, from the simplest building blocks, a complicated formula.

In order to formally specify the Gentzen calculus G—and indeed in order to specify *any* calculus—it is necessary to state the logical axioms and the inference rules from which its proofs are to be constructed. Although we have informally encountered the axioms and many of the inference rules of G in Example 5.1.1, we describe the formal calculus in its entirety now. As is customary, we write Φ, φ instead of $\Phi \cup \{\varphi\}$.

Definition 5.1.1

1. A *sequent* is an ordered pair $\langle \Phi, \Psi \rangle$ of sets of formulae. We usually write $\Phi \to \Psi$ for the sequent $\langle \Phi, \Psi \rangle$. If Φ is the empty set we write $\to \Psi$, and if Ψ is the empty set we write $\Phi \to$. The set Φ is called the *antecedent*, and Ψ is called the *succedent*, of the sequent.

2. The *Gentzen calculus G* is the calculus whose axioms are all sequents of the form $\Phi \to \Psi$ such that $\Phi \cap \Psi \neq \emptyset$, and whose inference rules are those given in Table 5.3.

If, as indicated in the above discussion, we regard the sequent $\Phi \to \Psi$ as a set Φ of formulae to be satisfied and a set Ψ of formulae to be falsified, then the axioms of G represent contradictions. Since our calculus is a negative Gentzen calculus, we seek to produce a contradiction from the negation of a formula to be proved from a set of axioms. In thinking of proofs synthetically, therefore, sequents representing contradictions are precisely what we should take as axioms for G.

The sequents appearing under the lines in the inference rules of Table 5.3 are called the *conclusions* of the rules, and those appearing above the line are called *premises*. Note that the rules of G are nondeterministic, in the sense that the order of application of the rules is not specified, and that the term t in the rule ($\forall$-left) and in the rule ($\exists$-right) is unspecified. Deduction in the Gentzen calculus G can therefore be implemented by a wide variety of concrete algorithms.

The variable y in the rule ($\exists$-left) and in the rule ($\forall$-right) is called the *eigenvariable* of the rule, and the condition that y is free for x in φ and that $y \notin (FV(\Phi) \cup FV(\Psi) \cup FV(\varphi)) - \{x\}$ is called the *eigenvariable condition*. The idea behind the eigenvariable condition is that since the variable y does not occur in formulae appearing in the given deduction, it behaves like an "arbitrary constant." Thus in applying the rule ($\forall$-right), once φ has been shown to hold for the specific variable y we may deduce that φ holds for all x. Similarly, in applying the rule ($\exists$-left), if we know that there exists a y satisfying φ and have made no assumptions about y (i.e., y is not in $(FV(\Phi) \cup FV(\Psi) \cup FV(\varphi)) - \{x\}$), then we know that $\exists x \, \varphi$ holds.

It is at first surprising that the formula $\forall x \, \varphi$ in the conclusion of the rule ($\forall$-left) also appears among its premises, and similarly for $\exists x \, \varphi$ in the rule ($\exists$-right). These repeated occurrences underscore the nondeterminism of the inference rules: the same rule can be applied over and over again to the same premise. Example 5.1.2 illustrates the utility of these inference rules. In that example, the elements of antecedents and succedents of sequents are listed without set brackets. We will follow this convention throughout this book.

Example 5.1.2   Let $\varphi = \exists x \, (P(x) \Rightarrow \forall y \, P(y))$. The formula φ is universally valid (the reader will want to verify this). The following tree constitutes a proof for φ.

TABLE 5.3.

- *Conjunction* (∧-left, ∧-right):

$$\frac{\Phi, \varphi, \psi \;\rightarrow\; \Psi}{\Phi, \varphi \wedge \psi \;\rightarrow\; \Psi} \qquad \frac{\Phi \;\rightarrow\; \Psi, \varphi \qquad \Phi \;\rightarrow\; \Psi, \psi}{\Phi \;\rightarrow\; \Psi, \varphi \wedge \psi}$$

- *Disjunction* (∨-left, ∨-right):

$$\frac{\Phi, \varphi \;\rightarrow\; \Psi \qquad \Phi, \psi \;\rightarrow\; \Psi}{\Phi, \varphi \vee \psi \;\rightarrow\; \Psi} \qquad \frac{\Phi \;\rightarrow\; \Psi, \varphi, \psi}{\Phi \;\rightarrow\; \Psi, \varphi \vee \psi}$$

- *Implication* (⇒-left, ⇒-right):

$$\frac{\Phi \;\rightarrow\; \Psi, \varphi \qquad \Phi, \psi \;\rightarrow\; \Psi}{\Phi, \varphi \Rightarrow \psi \;\rightarrow\; \Psi} \qquad \frac{\Phi, \varphi \;\rightarrow\; \Psi, \psi}{\Phi \;\rightarrow\; \Psi, \varphi \Rightarrow \psi}$$

- *Equivalence* (⇔-left, ⇔-right):

$$\frac{\Phi \;\rightarrow\; \Psi, \varphi, \psi \qquad \Phi, \varphi, \psi \;\rightarrow\; \Psi}{\Phi, \varphi \Leftrightarrow \psi \;\rightarrow\; \Psi} \qquad \frac{\Phi, \varphi \;\rightarrow\; \Psi, \psi \qquad \Phi, \psi \;\rightarrow\; \Psi, \varphi}{\Phi \;\rightarrow\; \Psi, \varphi \Leftrightarrow \psi}$$

- *Negation* (¬-left, ¬-right):

$$\frac{\Phi \;\rightarrow\; \Psi, \varphi}{\Phi, \neg\varphi \;\rightarrow\; \Psi} \qquad \frac{\Phi, \varphi \;\rightarrow\; \Psi}{\Phi \;\rightarrow\; \Psi, \neg\varphi}$$

- *Universal Quantification* (∀-left, ∀-right):

$$\frac{\Phi, \varphi\{x \leftarrow t\}, \forall x\, \varphi \;\rightarrow\; \Psi}{\Phi, \forall x\, \varphi \;\rightarrow\; \Psi} \qquad \frac{\Phi \;\rightarrow\; \Psi, \varphi\{x \leftarrow y\}}{\Phi \;\rightarrow\; \Psi, \forall x\, \varphi}$$

- *Existential Quantification* (∃-left, ∃-right):

$$\frac{\Phi, \varphi\{x \leftarrow y\} \;\rightarrow\; \Psi}{\Phi, \exists x\, \varphi \;\rightarrow\; \Psi} \qquad \frac{\Phi \;\rightarrow\; \Psi, \varphi\{x \leftarrow t\}, \exists x\, \varphi}{\Phi \;\rightarrow\; \Psi, \exists x\, \varphi}$$

In the quantification rules, y is assumed to be free for x in φ and is assumed not to appear in $(FV(\Phi) \cup FV(\Psi) \cup FV(\varphi)) - \{x\}$. The term t is an arbitrary term which is free for x in φ.

$$\frac{P(u), P(z) \;\rightarrow\; \exists x\,(P(x) \Rightarrow \forall y\, P(y)), \forall y\, P(y), P(z)}{P(u) \;\rightarrow\; \exists x\,(P(x) \Rightarrow \forall y\, P(y)), P(z) \Rightarrow \forall y\, P(y), P(z)}$$ $(\Rightarrow\text{-right})$

$$\frac{}{P(u) \;\rightarrow\; \exists x\,(P(x) \Rightarrow \forall y\, P(y)), P(z)}$$ $(\exists\text{-right})$

$$\frac{}{P(u) \;\rightarrow\; \exists x\,(P(x) \Rightarrow \forall y\, P(y)), \forall y\, P(y)}$$ $(\forall\text{-right})$

$$\frac{}{\rightarrow\; \exists x\,(P(x) \Rightarrow \forall y\, P(y)), P(u) \Rightarrow \forall y\, P(y)}$$ $(\Rightarrow\text{-right})$

$$\frac{}{\rightarrow\; \exists x\,(P(x) \Rightarrow \forall y\, P(y))}$$ $(\exists\text{-right})$

If, in the first step reading bottom-to-top, we had simply derived the sequent $\rightarrow\;\; P(u) \Rightarrow \forall y\, P(y)$, then the above proof would have been impossible since the substitution $\{y \leftarrow u\}$ is not permitted in applying the rule ($\forall$-right).   .

Although in practice they are almost always derived in a bottom-to-top (i.e., analytic) manner, as mentioned after Example 5.1.1, proof trees may also be considered as having been synthesized top-to-bottom. Having discussed them informally at some length, we now formally define the proof trees of G.

Definition 5.1.2 Let φ be a formula. A *proof tree (in G) for* φ is a finite labeled tree whose nodes are labeled with sequents, whose root is labeled with $\rightarrow \varphi$, and all of whose leaves are labeled with axioms of G. If a node k is labeled with $\Phi \rightarrow \Psi$, then the children of k must be labeled with the premises from which $\Phi \rightarrow \Psi$ follows by one of the inference rules of G. A formula φ is said to be *provable* (in G) if there is a proof tree (in G) for φ.

We usually draw proof trees "upside down," so that the leaves of the tree are above its root on the written page.

Example 5.1.3 Let $\varphi = (\forall x\, P(x) \wedge \exists y\, Q(y)) \Rightarrow (P(f(v)) \wedge \exists z\, Q(z))$. One possible proof tree for φ is given below.

$$\frac{\forall x\, P(x), Q(u) \;\rightarrow\; \exists z\, Q(z), Q(u)}{\forall x\, P(x), Q(u) \;\rightarrow\; \exists z\, Q(z)}$$

$$\frac{\forall x\, P(x), P(f(v)), \exists y\, Q(y) \;\rightarrow\; P(f(v))}{\forall x\, P(x), \exists y\, Q(y) \;\rightarrow\; P(f(v))} \qquad \frac{}{\forall x\, P(x), \exists y\, Q(y) \;\rightarrow\; \exists z\, Q(z)}$$

$$\frac{\forall x\, P(x), \exists y\, Q(y) \;\rightarrow\; P(f(v)) \wedge \exists z\, Q(z)}{\forall x\, P(x) \wedge \exists y\, Q(y) \;\rightarrow\; P(f(v)) \wedge \exists z\, Q(z)}$$

$$\frac{}{\rightarrow\; (\forall x\, P(x) \wedge \exists y\, Q(y)) \Rightarrow (P(f(v)) \wedge \exists z\, Q(z))}$$

The rule ($\exists$-left) is used in the first inference of the left fork of the proof tree, and the rules ($\exists$-right) and ($\forall$-left) are used in the first two inferences of the right fork of the proof tree. The rules ($\wedge$-right), ($\wedge$-left), and ($\Rightarrow$-right) are used in the remaining derivation steps.

Observe that in the application of the rules ($\forall$-left) and ($\exists$-right), the terms $f(v)$ and u must be substituted for the bound variable x so that the resulting sequents are axioms. Below we will develop a procedure for carrying out such substitutions systematically.

In proving the completeness of the Gentzen calculus G we will need to generalize the notion of a proof tree. The next definition is adequate for our purposes. Note that, by contrast with proof trees, the derivation trees of the next definition may be infinite, and their leaves, if indeed they have any, need not be labeled with axioms.

Definition 5.1.3 A labeled tree T is a *derivation tree (in G)* if its nodes are labeled with sequents, and if for each node k labeled with $\Phi \to \Psi$, the children of k are labeled with the premises from which $\Phi \to \Psi$ follows by one of the inference rules of G. If the root of T is labeled with the sequent $\to \varphi$, then T is a *derivation tree (in G) for φ*.

Like proof trees, derivation trees are drawn "upside down." We will also need to extend Definition 4.1.5 to sequents.

Definition 5.1.4 (Model relationship for sequents) Let $\mathcal{I}$ be an interpretation. Then $\mathcal{I}$ *satisfies* the sequent $\Phi \to \Psi$, denoted $\mathcal{I} \models \Phi \to \Psi$, if either $\mathcal{I} \not\models \varphi$ for some $\varphi \in \Phi$ or $\mathcal{I} \models \psi$ for some $\psi \in \Psi$; in this case the sequent $\Phi \to \Psi$ is said to be *satisfiable*. The interpretation $\mathcal{I}$ *falsifies* a sequent if $\mathcal{I}$ does not satisfy it. The sequent $\Phi \to \Psi$ is *universally valid* if every interpretation satisfies it. An interpretation $\mathcal{I}$ satisfies a set S of sequents precisely when it satisfies every sequent in S.

For any sequent $\Phi \to \Psi$, this definition says that if $\mathcal{I}$ satisfies $\Phi \to \Psi$ and also satisfies all formulae in Φ, then it must satisfy at least one formula in Ψ. We may therefore think of a set Φ on the left side of a sequent as representing the conjunction of its constituent formulae and a set Ψ on the right side as representing the disjunction of its constituent formulae. That is, if Φ is a set of formulae, and if we let

$$\bigwedge \Phi = \bigwedge_{\varphi \in \Phi} \varphi \quad \text{and} \quad \bigvee \Phi = \bigvee_{\varphi \in \Phi} \varphi,$$

then for any interpretation $\mathcal{I}$ we have

$$\mathcal{I} \models \Phi \to \Psi \quad \text{iff } \mathcal{I} \models \bigwedge \Phi \Rightarrow \bigvee \Psi.$$

The sequent $\Phi \to \Psi$ and the formula $\bigwedge \Phi \Rightarrow \bigvee \Psi$ are therefore semantically equivalent. In particular, the sequent $\to \psi$ is semantically equivalent to the formula ψ and the sequent $\varphi \to$ is semantically equivalent to $\neg\varphi$; we often blur the distinction between these sequents and the formulae corresponding to them.

Example 5.1.4   Let $S = \{(P \Rightarrow Q) \to \neg Q \Rightarrow \neg P\}$. Then S is semantically equivalent to the formula $(P \Rightarrow Q) \Rightarrow (\neg Q \Rightarrow \neg P)$.

The remainder of this section is devoted to proving the soundness of the Gentzen calculus G, i.e., to proving that every sequent provable in G is universally valid. We first show that the axioms enjoy this property.

Lemma 5.1.1   *Every axiom of G is a universally valid sequent.*

Proof. Every axiom is of the form $\Phi, \varphi \to \varphi, \Psi$. If there were some interpretation $\mathcal{I}$ falsifying this sequent, then $\mathcal{I}$ would be such that $\mathcal{I} \models \varphi$ and simultaneously $\mathcal{I} \not\models \varphi$. Clearly there cannot be any such interpretation. □

To see that the inference rules of G preserve validity, we will need to know that replacement by free variables does likewise.

Lemma 5.1.2   *Suppose $y \notin FV(\varphi) - \{x\}$ and y is free for x in φ. Then*

$$\mathcal{I}[x \to a] \models \varphi \text{ iff } \mathcal{I}[y \to a] \models \varphi\{x \leftarrow y\}.$$

Proof. Exercise. □

Lemma 5.1.3   *The conclusion of each inference rule of G is universally valid iff each of its premises is.*

Proof. For each inference rule of G we show that an interpretation $\mathcal{I} = \langle \mathcal{M}, \beta \rangle$ falsifies the conclusion of the rule iff some interpretation $\mathcal{I}' = \langle \mathcal{M}, \beta' \rangle$ falsifies its premises. The lemma follows directly from this assertion.

We prove the assertion for the cases when the inference rule in question is the rule ($\wedge$-left), ($\wedge$-right), ($\forall$-left), or ($\forall$-right); the other cases are left as exercises for the reader.

- ($\wedge$-left): We have

$$\mathcal{I} \not\models \Phi, \varphi, \psi \to \Psi \quad \text{iff} \quad \mathcal{I} \not\models \bigwedge \Phi \wedge \varphi \wedge \psi \to \bigvee \Psi$$
$$\text{iff} \quad \mathcal{I} \not\models \Phi, \varphi \wedge \psi \to \Psi.$$

Thus $\mathcal{I}$ falsifies the conclusion of the rule ($\wedge$-left) iff $\mathcal{I}$ also falsifies its premise.

- ($\wedge$-right): We have

$$\mathcal{I} \not\models \Phi \;\rightarrow\; \Psi, \varphi \wedge \psi$$

iff $\quad \mathcal{I} \models \bigwedge \Phi$ and $\mathcal{I} \not\models \bigvee \Psi$ and $\mathcal{I} \not\models \varphi \wedge \psi$

iff $\quad \mathcal{I} \models \Phi$ and $\mathcal{I} \not\models \bigvee \Psi$ and either $\mathcal{I} \not\models \varphi$ or $\mathcal{I} \not\models \psi$

iff $\quad \mathcal{I} \not\models \Phi \;\rightarrow\; \Psi, \varphi$ or $\mathcal{I} \not\models \Phi \;\rightarrow\; \Psi, \psi$.

Thus $\mathcal{I}$ falsifies the conclusion of the rule ($\wedge$-right) iff $\mathcal{I}$ also falsifies its premise.

- ($\forall$-left): If $\mathcal{I}$ falsifies the premise of the ($\forall$-left) rule then

$$\mathcal{I} \not\models \Phi, \varphi\{x \leftarrow t\}, \forall x\, \varphi \;\rightarrow\; \Psi.$$

From this it follows that $\mathcal{I} \models \bigwedge \Phi \wedge \varphi\{x \leftarrow t\} \wedge \forall x\, \varphi$ and $\mathcal{I} \not\models \bigvee \Psi$. Thus $\mathcal{I} \models \bigwedge \Phi \wedge \forall x\, \varphi$ and $\mathcal{I} \not\models \bigvee \Psi$, so that $\mathcal{I} \not\models \Phi, \forall x\, \varphi \;\rightarrow\; \Psi$. That is, $\mathcal{I}$ falsifies the conclusion of the rule as well.

If, conversely, $\mathcal{I} \not\models \Phi, \forall x\, \varphi \;\rightarrow\; \Psi$, then $\mathcal{I} \models \Phi, \forall x\, \varphi$ and $\mathcal{I} \not\models \Psi$ follow. Since $\mathcal{I} \models \forall x\, \varphi$, by Corollary 4.2.1 we have $\mathcal{I} \models \varphi\{x \leftarrow t\}$ provided t is free for x in φ. We therefore have that $\mathcal{I} \not\models \Phi, \varphi\{x \leftarrow t\}, \forall x\, \varphi \;\rightarrow\; \Psi$, i.e., $\mathcal{I}$ falsifies the premise of the rule.

- ($\forall$-right): From $\mathcal{I} \not\models \Phi \;\rightarrow\; \Psi, \forall x\, \varphi$ follows $\mathcal{I} \models \bigwedge \Phi$, $\mathcal{I} \not\models \forall x\, \varphi$, and $\mathcal{I} \not\models \bigvee \Psi$. In particular there exists an $a \in M$ such that $\mathcal{I}[x \rightarrow a] \not\models \varphi$. Define the interpretation $\mathcal{I}'$ by $\mathcal{I}' = \mathcal{I}[y \rightarrow a]$, where $y \notin FV(\Phi) \cup FV(\Psi) \cup FV(\varphi)$ is a variable which is distinct from x and free for x in φ. By the previous lemma we have $\mathcal{I}' \not\models \varphi\{x \leftarrow y\}$. In addition, $\mathcal{I}' \models \bigwedge \Phi$ and $\mathcal{I}' \not\models \bigvee \Psi$ since $y \notin FV(\Phi) \cup FV(\Psi)$, and therefore $\mathcal{I}' \not\models \Phi \;\rightarrow\; \Psi, \varphi\{x \leftarrow y\}$. That is, the conclusion of the rule is falsifiable by an interpretation over the structure $\mathcal{M}$ whenever the premise of the rule is falsified by an interpretation over $\mathcal{M}$.

Now let $\mathcal{I}$ be an interpretation falsifying the conclusion of the rule ($\forall$-right), i.e., let $\mathcal{I}$ be such that $\mathcal{I} \not\models \Phi \;\rightarrow\; \Psi, \varphi\{x \leftarrow y\}$. Then we have $\mathcal{I} \models \bigwedge \Phi$ and $\mathcal{I} \not\models \bigvee \Psi$ and $\mathcal{I} \not\models \varphi\{x \leftarrow y\}$. By the Substitution Lemma, $\mathcal{I}[x \rightarrow \mathcal{I}(y)] \not\models \varphi$ follows, so that $\mathcal{I}$ falsifies $\forall x\, \varphi$ and therefore also falsifies the premise of the rule. $\quad\square$

In fact Lemma 5.1.3 is stronger than we need for proving the soundness of the Gentzen calculus G, since soundness requires only that the conclusion of an inference rule be valid if its premises are, and not necessarily conversely.

Theorem 5.1.1   *(Soundness of G) Every sequent provable in G is universally valid.*

> **Proof.** This follows from Lemma 5.1.3 by induction on the structure of the proof tree for the sequent under consideration, using the fact that the axioms of G are universally valid. □

> The soundness of the calculus G was relatively easy to show. In the next section we will prove the completeness of G, but rather than showing directly that a refutation of $\neg\varphi$ exists for each universally valid formula φ, we will demonstrate the contrapositive, namely, that if a refutation search for $\neg\varphi$ fails then φ is falsifiable.

5.2 Completeness of G

> In this section we will show the existence of an algorithm based on the calculus G for constructing for each universally valid formula φ a proof tree for φ. First recall that the calculus G comprises a set of axioms and a set of inference rules, and can therefore be viewed as containing a nondeterministic rule system, i.e., as containing a rule system specifying neither the order in which rules are to be applied, nor which terms are to be substituted for the bound variable x when applying the rules ($\forall$-left) and ($\exists$-right). In particular, there is nothing to preclude the existence of derivations which never expand certain nodes, or which do not consider all possible instantiations of quantified formulae, as demonstrated by the next example.

Example 5.2.1

> 1. Let φ be the valid formula $(Q \wedge \neg Q) \Rightarrow \exists x\, P(f(x))$. The following is an infinite derivation tree in G for φ:

$$\vdots$$

$$\frac{\dfrac{\dfrac{\dfrac{(Q \wedge \neg Q) \;\to\; \exists x\, P(f(x)), P(f(f(y))), P(f(y))}{(Q \wedge \neg Q) \;\to\; \exists x\, P(f(x)), P(f(y))}}{(Q \wedge \neg Q) \;\to\; \exists x\, P(f(x))}}{\to\; (Q \wedge \neg Q) \Rightarrow \exists x\, P(f(x))}$$

(right side labels: $(\exists$-right$)$, $(\exists$-right$)$, $(\Rightarrow$-right$)$)

> 2. Let φ be the valid formula $P(f(a)) \Rightarrow \exists x\, P(f(x))$. The following is an infinite derivation tree in G for φ:

$$\vdots$$

$$\frac{\frac{\frac{\frac{}{P(f(a)) \;\to\; \exists x\, P(f(x)), P(f(f(f(a)))), P(f(f(a)))}}{P(f(a)) \;\to\; \exists x\, P(f(x)), P(f(f(a)))}}{P(f(a)) \;\to\; \exists x\, P(f(x))}}{\to\; P(f(a)) \Rightarrow \exists x\, P(f(x))}$$

(∃-right)

(∃-right)

(⇒ -right)

The first part of Example 5.2.1 is concerned with the order of the application of rules. In the given derivation, the rule (⇒-right) is applied, after which only the rule (∃-right) is applied. It is clear that φ can never be proved in this manner, since the antecedent is never expanded. A derivation strategy such as this, in which certain nodes of a derivation tree are never expanded, is in a certain sense "unfair." A fair strategy would require that every possible rule application is eventually carried out; thus if a proof tree for a given formula exists, then applying rules according to a fair strategy will eventually produce one.

The second part of the example is concerned with the question of which terms are substituted in an application of the rule (∃-right). The failure of the proof search in this example is based on the fact that the essential term a is never substituted for x. This strategy is also "unfair" in some sense. A fair strategy would require that every possible term is eventually substituted in the rule (∃-right), again guaranteeing that if a proof of a given formula exists then applying the rules according to a fair strategy will eventually find one.

The next definitions are used to formalize the fairness criterion for derivations.

Definition 5.2.1 For any set S of formulae, define $\mathcal{F}_S$ to be the set of function symbols occurring in formulae in S and define $\mathcal{V}_S$ to be the set of variables occurring free in formulae in S (an "extra" constant symbol is added to $\mathcal{F}_S$ if none appear in the formulae in S). If $H_S = \mathcal{T}(\mathcal{F}_S, \mathcal{V}_S)$, then H_S is the set of terms over the symbols occurring free in formulae in S, and is called a *Herbrand universe* for S.

Definition 5.2.2 Let $\Sigma = \langle \mathcal{F}, \mathcal{P} \rangle$ be a signature, let T be a derivation tree in G, and let S be the set of all formulae over Σ occurring in the sequents labeling the nodes of T. If $\Phi_1, \Phi_2, \ldots$ is any sequence of sets, then define

$$\Phi^\infty = \bigcap_{j \geq 0} \bigcup_{i \geq j} \Phi_i.$$

The derivation tree T is *fair* if every leaf of T is labeled with an axiom, and if for every infinite branch $\mathcal{B} = k_0, k_1, \ldots$ such that k_i is labeled with the sequent $\Phi_i \to \Psi_i$, each of the following hold:

1. Every formula in Φ^∞ is either atomic or of the form $\forall x\, \varphi$ for some $x \in \mathcal{V}$.

2. Every formula in Ψ^∞ is either atomic or of the form $\exists x\, \varphi$ for some $x \in \mathcal{V}$.

3. If $\forall x\, \varphi \in \bigcup_{i \geq 0} \Phi_i$ and $t \in H_S$ is free for x in φ, then $\varphi\{x \leftarrow t\} \in \bigcup_{i \geq 0} \Phi_i$.

4. If $\exists x\, \varphi \in \bigcup_{i \geq 0} \Psi_i$ and $t \in H_S$ is free for x in ψ, then $\psi\{x \leftarrow t\} \in \bigcup_{i \geq 0} \Psi_i$.

It is easy to see that the strategies of Example 5.2.1 are not fair. In the first part of that example the first condition for fairness is violated, and in the second part the fourth condition is violated.

As a special case of Definition 5.2.2 we observe that a finite derivation tree is fair iff all of its leaves are labeled with axioms. In the following we will always assume that every node of a fair derivation tree that is labeled with an axiom is a leaf, i.e., that no inference rule is ever applied to a sequent which is already an axiom.

Definition 5.2.2 may at first seem very abstract. Somewhat more clearly (albeit less precisely) formulated, the first and second conditions for fairness say that if a rule is applicable to a formula φ in node k_i on a branch $\mathcal{B}$, then that rule is actually applied to φ in some $k_j \in \mathcal{B}$ with $j \geq i$. The third and fourth conditions say that if φ occurs in a node k_i to which the rule ($\exists$-right) or rule ($\forall$-left) is applicable, then the appropriate rule is eventually applied with all possible terms from H_S.

Although we will not provide an algorithm which produces a fair derivation tree for each formula, one can be found, for example, on page 209 of [Gal86]. Our proof of the completeness of G will make use of the fact that such an algorithm exists.

The following lemma provides a characterization of fairness.

Lemma 5.2.1 *Let T be a fair derivation tree in G, let S be the set of all formulae occurring in the sequents of T, and let $\mathcal{B} = k_0, k_1, \ldots$ be an infinite branch of T such that each node k_i is labeled with the sequent $\Phi_i \to \Psi_i$. Moreover, let*

$$\Phi = \bigcup_{i \geq 0} \Phi_i \ \text{ and } \ \Psi = \bigcup_{i \geq 0} \Psi_i.$$

Then the following hold:

1. $\Phi \cap \Psi$ *contains no atomic formulae.*

2. *If* $\varphi \wedge \psi \in \Phi$ *then* $\varphi \in \Phi$ *and* $\psi \in \Phi$. *If* $\varphi \wedge \psi \in \Psi$ *then* $\varphi \in \Psi$ *or* $\psi \in \Psi$.

3. *If* $\varphi \vee \psi \in \Phi$ *then* $\varphi \in \Phi$ *or* $\psi \in \Phi$. *If* $\varphi \vee \psi \in \Psi$ *then* $\varphi \in \Psi$ *and* $\psi \in \Psi$.

4. *If* $\varphi \Rightarrow \psi \in \Phi$ *then* $\varphi \in \Psi$ *or* $\psi \in \Phi$. *If* $\varphi \Rightarrow \psi \in \Psi$ *then* $\varphi \in \Phi$ *and* $\psi \in \Psi$.

5. *If* $\varphi \Leftrightarrow \psi \in \Phi$ *then* $\{\varphi, \psi\} \subseteq \Psi$ *or* $\{\varphi, \psi\} \subseteq \Phi$. *If* $\varphi \Leftrightarrow \psi \in \Psi$ *then* $\varphi \in \Phi$ *and* $\psi \in \Psi$ *or* $\varphi \in \Psi$ *and* $\psi \in \Phi$.

6. *If* $\neg\varphi \in \Phi$ *then* $\varphi \in \Psi$. *If* $\neg\varphi \in \Psi$ *then* $\varphi \in \Phi$.

7. *If* $\exists x\, \varphi \in \Phi$ *then* $\varphi\{x \leftarrow y\} \in \Phi$ *for some variable* y. *If* $\forall x\, \psi \in \Psi$ *then* $\psi\{x \leftarrow y\} \in \Psi$ *for some variable* y.

8. *If* $\forall x\, \varphi \in \Phi$ *and if* $t \in H_S$ *is free for* x *in* φ, *then* $\varphi\{x \leftarrow t\} \in \Phi$. *If* $\exists x\, \psi \in \Psi$ *and if* $t \in H_S$ *is free for* x *in* ψ, *then* $\psi\{x \leftarrow t\} \in \Psi$.

Proof.

1. Let $\varphi \in \Phi$ be an atomic formula. Then there exists an $i \geq 0$ such that $\varphi \in \Phi_i$. Since φ is atomic, it appears in the antecedent of every node k_j for $j \geq i$, i.e., $\varphi \in \bigcap_{j \geq i} \Phi_j$. Similarly, if $\varphi \in \Psi$ holds, then there exists an $i' \geq 0$ such that $\varphi \in \bigcap_{j' \geq i'} \Psi_{j'}$. Assume, without loss of generality, that $i' \geq i$. Then we have $\varphi \in \Phi_{i'} \cap \Psi_{i'}$, and so the node $k_{i'}$ must be labeled with an axiom, contradicting the assumption that $\mathcal{B}$ is an infinite branch in T.

2. Let $\varphi \wedge \psi \in \Phi$. Then there exists an $i \geq 0$ such that $\varphi \wedge \psi \in \Phi_i$. Since $\varphi \wedge \psi$ is neither atomic nor of the form $\forall x\, \chi$, by the definition of fairness we have $\varphi \wedge \psi \notin \Phi^\infty$. Thus there is some $j > i$ so that $\varphi \wedge \psi \notin \Phi_j$. Let j be minimal with this property. Then $\varphi \wedge \psi \in \Phi_{j-1}$ and $\varphi \wedge \psi \notin \Phi_j$. The only way that the formula $\varphi \wedge \psi$ can disappear is through the application of the rule ($\wedge$-left) to node k_{j-1}. But then $\varphi \in \Phi_j$ and $\psi \in \Phi_j$. Thus $\varphi \in \Phi$ and $\psi \in \Phi$ as desired. The second half of the assertion is proved similarly.

3. Parts 3 through 7 are left as exercises.

8. Let $\forall x\, \varphi \in \Phi$ and let $t \in H_S$ be free for x in φ. Then by the third clause of the definition of fairness, we have $\varphi\{x \leftarrow t\} \in \Phi$. If $\exists x\, \psi \in \Psi$ and $t \in H_S$ is free for x in ψ, then by the fourth clause of the definition of fairness we have $\psi\{x \leftarrow t\} \in \Psi$. $\square$

We will now see that fairness guarantees the completeness of a proof strategy. If T is an infinite derivation tree for φ, then we can construct an interpretation which falsifies φ. For the construction we require a famous lemma due to König. We say that a tree T is *finitely branching* if each node in T has only finitely many children.

Lemma 5.2.2   *(König's Lemma) If T is a finitely branching infinite tree then T has an infinite branch.*

Proof. Let k_0 be the root of T. Since T is finite branching k_0 has only finitely many children. Thus there exists a child k_1 of k_0 which is the root of an infinite subtree T_1 of T, since if all children of k_0 were roots of finite subtrees of T then T would be finite. Repeatedly applying the same argument we find a child k_2 of k_1 which is the root of an infinite subtree T_2 of T_1, and so on. Clearly then the sequence $k_0, k_1, k_2, \ldots$ determines an infinite branch of T. □

To prove that the Gentzen calculus G is complete, we must show that every universally valid formula can be proved in G. We will show a stronger result, however, namely, that every universally valid formula can be proved using a *fair* derivation in G by establishing that every formula admitting no proof via a fair derivation in G is falsifiable. For this we will actually construct an explicit interpretation which falsifies the formula. Before making our method precise we illustrate it with the following example.

Example 5.2.2   1. Let $\varphi = (P \Rightarrow Q) \Rightarrow (Q \Rightarrow P)$. We show that φ is falsifiable by constructing a derivation in G, this time in table form.

In the last step we have selected only the second of the two premises of the rule ($\Rightarrow$-left). The attempt to prove the original formula is thwarted, and it is easy to find an interpretation $\mathcal{I}$ falsifying the original formula: any interpretation $\mathcal{I}$ satisfying Q and falsifying P satisfies all formulae in the left column and falsifies all formulae in the right column, and in particular satisfies the original formula.

2. Let $\varphi = P(a) \Rightarrow \exists x\, P(f(x))$. We construct the infinite table appearing

TABLE 5.4.

TRUE	FALSE
	$(P \Rightarrow Q) \Rightarrow (Q \Rightarrow P)$
$P \Rightarrow Q$	$Q \Rightarrow P$
$P \Rightarrow Q, Q$	P
Q	P

TABLE 5.5.

TRUE	FALSE
	$P(a) \Rightarrow \exists x\, P(f(x))$
$P(a)$	$\exists x\, P(f(x))$
$P(a)$	$\exists x\, P(f(x)), P(f(a))$
$P(a)$	$\exists x\, P(f(x)), P(f(a)), P(f(f(a)))$
$\vdots$	$\vdots$

above as Table 5.5:

In this infinite derivation tree no variables occur free and so $H_S = \{a, f(a), f(f(a)), \ldots\}$, where S is the set of all formulae occurring in the tree. The derivation is fair since every term in H_S is substituted for x in the formula $\exists x\, P(f(x))$. Let $\mathcal{I}$ be any interpretation satisfying the formula $P(a)$ in the left column and falsifying all formulae, including $P(f(a)), P(f(f(a))), \ldots$ in the right column. For the specification of the interpretation $\mathcal{I}$, the interpretations of the individual terms are not important—it is sufficient that each term in H_S have a distinct interpretation under $\mathcal{I}$. For concreteness, we can take $\mathcal{I}$ to be any interpretation with carrier H_S and such that $\mathcal{I}(t) = t$ for every term $t \in H_S$, since every such interpretation clearly has this property.

An interpretation such as that introduced in the second part of the last example is rather specialized, but these turn out to be precisely the most advantageous interpretations to consider.

Definition 5.2.3

1. Let S be any set of formulae. A *Herbrand structure* for S is a structure $\mathcal{H}$ with carrier H_S such that $f^{H_S}(t_1, \ldots t_n) = f t_1 \ldots t_n$ for all $f \in \mathcal{F}_n$.

2. A *Herbrand interpretation* for S is an interpretation $\mathcal{I}_S = \langle \mathcal{H}, \beta \rangle$ such that $\mathcal{H}$ is a Herbrand structure for S and $\beta(x) = x$ for all $x \in \mathcal{V}_S$.

Lemma 5.2.3 *If $\mathcal{I}_S$ is a Herbrand interpretation, then for each $t \in H_S$, $\mathcal{I}_S(t) = t$.*

Proof. By the Principle of Structural Induction for terms. □

With the notion of a Herbrand interpretation in hand we are ready to prove the completeness of the Gentzen calculus.

Theorem 5.2.1 *Let T be a fair derivation tree in G for φ_0. If φ_0 is universally valid, then T is a proof tree for φ_0.*

Proof. Let φ_0 be a formula, and assume that T is a fair derivation tree in G for φ_0 which is not a proof tree for φ_0. There are two possibilities. If T

possesses a leaf that is not labeled with an axiom, then let B be the branch of T leading from the root of T to this leaf. If there is no such leaf, then T is infinite, and so by König's Lemma T has an infinite branch B starting from the root. In either case, let $B = k_0, k_1, \ldots$, where k_0 is the root of T, and suppose that each node k_i is labeled with the sequent $\Phi_i \to \Psi_i$.

Let $\Phi = \bigcup_{i \geq 0} \Phi_i$ be the set of formulae appearing in antecedents of sequents in B, and $\Psi = \bigcup_{i \geq 0} \Psi_i$ be the set of formulae appearing in sequents in B. Note that $\varphi_0 \in \Psi$. We construct an interpretation falsifying φ_0.

Let S be the set of formulae occurring in $\Phi \cup \Psi$, and consider the Herbrand structure $\mathcal{H}$ satisfying

$$P^{H_S} = \{\langle t_1, \ldots, t_n \rangle \mid Pt_1 \ldots t_n \in \Phi\}$$

for every n-ary predicate symbol P. For this $\mathcal{H}$, let $\mathcal{I}_S = \langle \mathcal{H}, \beta \rangle$ be a Herbrand interpretation for S. We will show by induction on the rank of formulae that $\mathcal{I}_S$ satisfies all formulae in Φ and falsifies all formulae in Ψ. In particular, then $\mathcal{I}_S$ will falsify φ_0.

If $Pt_1 \ldots t_n \in \Phi$ is an atomic formula, then $\langle t_1, \ldots, t_n \rangle \in P^{H_S}$, from which it follows that $\langle \mathcal{I}_S(t_1), \ldots, \mathcal{I}_S(t_n) \rangle \in P^{H_S}$, i.e., that $\mathcal{I}_S \models Pt_1 \ldots t_n$. If $Pt_1 \ldots t_n \in \Psi$ is an atomic formula then by the first part of Lemma 5.2.1 we have $Pt_1 \ldots t_n \notin \Phi$. Then $\langle t_1, \ldots, t_n \rangle \notin P^{H_S}$ and so $\langle \mathcal{I}_S(t_1), \ldots, \mathcal{I}_S(t_n) \rangle \notin P^{H_S}$, i.e., $\mathcal{I}_S \not\models Pt_1 \ldots t_n$.

Now let $\varphi \in \Phi \cup \Psi$ be a nonatomic formula. We show the assertion for the cases when $\varphi = \psi \wedge \chi \in \Phi$, $\varphi = \psi \wedge \chi \in \Psi$, and $\varphi = \forall x \psi \in \Phi$. The proofs in the remaining cases are analogous.

If $\varphi = \psi \wedge \chi \in \Phi$, then by the second part of Lemma 5.2.1 we have $\psi \in \Phi$ and $\chi \in \Phi$. By the induction hypothesis, $\mathcal{I}_S \models \psi$ and $\mathcal{I}_S \models \chi$, and so $\mathcal{I}_S \models \psi \wedge \chi$.

If $\varphi = \psi \wedge \chi \in \Psi$, then by the second part of Lemma 5.2.1 we have $\psi \in \Psi$ or $\chi \in \Psi$. By the induction hypothesis, $\mathcal{I}_S \not\models \psi$ or $\mathcal{I}_S \not\models \chi$, and so $\mathcal{I}_S \not\models \psi \wedge \chi$.

Finally, let $\varphi = \forall x \, \psi \in \Phi$, and let $t \in H_S$ be an arbitrary term which is free for x in ψ. By the last part of Lemma 5.2.1 we have $\psi\{x \leftarrow t\} \in \Phi$. Since $rank(\psi\{x \leftarrow t\}) = rank(\psi) < rank(\varphi)$, the induction hypothesis gives $\mathcal{I}_S \models \psi\{x \leftarrow t\}$ and the Substitution Lemma yields $\mathcal{I}_S[x \to \mathcal{I}_S(t)] \models \psi$. Since $\mathcal{I}_S$ is a Herbrand interpretation we must have $\mathcal{I}_S(t) = t$, and so $\mathcal{I}_S[x \to t] \models \psi$. Since t was chosen arbitrarily in H_S it follows that $\mathcal{I}_S \models \forall x \, \psi$.

We have shown that if T is a fair derivation tree which is not a proof tree in G for φ_0, then the Herbrand interpretation $\mathcal{I}_S$ satisfies the set of formulae Φ and falsifies the set of formulae Ψ. In particular, since $\varphi_0 \in \Psi$, $\mathcal{I}_S$ falsifies φ_0. That is, we have shown that if φ_0 is valid and if T is a fair derivation tree in G for φ_0, then T must actually be a proof tree in G for φ_0. □

Corollary 5.2.1   *A formula is universally valid iff it is provable in the calculus G.*

Proof. This follows from Theorems 5.1.1 and 5.2.1, and the fact that a fair derivation tree exists for every formula. □

Corollary 5.2.2   *The universal validity of quantifier-free formulae is decidable.*

Proof. Note that only the connectives $\vee$, $\wedge$, $\Rightarrow$, $\Leftrightarrow$, and $\approx$ and the negation symbol $\neg$ appear in quantifier-free formulae. In the bottom-to-top construction of a derivation tree for such a formula, each application of a rule for one of these connectives reduces the number of connectives in a given sequent, and so any sequence of applications of these rules must terminate. If the resulting finite tree is a proof tree, i.e., if all its leaves are labeled with axioms, then the original formula is universally valid; otherwise the original formula is falsifiable. □

Corollary 5.2.3   *The universal validity of formulae of the form $\forall x_1 \ldots \forall x_n\, \varphi$, where φ is quantifier free, is decidable.*

Proof. Let T be an arbitrary derivation tree with root $\rightarrow \forall x_1 \ldots \forall x_n\, \varphi$. Then T necessarily has the following shape, since the rule ($\forall$-right) is the only rule which applies to produce a formula of the form $\forall y_1 \ldots \forall y_m\, \psi$:

$$
\vdots
$$
$$
\frac{}{\rightarrow\ \varphi\{x_1 \leftarrow y_1\} \ldots \{x_n \leftarrow y_n\}} \quad (\forall\text{-right})
$$
$$
\vdots
$$
$$
\frac{\rightarrow\ \forall x_2 \ldots \forall x_n\, \varphi\{x_1 \leftarrow y_1\}}{\rightarrow\ \forall x_1 \forall x_2 \ldots \forall x_n\, \varphi} \quad \begin{array}{l}(\forall\text{-right})\\[4pt](\forall\text{-right})\end{array}
$$

The sequent $\rightarrow\ \varphi\{x_1 \leftarrow y_1\} \ldots \{x_n \leftarrow y_n\}$ is quantifier free and, by the argument used in the proof of Corollary 5.2.2, the tree T' whose root is $\rightarrow\ \varphi\{x_1 \leftarrow y_1\} \ldots \{x_n \leftarrow y_n\}$ is finite. Thus T is also finite. The formula $\forall x_1 \ldots \forall x_n\, \varphi$ is universally valid if T is a proof tree (i.e., if the leaves of T', and hence of T, are labeled with axioms), and is falsifiable otherwise. □

As indicated in the introduction to this chapter, there is no decision procedure for semantic consequence, and therefore none for universal validity, of arbitrary first-order formulae. This was proved in 1936 by the logician Alonzo Church ([Chu36]).

6

Normal Forms and Herbrand's Theorem

The Gentzen calculus introduced in the last chapter provides a relatively straightforward method for demonstrating validity of first-order formulae, and one whose completeness can be proved directly. But—practically speaking—Gentzen calculi suffer quite serious disadvantages, unfortunately rendering them unsuitable for use in mechanizing proofs without extensive modification. The primary obstacles to their efficient automation are the nondeterminism, at any given stage of proof development, of the choice of rule to be applied as well as of the formula to which to apply it, and the unguided consideration of all terms for substitution in applications of the quantifier rules. In a derivation it is possible, for example, that the quantifier rules can be applied repeatedly to the same formula to the exclusion of applications of other rules needed for the successful development of a proof, or that in applying a quantifier rule, the bound variables of the formula will never be instantiated by the "right" substitution terms. We will see in Theorems 6.2.1 and 6.3.2 that restricting the syntactic forms that formulae to be proved may have, and then showing that every formula can be converted to a semantically equivalent formula meeting these syntactic requirements, will allow us to correspondingly restrict the structure of proof trees for valid formulae. From such proof trees in "standard form" we may derive significantly simpler formulae provable iff the original formulae are. This "preprocessing" of formulae in the Gentzen calculus thus emerges as a basis for deriving quite effective calculi for automating deduction. In this book, Gentzen calculi will serve primarily as a point of departure for discussing one particular class of such calculi, namely, resolution calculi, and for discussing Herbrand's Theorem, the foundation for proving the refutation completeness of such calculi.

Because resolution calculi and most other effective calculi used in automating deduction derive their success in part from the fact that they are applied only to formulae with certain syntactic properties (i.e., to so-called *normal forms*), they are considerably less transparent for human comprehension than are Gentzen calculi. That is, Gentzen calculi, which typically comprise only a few logical axioms and some easily understandable rules of inference, are regarded as "human oriented," while resolution calculi are considered to be "machine oriented" for reasons that will become clearer in Chapter 7. But of course human amenability is not necessary for calculi to be used in mechanical theorem proving, and it is even reasonable to expect that calculi which humans can efficiently manipulate may differ significantly from calculi which can be mechanized effectively. After all, automated proofs are not guided by "intuition," as are most human-produced proofs, and so must resort to some variation on or restriction of the method of exhaustion (also called the British museum method) for their construction.

We begin this chapter by investigating various methods for simplifying formulae for deduction efficiency, and thereby arrive at the normal forms with which Herbrand's Theorem and resolution calculi are concerned.

6.1 Normal Forms

To overcome difficulties resulting from the unchecked application of quantifier rules in G, we may require, in the (bottom-up) construction of a proof tree for a given formula, that all quantifier rules to be applied actually be applied before other rules are. Note in particular that this precludes the first kind of problematic quantifier application mentioned in the introduction to this chapter. To overcome the second kind, i.e., to ensure that a quantifier rule's bound variable is eventually instantiated by an appropriate term, is somewhat more difficult; this problem is taken up in Section 6.3.

If we are to improve the efficiency of Gentzen calculi by showing that every formula provable in G has a proof in which all applications of quantifier rules precede all applications of other rules, it will be helpful to know that for every formula (provable in G or not) there exists a semantically equivalent formula all of whose quantifiers appear "at the front" of the formula, in the sense of the next definition.

Definition 6.1.1   A formula $\varphi = Q_1 x_1 \ldots Q_n x_n \, \psi$ is said to be in *prenex normal form* provided ψ is quantifier free. The sequence $Q_1 x_1 \ldots Q_n x_n$ is called the *prefix* of φ, and ψ is called the *matrix* of φ.

In Theorem 6.1.2 we will describe an algorithm for converting each formula to a semantically equivalent formula in prenex normal form. To specify this algorithm we first introduce a variant G' of the Gentzen calculus G and prove that, although G' is easier to work with in practice, it is equivalent to G in the sense that every proof in G can be transformed into a proof in G' and vice versa. We then use G' to prove—more simply than would be possible in G itself—a set of semantic equivalences from which rewrite rules for converting formulae to prenex normal form can be extracted.

Definition 6.1.2   1. The inference rules of G' are the rules of G together with the *weakening rules*

$$\frac{\Phi \rightarrow \Psi}{\Phi, \varphi \rightarrow \Psi} \qquad \text{and} \qquad \frac{\Phi \rightarrow \Psi}{\Phi \rightarrow \Psi, \varphi}$$

2. The axioms of G' are all sequents of the form $\varphi \rightarrow \varphi$.

We define proof trees and derivation trees in G' by analogy with Definitions 5.1.2 and 5.1.3. It is not hard to see that G and G' are equivalent:

Theorem 6.1.1   *Let φ be a formula. Then the following are equivalent:*

1. *φ is provable in the calculus G'.*

2. *φ is provable in the calculus G.*

Proof. To prove that the first statement implies the second, we give a transformation from proof trees in G' to proof trees in G which first moves all applications of weakening rules toward the leaves and then eliminates them completely. Let T be a proof tree in G' for φ and let k and k' be nodes in T such that k' is the parent of k, and such that, in the bottom-up construction of T, a rule from G is applied to k and a weakening rule is applied to k'. We show by example how we may always interchange applications of rules of G with applications of the weakening rules. The transformation of proof trees in G' which accomplishes the desired interchange for the rule ($\wedge$-left) is given by

$$\frac{\dfrac{\Phi, \varphi, \psi \;\rightarrow\; \Psi}{\Phi, \varphi \wedge \psi \;\dashrightarrow\; \Psi}}{\Phi, \varphi \wedge \psi \;\rightarrow\; \chi, \Psi} \qquad \frac{\dfrac{\Phi, \varphi, \psi \;\rightarrow\; \Psi}{\Phi, \varphi, \psi \;\rightarrow\; \chi, \Psi}}{\Phi, \varphi \wedge \psi \;\rightarrow\; \chi, \Psi}$$

Clearly there are analogous transformations for the other rules in G'. Repeatedly interchanging rules in G with applications of weakening rules

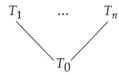

FIGURE 6.1.

until this can no longer be done, we may transform T into a proof tree in G' for φ as in Figure 6.1, in which only rules of G are applied in T_0 and only weakening rules are applied in $T_1, \ldots, T_n$. Since the leaves of T_0 are axioms of G, and since T_0 is finite because T is, we have that T_0 is a proof tree in G for φ.

To prove that the second statement implies the first, we give a transformation from proof trees in G to proof trees in G'. Let $\Phi, \psi \to \psi, \Psi$ be an axiom of G appearing in a proof T in G for φ. By repeatedly applying the weakening rule to formulae from Φ and Ψ, a proof tree in G' for $\Phi, \psi \to \psi, \Psi$ can be derived from the axiom $\psi \to \psi$ as indicated below:

$$\Phi, \psi \ \to \ \psi, \Psi \qquad \qquad \frac{\dfrac{\psi \ \to \ \psi}{\vdots}}{\Phi, \psi \ \to \ \psi, \Psi} \ \text{(Weakening)}$$

Applying weakening rules in this manner to each leaf of T yields a new tree T' which is indeed a proof tree in G' for φ. □

The next lemma indicates the semantic equivalences which will provide the foundation for the rewrite rules for converting formulae into prenex normal forms.

Lemma 6.1.1 *The following semantic equivalences hold.*

$\quad$ *1.* • $(\forall x \, \varphi) \wedge (\forall x \, \psi) \simeq \forall x \, (\varphi \wedge \psi)$ $\hfill$ (1)

$\qquad$ • $(\exists x \, \varphi) \vee (\exists x \, \psi) \simeq \exists x \, (\varphi \vee \psi)$ $\hfill$ (2)

$\quad$ *2. If $x \notin FV(\psi)$, then*

$\qquad$ • $((\exists x \, \varphi) \Rightarrow \psi) \simeq \forall x \, (\varphi \Rightarrow \psi)$ $\hfill$ (3)

$\qquad$ • $((\forall x \, \varphi) \Rightarrow \psi) \simeq \exists x \, (\varphi \Rightarrow \psi)$ $\hfill$ (4)

$\quad$ *3. If $x \notin FV(\varphi)$, then*

$\qquad$ • $(\varphi \Rightarrow \forall x \, \psi) \simeq \forall x \, (\varphi \Rightarrow \psi)$ $\hfill$ (5)

$\qquad$ • $(\varphi \Rightarrow \exists x \, \psi) \simeq \exists x \, (\varphi \Rightarrow \psi)$ $\hfill$ (6)

4. If $x \notin FV(\psi)$, then

- $(\exists x\, \varphi \Leftrightarrow \psi) \simeq (\forall x\, (\varphi \Rightarrow \psi)) \wedge (\exists x\, (\psi \Rightarrow \varphi))$ (7)

- $(\forall x\, \varphi \Leftrightarrow \psi) \simeq (\exists x\, (\varphi \Rightarrow \psi)) \wedge (\forall x\, (\psi \Rightarrow \varphi))$ (8)

5. If $x \notin FV(\varphi)$, then

- $\neg \forall x\, \varphi \simeq \exists x\, \neg\varphi$ (9)

- $\neg \exists x\, \varphi \simeq \forall x\, \neg\varphi$ (10)

- $\varphi * Qx\, \psi \simeq Qx\, (\varphi * \psi)$ for $* \in \{\wedge, \vee\}$ and $Q \in \{\forall, \exists\}$ (11)

6. If $y \notin FV(\varphi) - \{x\}$ and y is free for x in φ, then

- $Qx\, \varphi \simeq Qy\, \varphi\{x \leftarrow y\}$ for $Q \in \{\forall, \exists\}$ (12)

Proof. Each of these equivalences, of the form $\varphi \simeq \psi$, is shown by constructing proof trees in G' first for $\varphi \Rightarrow \psi$ and then for $\psi \Rightarrow \varphi$. We prove (3) and one direction of (9).

- The following is a proof for $\forall x\, (\varphi \Rightarrow \psi) \Rightarrow ((\exists x\, \varphi) \Rightarrow \psi)$. Here, y is any variable which is free for x in φ and which satisfies the appropriate eigenvariable condition. In applying the rule ($\forall$-left) we use the fact that $\psi\{x \leftarrow y\} = \psi$ since $x \notin FV(\psi)$.

$$
\begin{array}{l}
\dfrac{\dfrac{\varphi\{x \leftarrow y\} \;\to\; \varphi\{x \leftarrow y\}}{\varphi\{x \leftarrow y\} \;\to\; \psi, \varphi\{x \leftarrow y\}} \qquad \dfrac{\dfrac{\psi \;\to\; \psi}{\varphi\{x \leftarrow y\}, \psi \;\to\; \psi}}{}}{\dfrac{\varphi\{x \leftarrow y\}, (\varphi\{x \leftarrow y\} \Rightarrow \psi) \;\to\; \psi}{\dfrac{\varphi\{x \leftarrow y\}, \forall x\, (\varphi \Rightarrow \psi), (\varphi\{x \leftarrow y\} \Rightarrow \psi) \;\to\; \psi}{\dfrac{\varphi\{x \leftarrow y\}, \forall x\, (\varphi \Rightarrow \psi) \;\to\; \psi}{\dfrac{\exists x\, \varphi, \forall x\, (\varphi \Rightarrow \psi) \;\to\; \psi}{\dfrac{\forall x\, (\varphi \Rightarrow \psi) \;\to\; (\exists x\, \varphi) \Rightarrow \psi}{\to\; \forall x\, (\varphi \Rightarrow \psi) \Rightarrow ((\exists x\, \varphi) \Rightarrow \psi)}}}}}}
\end{array}
$$

(Weakening)
($\Rightarrow$-left)
(Weakening)
($\forall$-left)
($\exists$-left)
($\Rightarrow$-right)
($\Rightarrow$-right)

Let y and z be any variables which are free for x in $\varphi \Rightarrow \psi$ and which satisfy the appropriate eigenvariable conditions. The following proof that $((\exists x\, \varphi) \Rightarrow \psi) \Rightarrow \forall x(\varphi \Rightarrow \psi)$ also uses the fact that $\psi\{x \leftarrow y\} = \psi$ since $x \notin FV(\psi)$.

$$\frac{\varphi\{x \leftarrow z\} \ \rightarrow \ \varphi\{x \leftarrow z\}}{\cfrac{\varphi\{x \leftarrow z\} \ \rightarrow \ \varphi\{x \leftarrow z\}, \exists x\, \varphi}{\cfrac{\varphi\{x \leftarrow z\} \ \rightarrow \ \varphi\{x \leftarrow z\}, \psi, \exists x\, \varphi}{\cfrac{\rightarrow \ \varphi\{x \leftarrow z\}, (\varphi\{x \leftarrow z\} \Rightarrow \psi), \exists x\, \varphi}{\rightarrow \ (\varphi\{x \leftarrow z\} \Rightarrow \psi), \exists x\, \varphi}}}}$$

$$\cfrac{\cfrac{\psi \ \rightarrow \ \psi}{\cfrac{\psi, \varphi\{x \leftarrow y\} \ \rightarrow \ \psi}{\cfrac{\psi \ \rightarrow \ \varphi\{x \leftarrow y\} \Rightarrow \psi}{\psi \ \rightarrow \ \forall x(\varphi \Rightarrow \psi)}}} \qquad \rightarrow \ \exists x\, \varphi, \forall x\,(\varphi \Rightarrow \psi)}{\cfrac{(\exists x\, \varphi) \Rightarrow \psi \ \rightarrow \ \forall x\,(\varphi \Rightarrow \psi)}{\rightarrow \ ((\exists x\, \varphi) \Rightarrow \psi) \Rightarrow \forall x\,(\varphi \Rightarrow \psi)}}$$

Here the rules (Weakening), ($\Rightarrow$-right), and ($\forall$-right), respectively, are used in the left fork of the proof tree, the rules (Weakening), (Weakening), ($\Rightarrow$-right), ($\exists$-right), and ($\forall$-right), respectively, are used in its right fork, and the rules ($\Rightarrow$-left) and ($\Rightarrow$-right) are used in its trunk.

- The following is a proof that $\neg \forall x\, \varphi \Rightarrow \exists x\, \neg\varphi$. Let y be free for x in φ, and suppose y satisfies the appropriate eigenvariable condition. The proof that $\exists x\, \neg\varphi \Rightarrow \neg\forall x\, \varphi$ is similar.

$$\cfrac{\cfrac{\cfrac{\cfrac{\cfrac{\varphi\{x \leftarrow y\} \ \rightarrow \ \varphi\{x \leftarrow y\}}{\varphi\{x \leftarrow y\} \ \rightarrow \ \varphi\{x \leftarrow y\}, \exists x\, \neg\varphi}}{\rightarrow \ \neg\varphi\{x \leftarrow y\}, \varphi\{x \leftarrow y\}, \exists x\, \neg\varphi}}{\rightarrow \ \varphi\{x \leftarrow y\}, \exists x\, \neg\varphi}}{\rightarrow \ \forall x\, \varphi, \exists x\, \neg\varphi}}{\cfrac{\neg\forall x\, \varphi \ \rightarrow \ \exists x\, \neg\varphi}{\rightarrow \ \neg\forall x\, \varphi \Rightarrow \exists x\, \neg\varphi}}$$

with labels to the right:
(Weakening)
($\neg$-right)
($\exists$-right)
($\forall$-right)
($\neg$-left)
($\Rightarrow$-right)

The proofs in the remaining cases are left as an exercise. □

Lemma 6.1.2 *Let $\mathcal{R}_1$ be the rewrite system for formulae obtained by reading the equivalences (1) through (12) in Lemma 6.1.1 from left to right.*

1. *The system $\mathcal{R}_1$ is terminating.*

2. *If φ is a formula to which no rule in $\mathcal{R}_1$ applies, then φ is in prenex normal form.*

Proof. Each rule in $\mathcal{R}_1$ can be seen to decrease the measure μ where $\mu(\varphi)$ is the number of quantifiers occurring below a logical connective. Thus the rewrite system $\mathcal{R}_1$ is terminating. The proof of the second part of the theorem is not difficult and is left as an exercise. □

Theorem 6.1.2 *There exists an algorithm constructing from each formula φ a semantically equivalent formula φ' in prenex normal form.*

Proof. The algorithm consists in applying the rules of $\mathcal{R}_1$ to a formula φ as many times as possible. We assume that in any subformula of the form $\exists x\,\psi$ or $\forall x\,\psi$ of φ the variable x appears only in ψ, which can be ensured by renaming the finitely many bound variables of φ according to part (12) of Lemma 6.1.1 if necessary. By Lemma 6.1.2, any sequence of applications of rules in $\mathcal{R}_1$ terminates and the resulting formula φ' is in prenex normal form. Lemma 6.1.1 guarantees that φ and φ' are equivalent. □

Example 6.1.1 Let

$$\varphi = \forall x\,(P(x) \vee \neg \exists y\,(Q(y) \wedge R(x,y))) \;\vee\; \neg(P(y) \wedge \neg \forall x\,P(x)).$$

The following sequence of rule applications transforms φ into an equivalent formula in prenex normal form. For readability, the part of each formula to which a rule is applied is enclosed in a box.

$$\forall x\,(P(x) \vee \boxed{\neg \exists y\,(Q(y) \wedge R(x,y))}) \vee \neg(P(y) \wedge \neg \forall x\,P(x)) \qquad \simeq$$

$$\forall x\,\boxed{(P(x) \vee \forall y\,\neg(Q(y) \wedge R(x,y)))} \vee \neg(P(y) \wedge \neg \forall x\,P(x)) \qquad \simeq$$

$$\forall x \forall y\,(P(x) \vee \neg(Q(y) \wedge R(x,y))) \vee \neg(P(y) \wedge \boxed{\neg \forall x\,P(x)}) \qquad \simeq$$

$$\forall x \forall y\,(P(x) \vee \neg(Q(y) \wedge R(x,y))) \vee \neg \boxed{(P(y) \wedge \exists x\,\neg P(x))} \qquad \simeq$$

$$\forall x \forall y\,(P(x) \vee \neg(Q(y) \wedge R(x,y))) \vee \boxed{\neg \exists x\,(P(y) \wedge \neg P(x))} \qquad \simeq$$

$$\forall x \forall y\,(P(x) \vee \neg(Q(y) \wedge R(x,y))) \vee \boxed{\forall x\,\neg(P(y) \wedge \neg P(x))} \qquad \simeq$$

$$\forall x \forall y'\,\boxed{(P(x) \vee \neg(Q(y') \wedge R(x,y'))) \vee \forall x'\,\neg(P(y) \wedge \neg P(x'))} \qquad \simeq$$

$$\forall x \forall y' \forall x'\,(P(x) \vee \neg(Q(y') \wedge R(x,y')) \vee \neg(P(y) \wedge \neg P(x')))$$

We can further standardize the syntactic structure of formulae by specifying the form the matrices of formulae in prenex normal form must have.

Definition 6.1.3 A *literal* is a formula of the form φ or $\neg\varphi$, where φ is atomic. A quantifier-free formula φ is a *disjunction of literals* if it is of the form $\varphi_1 \vee \ldots \vee \varphi_n$, where $\varphi_1, \ldots, \varphi_n$ are all literals; φ is said to be in *conjunctive normal form* if it is of the form

$$\varphi = (\varphi_{11} \vee \ldots \vee \varphi_{1n_1}) \wedge \ldots \wedge (\varphi_{k1} \vee \ldots \vee \varphi_{kn_k}),$$

where each formula $\varphi_{i1} \vee \ldots \vee \varphi_{in_i}$ is a disjunction of literals.

We can also represent quantifier-free formulae in terms of sequents. A *clause* is a sequent $\Phi \to \Psi$, where Φ and Ψ are sets of atomic formulae; a *Horn clause* is a clause $\Phi \to \Psi$ for which Ψ contains at most one atom; a *propositional clause* is a clause all of whose atoms are (propositional) atoms. The *length* of a clause $\Phi \to \Psi$ is $|\Phi| + |\Psi|$, i.e., the length of a clause is the number of atoms appearing in it. If C is a clause, write $Var(C)$ for the set of variables occurring in C. In light of Definitions 4.1.5 and 5.1.4 the clause $\varphi_1, \ldots, \varphi_n \to \psi_1, \ldots, \psi_m$ is semantically equivalent to the formula $\neg\varphi_1 \vee \ldots \vee \neg\varphi_n \vee \psi_1 \vee \ldots \vee \psi_m$, and the set

$$S = \{\Phi_1 \to \Psi_1, \ldots, \Phi_1 \to \Psi_1\}$$

of clauses is semantically equivalent to the conjunctive normal form

$$\Phi_S = (\bigvee_{\varphi \in \Phi_1} \neg\varphi \vee \bigvee_{\psi \in \Psi_1} \psi) \wedge \ldots \wedge (\bigvee_{\varphi \in \Phi_n} \neg\varphi \vee \bigvee_{\psi \in \Psi_n} \psi).$$

We may therefore express quantifier-free formulae in either conjunctive normal form or in *clausal form* interchangeably.

The Gentzen calculi G and G' provide bases for natural algorithms for converting a given quantifier-free formula φ into an equivalent formula in clausal form (and so, effectively, into conjunctive normal form). This representation of formulae will be useful when discussing resolution calculi, which operate on clauses.

Lemma 6.1.3   *There exists an algorithm transforming any given quantifier-free formula φ into a semantically equivalent clause set S.*

Proof. We have already seen in the proof of Corollary 5.2.2 that any sequence of applications of rules of the Gentzen calculus G out of any quantifier-free formula must terminate. Let φ be a quantifier-free formula and let T be a derivation tree with root $\to \varphi$ to which no rule of G applies. The leaves of T are all labeled with clauses; let S be the set of all clauses labeling leaves of T and let $\mathcal{I}$ be an arbitrary interpretation. By the proof of Lemma 5.1.3, $\mathcal{I} \models \to \varphi$ iff $\mathcal{I} \models C$ for every $C \in S$, i.e., iff $\mathcal{I} \models S$. The sequent $\to \varphi$ is thus semantically equivalent to the set S of clauses, and so the formula φ is as well. $\square$

There exists an alternate method, based on a set of semantic equivalences like those for converting formulae to prenex normal form, for converting a quantifier-free formula to conjunctive normal form. Included among the equivalences are three indicating how to expand formulae containing the connective $\Leftrightarrow$. Note that the same literal can appear more than once in a given conjunct of a formula

$$\varphi = (\varphi_{11} \vee \ldots \vee \varphi_{1n_1}) \wedge \ldots \wedge (\varphi_{k1} \vee \ldots \vee \varphi_{kn_k})$$

in conjunctive normal form. Of course this kind of repetition is not possible in the clausal representation of φ since elements appear in sets are exactly once. The rules (9), (10), and (11) below formally justify the sequent representation of formulae in conjunctive normal form since associativity, commutativity, and idempotence are precisely the salient properties of the set operations.

Lemma 6.1.4 *The following semantic equivalences hold:*

(1) $(\varphi \Leftrightarrow \psi) \simeq (\neg\varphi \vee \psi) \wedge (\neg\psi \vee \varphi)$	(Equivalence)
(2) $\neg(\varphi \Leftrightarrow \psi) \simeq (\varphi \vee \psi) \wedge (\neg\psi \vee \neg\varphi)$	(Antivalence)
(3) $(\varphi \Rightarrow \psi) \simeq (\neg\varphi \vee \psi)$	(Implication)
(4) $\neg(\varphi \wedge \psi) \simeq (\neg\varphi \vee \neg\psi)$	(DeMorgan 1)
(5) $\neg(\varphi \vee \psi) \simeq (\neg\varphi \wedge \neg\psi)$	(DeMorgan 2)
(6) $\neg\neg\varphi \simeq \varphi$	(Double Negation)
(7) $\varphi \vee (\psi \wedge \chi) \simeq (\varphi \vee \psi) \wedge (\varphi \vee \chi)$	(Distributivity 1)
(8) $(\psi \wedge \chi) \vee \psi \simeq (\psi \vee \varphi) \wedge (\chi \vee \varphi)$	(Distributivity 2)
(9) $\varphi * \psi \simeq \psi * \varphi$ $\quad for * \in \{\wedge, \vee\}$	(Commutativity)
(10) $(\varphi * \psi) * \chi \simeq \varphi * (\psi * \chi)$ $\quad for * \in \{\wedge, \vee\}$	(Associativity)
(11) $\varphi * \varphi \simeq \varphi$ $\quad for * \in \{\wedge, \vee\}$	(Idempotence)

Proof. Exercise. $\square$

The equivalences (1) through (8) form the basis of a rewrite system for converting formulae to conjunctive normal form:

Lemma 6.1.5 *Let $\mathcal{R}_2$ be the rewrite system for quantifier-free formulae obtained by reading the equivalences (1) through (8) in Lemma 6.1.4 from left to right.*

1. *The system $\mathcal{R}_2$ is terminating.*

2. *If φ is a quantifier-free formula to which no rule in $\mathcal{R}_2$ applies, and if φ is of the form $\neg\psi$, then φ is a literal. If φ is of the form $\psi \vee \chi$, then φ is a disjunction of literals, and if φ is of the form $\psi \wedge \chi$, then*

φ *is in conjunctive normal form. Thus, if* φ *is* $\mathcal{R}_2$-*irreducible, it must be in conjunctive normal form.*

Proof.

1. Let the measure μ on formulae be defined by

$$\mu(\varphi) = \langle \mu_1(\varphi), \mu_2(\varphi), \mu_3(\varphi), \mu_4(\varphi), \mu_5(\varphi) \rangle,$$

where $\mu_1(\varphi)$ is the number of occurrences of $\Leftrightarrow$ in φ, $\mu_2(\varphi)$ is the number of occurrences of $\Rightarrow$ in φ, $\mu_3(\varphi)$ is the number of occurrences of $\neg$ appearing below an occurrence of $\wedge$ or $\vee$ in φ, $\mu_4(\varphi)$ is the number of occurrences of $\neg$ in φ, and $\mu_5(\varphi)$ is the number of occurrences of $\wedge$ occurring below an occurrence of $\vee$ in φ. Then the rules (Equivalence) and (Antivalence) decrease μ_1, the rule (Implication) decreases μ_2 and does not increase μ_1, the DeMorgan rules decrease μ_3 and increase neither μ_1 nor μ_2, the rule (Double Negation) decreases μ_4 and increases none of μ_1, μ_2, and μ_3, and the distributivity rules decrease μ_5 while increasing none of the other components of the measure μ.

2. By the Principle of Structural Induction for Formulae. Let φ be a formula to which no rule in $\mathcal{R}_2$ applies. First it is clear that φ contains only the connectives $\neg$, $\wedge$, and $\vee$, since otherwise one of the rules (Equivalence), (Antivalence), or (Implication) is applicable. If φ is atomic, there is nothing to prove. Otherwise, one of the following situations obtains.

   - If $\varphi = \neg\psi$, then ψ is atomic since otherwise one of the DeMorgan rules or (Double Negation) would apply. Thus φ is a literal, and therefore in conjunctive normal form.
   - If $\varphi = \psi \vee \chi$ and if ψ and χ are atomic, then φ is a disjunction of literals. If either ψ or χ is not atomic, then $\psi = \psi_1 \vee \psi_2$ or $\psi = \neg\psi_1$, since otherwise the second distributivity rule would apply; similarly for χ, since otherwise the first distributivity rule would apply. By the induction hypothesis, ψ and χ are both disjunctions of literals, and so φ is also a disjunction of literals.
   - If $\varphi = \psi \wedge \chi$, then by the induction hypothesis ψ and χ are both in conjunctive normal form since they are $\mathcal{R}_2$-irreducible, and so φ is also in conjunctive normal form. $\square$

Theorem 6.1.3 *The rewrite system* $\mathcal{R}_2$ *provides an algorithm constructing from each quantifier-free formula* φ *a semantically equivalent formula* φ' *in conjunctive normal form.*

Proof. Lemma 6.1.5 entails that we may convert a quantifier-free formula φ to conjunctive normal form by repeatedly rewriting φ according to the rules of $\mathcal{R}_2$ until no more applications of rules from $\mathcal{R}_2$ are possible. By the first part of that lemma any such sequence of applications of rules from $\mathcal{R}_2$ must terminate, and by the second part the resulting $\mathcal{R}_2$-irreducible formula must be in conjunctive normal form. $\square$

It follows from the results of this section that we may arrange that the matrix of any formula in prenex normal form is in conjunctive normal form. But as shown by the following example there are, in general, many possible sequences of $\mathcal{R}_2$-reductions available out of a given formula, each of which can result in quite a different normal form.

Example 6.1.2   Let P and Q be proposition symbols and let $\varphi = \neg(P \Leftrightarrow Q)$. We give a transformation of φ into conjunctive normal form. The parts of the formulae to which the rules are applied are enclosed in boxes to aid readability.

$$\neg \boxed{(P \Leftrightarrow Q)} \qquad\qquad \text{(Equivalence)}$$

$$\simeq \boxed{\neg((\neg P \vee Q) \wedge (\neg Q \vee P))} \qquad \text{(DeMorgan)}$$

$$\simeq (\boxed{\neg(\neg P \vee Q)} \vee \boxed{\neg(\neg Q \vee P)}) \qquad \text{(DeMorgan)}$$

$$\simeq (\boxed{\neg\neg P} \wedge \neg Q) \vee (\boxed{\neg\neg Q} \wedge \neg P) \qquad \text{(Double Negation)}$$

$$\simeq \boxed{(P \wedge \neg Q) \vee (Q \wedge \neg P)} \qquad\qquad \text{(Distributivity)}$$

$$\simeq (P \vee Q) \wedge (P \vee \neg P) \wedge (\neg Q \vee Q) \wedge (\neg Q \vee \neg P),$$

or, in clausal form,

$$\{\rightarrow P,Q, \ \ P \rightarrow P, \ \ Q \rightarrow Q, \ \ P,Q \rightarrow\}.$$

Alternatively, we can apply the rule (Antivalence) in the first step. The sequence of $\mathcal{R}'$-reductions then becomes

$$\boxed{\neg(P \Leftrightarrow Q)} \qquad\qquad \text{(Antivalence)}$$

$$\simeq (P \vee Q) \wedge (\neg Q \vee \neg P),$$

or, in clausal form,

$$\{\rightarrow P,Q, \ \ P,Q \rightarrow\}.$$

From Example 6.1.2 it is immediately clear that the representation of a formula in conjunctive normal form is not unique. The example also shows that the different possibilities of applications of rules can have dramatically different impacts on the size of the resulting formulae, as well as on the lengths of their derivations.

In general, an "outermost/innermost" strategy, i.e., a strategy which applies rules at the closest position possible from the root of the formula tree, is most effective. In Example 6.1.2 this is the rule (Antivalence), since it applies to the root of φ while the rule (Equivalence) applies to a deeper node. It is easy to convince oneself that such a strategy for transforming quantifier-free formulae into conjunctive normal forms is not essentially different from the application of the rules of the Gentzen calculus described in Lemma 6.1.3.

Finally, it must be mentioned that application of the transformations for converting formulae to conjunctive normal form is, in the worst case, of exponential complexity. That is, for a given formula with n connectives, a derived formula in conjunctive normal form can have as many as 2^n connectives. The responsibility for this explosion of connectives lies with rules (1), (2), (7), and (8), which essentially double the number of connectives in a formula.

6.2   Gentzen's Sharpened Hauptsatz

The main theorem of this chapter is Herbrand's Theorem (Theorem 6.3.2), which is the fundamental result of first-order logic as concerns automated deduction. It says, in essence, that through the application of appropriate substitutions, a quantifier-free provable formula can be obtained from any provable formula, and thus the provability of arbitrary formulae can be reduced to the provability of quantifier-free formulae. This observation is at the heart of completeness proofs for resolution calculi; it indicates the manner in which simple techniques—like the use of truth tables—for proving propositional validity can be used to accomplish the much more difficult task of establishing validity of first-order formulae.

Theorem 6.1.2 permits the transformation of a given formula into a semantically equivalent formula φ in prenex normal form (and we have seen that the matrix of φ may be taken to be in conjunctive normal form as well). The next step on the way to proving Herbrand's Theorem is to eliminate the prefix of φ. That is, we want to see that from φ a quantifier-free formula φ', provable iff φ is, can always be derived.

It is an immediate consequence of Gentzen's Sharpened Hauptsatz (Theorem 6.2.1) that for every formula φ such a provability-equivalent quantifier-free formula φ' is obtainable using the rules of the calculus G'. Gentzen's Sharpened Hauptsatz states that every proof tree in G' for a formula φ in prenex normal form can be transformed into a proof tree in G' for φ having nodes labeled with quantified sequents only from the root to some certain node k labeled with a quantifier-free sequent $\rightarrow \Psi$

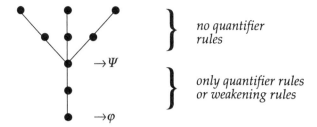

FIGURE 6.2.

(see Figure 6.2). That is, the resulting proof tree in G' for φ is such that the label of no descendant node of k is obtained from its parent by the application of a quantifier rule. It follows that for every provable formula φ there exists a provable quantifier-free formula φ' provability-equivalent to $\rightarrow \Psi$ from which φ can be obtained from φ' by repeated applications of quantifier and weakening rules.

We give a constructive proof of Gentzen's Sharpened Hauptsatz, specifying transformations on proof trees which move the applications of the quantifier rules in each such tree toward its root. To effect such a migration of applications of quantifier rules, we will need to know that applications of quantifier rules can be interchanged with applications of the other rules of the calculus. That interchanging rules requires some care is indicated in the following examples.

Example 6.2.1 Consider the following part of a derivation tree in G':

$$\frac{(\forall x\, Q(f(x))), Q(f(g(a))) \; \rightarrow \; Q(f(g(a)))}{} \quad (\forall\text{-left})$$

$$\frac{P(a) \; \rightarrow \; Q(f(g(a))) \qquad (\forall x\, Q(f(x))) \; \rightarrow \; Q(f(g(a)))}{P(a) \vee (\forall x\, Q(f(x))) \; \rightarrow \; Q(f(g(a)))} \quad (\vee\text{-left})$$

It is not possible here to interchange the order of application of the logical rules ($\forall$-left) and ($\vee$-right) since the former cannot be applied to the subformula $\forall x\, Q(f(x))$ of the antecedent of the sequent resulting from the application of the latter.

A further difficulty which may arise is illustrated by

Example 6.2.2 Consider the following part of a derivation tree, where y is free for x in $P(x)$ and satisfies the appropriate eigenvariable condition:

$$\frac{\rightarrow P(y), Q}{\rightarrow \forall x\, P(x), R(y) \qquad \rightarrow \forall x\, P(x), Q} \quad (\forall\text{-right})$$
$$\frac{}{\rightarrow \forall x\, P(x), Q \wedge R(y)} \quad (\wedge\text{-right})$$

Here the interchange of the ($\forall$-right) rule with the ($\wedge$-right) rule is not possible without violating the eigenvariable condition of the ($\forall$-right) rule. For this reason, the following tree is not a derivation tree in G'.

$$
\dfrac{
  \dfrac{\rightarrow \forall x\, P(x), R(y)}{\rightarrow P(y), \forall x\, P(x), R(y)} \qquad \dfrac{\rightarrow P(y), Q}{\rightarrow P(y), \forall x\, P(x), Q}
}{
  \dfrac{\rightarrow P(y), \forall x\, P(x), Q \wedge R(y)}{\rightarrow \forall x\, P(x), Q \wedge R(y)}
}
$$

(Weakening)

($\wedge$-right)

($\forall$-right)

It is easy to see that the problems encountered in Examples 6.2.1 and 6.2.2 are solvable simply by restricting our attention to formulae in prenex normal form and by renaming variables in the original formula, respectively. Theorem 6.1.2 provides full justification for the former; the need for the latter leads to the notion of a variable-pure proof tree.

Definition 6.2.1   A proof tree T in G' is *variable-pure* if every eigenvariable y introduced by the application of the rule ($\forall$-right) or the rule ($\exists$-left) to a node k in T appears only in the subtree of T with root k.

Of course, it makes sense to talk about variable-pure proof trees in G as well.

Lemma 6.2.1   *There exists a proof tree in G' for φ iff there exists a variable-pure proof tree in G' for φ.*

Proof. Sufficiency clearly holds. Necessity is proved by applying a suitable renaming of the eigenvariables occurring in any proof tree in G' for φ which is not variable-pure. $\square$

Lemma 6.2.2   *There exists a proof tree in G' for φ iff there exists a proof tree in G' for φ all of whose leaves are labeled with sequents of the form $\psi \rightarrow \psi$ with ψ atomic. Moreover, the latter proof tree with atomic leaves is variable-pure if the former is.*

Proof. Again, sufficiency is obvious. To establish necessity it suffices to show by induction on the structure of φ that for every axiom $\varphi \rightarrow \varphi$ in G' there exists a proof tree in G' with root $\varphi \rightarrow \varphi$ and leaves of the form $\psi \rightarrow \psi$ with ψ atomic. Then for each leaf labeled $\varphi \rightarrow \varphi$ in the original proof tree in G', the new proof tree in G' for $\varphi \rightarrow \varphi$ which is constructed can be appended to the original tree to obtain a proof tree in G' of the desired form. If φ is atomic then the assertion is trivially verified. If φ is of the form $\psi_1 \wedge \psi_2$, then we have

$$
\cfrac{
\cfrac{\psi_1 \to \psi_1}{\psi_1, \psi_2 \to \psi_1} \qquad \cfrac{\psi_2 \to \psi_2}{\psi_1, \psi_2 \to \psi_2}
}{
\cfrac{\psi_1, \psi_2 \to \psi_1 \wedge \psi_2}{\psi_1 \wedge \psi_2 \to \psi_1 \wedge \psi_2}
}
$$

$$
\begin{array}{l}
\text{(Weakening)} \\[4pt]
\text{($\wedge$-right)} \\[4pt]
\text{($\wedge$-left)}
\end{array}
$$

where, by the induction hypothesis, there are proof trees in G' for ψ_1 and ψ_2 of the desired form. The remaining cases are left as exercises. In all cases, it is a simple matter to see that variable-purity is preserved. □

Theorem 6.2.1 *(Gentzen's Sharpened Hauptsatz for prenex normal forms) Let φ be a formula in prenex normal form. Then φ is provable in G (and hence in G') iff there exists a proof tree T_0 in G' for φ and a node k in T_0 labeled with a sequent $\to \Psi$ such that*

- *every formula in Ψ is quantifier-free;*

- *if k' is a node of T_0 with $k > k'$ or $k = k'$, then either a weakening rule or a nonquantifier rule, i.e., a rule from G, is applied to k'; and*

- *if $k' > k$, then either a quantifier rule or a weakening rule is applied to node k'.*

Proof. We prove only necessity, since sufficiency is obvious. By assumption, φ is provable in G (and hence in G'), and so by Lemmas 6.2.1 and 6.2.2 there exists a variable pure proof tree T in G' for φ all of whose leaves are labeled with axioms of the form $\psi \to \psi$ with ψ atomic. We must transform the proof tree T so that nodes labeled with quantified sequents are moved toward the root.

Let $K(T)$ be the set of nodes of T, $K_Q(T)$ be the set of nodes to which a quantifier rule is applied, and $K_W(T)$ be the set of nodes to which a weakening rule is applied. If $k \in K(T)$, let $\mu_1(k, T)$ be the number of nodes among k and the ancestors of k to which neither a quantifier nor a weakening rule is applied, and let $\mu_2(k, T)$ be the number of ancestors of k to which a weakening rule is applied. That is, let

$$\mu_1(k, T) = |\{k' \in K(T) - (K_Q(T) \cup K_W(T)) \mid k' < k \text{ or } k = k'\}|$$

and

$$\mu_2(k, T) = |\{k' \in K_W(T) \mid k' < k\}|.$$

Define the complexity measure $\mu(T)$ for a tree T to be the ordered pair of multisets

$$\mu(T) = \langle \{\mu_1(k,T) \mid k \in K_Q(T)\}, \{\mu_2(k,T) \mid k \in K_Q(T)\}\rangle.$$

We define the ordering $>_2$ on ordered pairs of natural numbers to be the lexicographic extension of the multiset extension $>_{mul}$ of the usual greater-than ordering $>$ on the natural numbers.

We first show that if T is a proof tree in G' for φ such that $\mu(T) \neq 0$—i.e. such that $\mu_1(k,T) \neq 0$ or $\mu_2(k,T) \neq 0$ for some $k \in K_Q(T)$—then there exists a proof tree T' in G' for φ with $\mu(T) >_2 \mu(T')$. Clearly there exist in such a tree T nodes k and k' such that k is a child of k', a quantifier rule Q is applied to k, and a nonquantifier rule or a weakening rule R is applied to k'. By way of illustration, we generate T' from T for three choices of rules R and Q.

Case 1: Let R be the rule ($\wedge$-left) and let Q be the rule ($\forall$-left). From the proof tree T we construct a proof tree T' for which $\mu(T) >_2 \mu(T')$ holds as follows.

$$
\begin{array}{cc}
T & T' \\[2pt]
\vdots & \vdots
\end{array}
$$

$$
\dfrac{\dfrac{\forall x\,\varphi, \varphi\{x \leftarrow t\}, \psi_1, \psi_2, \Phi \;\rightarrow\; \Psi}{\forall x\,\varphi, \psi_1, \psi_2 \Phi \;\rightarrow\; \Psi}}{\forall x\,\varphi, \psi_1 \wedge \psi_2, \Phi \;\rightarrow\; \Psi}
\qquad
\dfrac{\dfrac{\forall x\,\varphi, \varphi\{x \leftarrow t\}, \psi_1, \psi_2, \Phi \;\rightarrow\; \Psi}{\forall x\,\varphi, \varphi\{x \leftarrow t\}, \psi_1 \wedge \psi_2, \Psi \;\rightarrow\; \Psi}}{\forall x\,\varphi, \psi_1 \wedge \psi_2, \Phi \;\rightarrow\; \Psi}
$$

Certainly $\mu_1(k',T') = \mu_1(k,T) - 1$, and for all nodes other than k and k', μ_1 is unchanged, i.e., $\mu_1(k'',T') = \mu_1(k'',T)$ for k'' distinct from k and k'. Since $k' \notin K_Q(T)$ and $k \notin K_Q(T')$, we have $\mu(T) >_2 \mu(T')$.

Case 2: Let R be the rule ($\vee$-left) and let Q be the rule ($\exists$-left). Then T has the following form:

$$
\begin{array}{cc}
\vdots & \vdots
\end{array}
$$

$$
\dfrac{\dfrac{\varphi\{x \leftarrow y\}, \psi_1, \Phi \;\rightarrow\; \Psi}{\exists x\,\varphi, \psi_1, \Phi \;\rightarrow\; \Psi} \qquad \exists x\,\varphi, \psi_2, \Phi \;\rightarrow\; \Psi}{\exists x\,\varphi, \psi_1 \vee \psi_2, \Phi \;\rightarrow\; \Psi}
$$

We construct a proof tree T' as follows:

$$
\begin{array}{cc}
\vdots & \vdots
\end{array}
$$

$$
\dfrac{\varphi\{x \leftarrow y\}, \psi_1, \Phi \;\rightarrow\; \Psi}{}
\qquad
\dfrac{\exists x\varphi, \psi_2, \Phi \;\rightarrow\; \Psi}{}
$$

$$\frac{\varphi\{x \leftarrow y\}, \exists x\, \varphi, \psi_1, \Phi \;\to\; \Psi \qquad \varphi\{x \leftarrow y\}, \exists x\, \varphi, \psi_2, \Phi \;\to\; \Psi}{\dfrac{\varphi\{x \leftarrow y\}, \exists x\, \varphi, \psi_1 \vee \psi_2, \Phi \;\to\; \Psi}{\exists x\, \varphi, \psi_1 \vee \psi_2, \Phi \;\to\; \Psi}}$$

Here the exchange of the rule ($\vee$-left) with the rule ($\exists$-left) requires two additional applications of weakening rules, but it is nevertheless clear that $\mu(T) >_2 \mu(T')$. Essential is the assumption that the eigenvariable y does not appear in ψ_2 since T is variable-pure.

Case 3: Let R be the first weakening rule and let Q be the rule ($\forall$-left). Then T has the form:

$$\vdots$$

$$\frac{\dfrac{\forall x\, \varphi, \varphi\{x \leftarrow t\}, \Phi \;\to\; \Psi}{\forall x\, \varphi, \Phi \;\to\; \Psi}}{\forall x\, \varphi, \Phi, \psi \;\to\; \Psi}$$

We construct a proof tree T':

$$\vdots$$

$$\frac{\dfrac{\forall x\, \varphi, \varphi\{x \leftarrow t\}, \Phi \;\to\; \Psi}{\forall x\, \varphi, \varphi\{x \leftarrow t\}, \Phi, \psi \;\to\; \Psi}}{\forall x\, \varphi, \Phi, \psi \;\to\; \Psi}$$

Here $\mu_1(k'', T') = \mu_1(k'', T)$ for all k'', including $k'' = k$ and $k'' = k'$. But since $k' \notin K_Q(T)$ and $k \notin K_Q(T')$, we have $\mu_2(k'', T') = \mu_2(k'', T)$ for $k'' \neq k$ and $\mu_2(k, T') = \mu_2(k, T) - 1$. Since in addition $\mu_2(k', T') = \mu_2(k, T')$, we have $\mu(T) >_2 \mu(T')$, as desired.

The remaining cases are proved analogously. We have thus shown that for every proof tree T in G for a given formula φ there exists a proof tree T' in G' for φ such that $\mu(T) >_2 \mu(T')$. Since the ordering $>_2$ is noetherian, there must therefore exist a proof tree T_1 in G' for φ such that $\mu_1(k, T_1) = 0$ and $\mu_2(k, T_1) = 0$ for all $k \in K_Q(T_1)$. For this proof tree we have that $k \in K_Q(T_1)$ implies $k' \in K_Q(T_1)$ for all $k' < k$, i.e., that only applications of quantifier rules occur directly below the root. Let k be the unique maximal node in $K_Q(T_1)$ and let k' be its (necessarily unique) child. The sequent $\to \Psi'$ which labels k' will, in general, contain quantified formulae. Let T' be the subtree of T_1 with root k'. Then T' is a proof tree for the sequent $\to \Psi'$. Since the leaves of T' are all labeled with quantifier-free sequents, by removing all quantified formulae in the proof tree T' we obtain a proof tree T'' for the quantifier-free sequent $\to \Psi$ obtained by removing all quantified formulae from $\to \Psi'$. We arrive at a proof tree T_0

for φ of the form

$$
\frac{\begin{array}{c} \vdots \\ \rightarrow\ \Psi \end{array}}{\begin{array}{c} \vdots \\ \hline \rightarrow\ \Psi' \\ \vdots \end{array}} \quad \text{(Weakening)}
$$

It is easy to see that the proof tree T_0 satisfies the requirements of the theorem. □

We say that a proof tree T is in *normal form* if it satisfies the conclusion of Gentzen's Sharpened Hauptsatz. The sequent $\rightarrow \Psi$ in its statement is called the *central sequent* of T_0.

Example 6.2.3   Let

$$\varphi = (\exists x \forall y\, P(x,y)) \Rightarrow (\forall v \exists w\, P(w,v)).$$

We must give a proof tree in G' for φ satisfying the conclusion of Gentzen's Sharpened Hauptsatz. First we must put φ into prenex normal form. By the rules of Lemma 6.1.1 we obtain

$$\varphi' = \forall x \forall v\, \exists y \exists w\, (P(x,y) \Rightarrow P(w,v)).$$

(There are other possibilities, such as $\forall x \exists y \forall v \exists w\, (P(x,y) \Rightarrow P(w,v))$). The following proof tree is in normal form.

$$
\frac{\dfrac{\dfrac{\dfrac{\dfrac{\dfrac{P(x,v)\ \rightarrow\ P(x,v)}{\rightarrow\ P(x,v) \Rightarrow P(x,v)}}{\rightarrow\ \exists w\,(P(x,v) \Rightarrow P(w,v))}}{\rightarrow\ \exists y \exists w\,(P(x,y) \Rightarrow P(w,v))}}{\rightarrow\ \forall v \exists y \exists w\,(P(x,y) \Rightarrow P(w,v))}}{\rightarrow\ \forall x \forall v \exists y \exists w\,(P(x,y) \Rightarrow P(w,v))}
$$

$(\Rightarrow\text{-right})$

$(\exists\text{-right and Weakening})$

$(\exists\text{-right and Weakening})$

$(\forall\text{-right})$

$(\forall\text{-right})$

6.3   Skolemization and Herbrand's Theorem

One consequence of Gentzen's Sharpened Hauptsatz is that it is possible, for every formula φ, to derive in the calculus G (and hence in G') a quantifier-free formula which is provable iff φ is. The proof that this is possible is, however, not constructive, since the calculi G and G' in no way indicate which eigenvariables and terms are to appear in applications of the quantifier rules. In this section we will learn how to *construct*, for each formula φ, a variable-pure formula φ' containing no existential quantifiers and such that φ is provable iff φ' is. That is, by relaxing the requirement that the validity-equivalent formula φ' to be derived from φ be quantifier-free, and stipulating only that it contain no existential quantifiers, we regain the ability to provide a constructive determination of φ' from φ. Of course this raises the issue of how to work with such an arbitrary variable-pure universally quantified formula.

Recall that negative calculi in general, and resolution calculi in particular, prove the validity of a formula ψ by establishing the unsatisfiability of $\neg\psi$; negative calculi are thus not concerned with actually *producing* a proof of ψ, but rather only with demonstrating that one *exists*. Given a formula ψ to prove—and hence a formula $\neg\psi$ to refute—we begin by letting φ stand for $\neg\psi$ and converting φ to prenex normal form as described in Section 6.1. We then eliminate all existential quantifiers from φ to arrive at a formula φ' which is not necessarily semantically equivalent to φ, but which is satisfiable iff φ is. This is accomplished in part by extending the signature over which φ is considered to be defined; the method we employ is constructive, and is called *skolemization* after the Norwegian mathematician Thoralf Skolem. The upshot here is that since the formula φ is satisfiable iff φ' is, we may refute φ by refuting φ'—i.e., we may demonstrate that φ is unsatisfiable by showing that φ' is—and so we see that ψ is valid iff φ' is unsatisfiable. We therefore see that the problem of proving arbitrary first-order formulae can be *effectively* reduced to the considerably easier problem of refuting formulae containing no existential quantifiers. This is the fundamental observation underlying the development of resolution calculi, which seek to prove arbitrary first-order formulae by refuting the associated formulae without existential quantifiers obtained from them as described in this section.

We first show how to derive for each formula in prenex normal form a validity-equivalent formula without existential quantifiers, i.e., we show how we may eliminate existential quantifiers from formulae while preserving their satisfiability or unsatisfiability.

Definition 6.3.1 Let $\Sigma = \langle \mathcal{F}, \mathcal{P} \rangle$ be a signature.

1. The *skolemization rule for formulae in the antecedent* is

$$\frac{\Phi, \forall x_1 \dots \forall x_n \exists y\, \psi \to \Psi}{\Phi, \forall x_1 \dots \forall x_n\, \psi\{y \leftarrow f_y x_1 \dots x_n\} \to \Psi}$$

where the conclusion of the rule is a formula over the signature Σ' obtained by extending Σ by the n-ary function symbol f_y.

2. The *skolemization rule for formulae in the succedent* is

$$\frac{\Phi \to \exists x_1 \ldots \exists x_n \forall y \, \psi, \Psi}{\Phi \to \exists x_1 \ldots \exists x_n \, \psi\{y \leftarrow f_y x_1 \ldots x_n\}, \Psi}$$

where the conclusion of the rule is a formula over the signature Σ' obtained by extending Σ by the n-ary function symbol f_y.

The function symbol f_y introduced by a skolemization rule is called a *skolem function symbol* and a term $f_y x_1 \ldots x_n$ introduced by a skolemization rule is called a *skolem term*.

The idea of skolemization is to replace an existentially quantified variable with a term representing one of the objects whose existence it asserts. The arguments to the skolem function symbols indicate the dependence of the objects referred to by the existential quantifiers they replace on the objects referred to by preceding universal quantifiers. *Skolemization* is the process of repeatedly applying skolemization rules to formulae; it can be thought of as the process of deleting each existential quantifier of a formula φ and its attached variable from the prefix of φ and replacing the resulting free variables occurring in the matrix of φ by skolem terms. Because we will be concerned in the next chapter with negative calculi, we require skolemization only in the antecedent.

The idea of skolemization is illustrated in the following example:

Example 6.3.1 If

$$\varphi = \forall x \, \exists y (y > x),$$

then skolemization of φ gives the formula

$$\varphi' = \forall x \, (f(x) > x).$$

The skolemization function f may be interpreted as the successor function.

We write $\Phi \Rightarrow_S \Phi'$ if $\Phi' \to$ is obtained from $\Phi \to$ by skolemization in the antecedent. Let Φ be a set of prenex normal forms. The *functional form* $F(\Phi)$ of Φ is the unique normal form of Φ with respect to $\Rightarrow_S$, i.e., $F(\Phi)$ is the unique set of formulae which is free of existential quantifiers and which is such that $\Phi \Rightarrow_S^* F(\Phi)$. We write $F(\varphi)$ in place of $F(\{\varphi\})$. The terminology "functional form" refers to the fact that skolemization introduces function symbols. Write $\widehat{\Phi}$ for the set of all matrices of formulae in $F(\Phi)$, and $\widehat{\varphi}$ when Φ is the singleton $\{\varphi\}$.

Example 6.3.2   Let

$$\Phi = \forall x \exists y \, \neg P(x,y), \, \exists u \forall v \, P(u,v) \rightarrow \, .$$

We define a unary skolem function symbol f for the variable y and a skolem constant symbol a for the variable u and obtain

$$\widehat{\Phi} = \{\neg P(x, f(x)), P(a,v)\}.$$

The formula $\Phi = (\forall x \exists y \, \neg P(x,y)) \wedge (\exists u \forall v P(u,v))$ is refutable iff the sequent $\Phi \rightarrow$ is provable. One possible proof in normal form is as follows:

$$
\cfrac{
\cfrac{
\cfrac{
\cfrac{
\cfrac{P(u,y) \; \rightarrow \; P(u,y)}{\neg P(u,y), P(u,y) \; \rightarrow}
}{\neg P(u,y), \forall v \, P(u,v) \; \rightarrow}
}{\exists y \, \neg P(u,y), \forall v \, P(u,v) \; \rightarrow}
}{\forall x \exists y \, \neg P(x,y), \forall v \, P(u,v) \; \rightarrow}
}{\forall x \exists y \, \neg P(x,y), \exists u \forall v \, P(u,v) \; \rightarrow}
$$

(¬-left)

(∀-left and Weakening)

(∃-left)

(∀-left and Weakening)

(∃-left)

We can modify this proof in the following way. In an application of the rule (∃-left) with bound variable w, we substitute for w the skolem term corresponding to w. Note that this is not a valid application of a quantifier rule over the original signature (since the skolem term is not a term over the original signature), but it *is* a valid application of a quantifier rule over the signature obtained by extending the original signature with the skolem function symbols for the bound variables in the original formula to be proved. Moreover, as in the proof tree below, the appearance of skolem terms can help determine the terms by which universally quantified variables should be instantiated for successful proof development. For the formula above, we obtain the following proof:

$$
\cfrac{
\cfrac{
\cfrac{
\cfrac{
\cfrac{P(a,f(a)) \; \rightarrow \; P(a,f(a))}{\neg P(a,f(a)), P(a,f(a)) \; \rightarrow}
}{\neg P(a,f(a)), \forall v \, P(a,v) \; \rightarrow}
}{\exists y \, \neg P(a,y), \forall v \, P(a,v) \; \rightarrow}
}{\forall x \exists y \, \neg P(x,y), \forall v \, P(a,v) \; \rightarrow}
}{\forall x \exists y \, \neg P(x,y), \exists u \forall v \, P(u,v) \; \rightarrow}
$$

(¬-left)

(∀-left and Weakening)

(∃-left)

(∀-left and Weakening)

(∃-left)

This discussion foreshadows the conclusion of Herbrand's Theorem (Theorem 6.3.2): the substitution $\sigma = \{x \leftarrow a, y \leftarrow f(a), u \leftarrow a, v \leftarrow f(a)\}$, which introduces ground terms over the extended Herbrand universe, instantiates the original formula to obtain a refutable variable-free formula. Since we are working in classical logic, the process outlined above requires that the given signature contains at least one constant symbol (consider the classically valid formula $\forall x\,(P(x) \vee \neg P(x))$ which is trivially satisfiable in a signature with empty carrier). We always assume this in what follows.

The functional form of a formula φ will not necessarily be semantically equivalent to φ, i.e., it will not necessarily have precisely the same models as φ. There exist, for example, interpretations which satisfy the formula $\exists x\,P(x)$ but not $P(a)$, and so skolemization can be regarded as a way of restricting models of formulae. But skolemization *does* preserve satisfiability, if not semantic equivalence, in the sense that a formula φ is satisfiable iff its functional form $F(\varphi)$ is. And since negative calculi, like resolution calculi, are concerned with determining only that a proof of a given formula *exists*, the fact that skolemization is satisfiability-preserving is sufficient for our purposes.

Note that ψ need not be quantifier-free in

Lemma 6.3.1   *The formula $\forall x_1 \ldots \forall x_n \exists y\, \psi$ is satisfiable iff $\forall x_1 \ldots \forall x_n\, \psi\{y \leftarrow f_y x_1 \ldots x_n\}$ is satisfiable, where f_y is the skolem function symbol associated with y.*

Proof. One direction is immediate. For the other, let Σ be the original signature, and let Σ' be its extension by the function symbol f_y. Let $\mathcal{I} = \langle \mathcal{M}, \beta \rangle$ be a model of $\forall x_1 \ldots \forall x_n \exists y\, \psi$ and let $a_1, \ldots, a_n \in M$ be arbitrary. Then $\mathcal{I}' = \mathcal{I}[x_1 \to a_1, \ldots, x_n \to a_n] \models \exists y\, \psi$. Thus there exists an $a \in M$ such that $\mathcal{I}'[y \to a] \models \psi$. We extend the Σ-interpretation $\mathcal{I}$ to a Σ'-interpretation $\mathcal{I}_1$ by defining $\mathcal{I}_1(f_y) = f^a$, where f^a is any function such that $f^a(\langle a_1, \ldots, a_n \rangle) = a$. Let $\mathcal{I}_2 = \mathcal{I}_1[x_1 \to a_1, \ldots, x_n \to a_n]$. Then

$$
\begin{aligned}
\mathcal{I}_2[y \to \mathcal{I}_2(f_y x_1 \ldots x_n)] &= \mathcal{I}_2[y \to f^a(\mathcal{I}_2(x_1), \ldots, \mathcal{I}_2(x_n))] \\
&= \mathcal{I}_2[y \to f^a(\langle a_1, \ldots, a_n \rangle)] \\
&= \mathcal{I}_2[y \to a].
\end{aligned}
$$

Since the formula ψ does not contain the symbol f_y, it follows from $\mathcal{I}'[y \to a] \models \psi$ that $\mathcal{I}_2[y \to a] \models \psi$, and thus that $\mathcal{I}_2[y \to \mathcal{I}_2(f_y x_1 \ldots x_n)] \models \psi$. By the Substitution Lemma (Lemma 4.2.2), we have $\mathcal{I}_2 \models \psi\{y \leftarrow f_y x_1 \ldots x_n\}$. Since $a_1, \ldots, a_n$ were chosen arbitrarily in M, we have $\mathcal{I}_1 \models \forall x_1 \ldots \forall x_n\, \psi\{y \leftarrow f_y x_1 \ldots x_n\}$. $\square$

Lemma 6.3.1 implies that φ is satisfiable iff $F(\varphi)$ is. This in turn implies that φ is unsatisfiable iff $F(\varphi)$ is, and therefore that $\varphi \to$ is valid iff $F(\varphi) \to$ is. That is, if $F(\Phi) = \{\varphi_1, \ldots, \varphi_n\}$ then $\neg\varphi$ is valid iff $\neg(\varphi_1 \wedge \ldots \wedge \varphi_n)$ is. We record a more general version of this latter observation as

Theorem 6.3.1   *Let Φ be a set of formulae in prenex normal form. Then $\Phi \to$ is valid iff $F(\Phi) \to$ is.*

The proof of the main result of this chapter makes use of the following observation. Since, for any formula φ and any $x \in FV(\varphi)$, φ is valid iff $\forall x\, \varphi$ is, when considering validity of formulae we may assume without loss of generality that for any set Φ of formulae in prenex normal form, $F(\Phi) = \{\forall x_1^1 \ldots \forall x_1^{k_1} \psi_1, \ldots, \forall x_n^1 \ldots \forall x_n^{k_n} \psi_n\}$, where $\widehat{\Phi} = \{\psi_1, \ldots, \psi_n\}$ and $FV(\psi_i) = \{x_i^1, \ldots, x_i^{k_i}\}$. In particular, when considering validity, we may assume without loss of generality that formulae are closed. Because a formula φ is satisfiable iff $\exists x\, \varphi$ is, when considering satisfiability we may likewise assume without loss of generality that formulae are closed.

Finally, we have

Theorem 6.3.2   *(Herbrand's Theorem for prenex normal forms) Let Φ be a set of formulae in prenex normal form. The sequent $\Phi \to$ is provable iff there exist ground instances $\varphi_1, \ldots, \varphi_n$ of formulae in the set $\widehat{\Phi}$ such that the sequent $\varphi_1, \ldots, \varphi_n \to$ is provable. Moreover, for $i = 1, \ldots, n$, if $\varphi_i = \sigma(\psi)$ for some $\psi \in \widehat{\Phi}$, then the terms in $Cod(\sigma)$ are ground terms over the signature obtained by extending the original signature by the skolem function symbols in $\widehat{\Phi}$.*

Proof. First suppose that the sequent $\Phi \to$ is provable, and that all of the formulae in Φ are closed. By Gentzen's Sharpened Hauptsatz (Theorem 6.2.1) we may assume that there is a proof tree T in G' in normal form, and that the central sequent of this proof tree is $\Phi_0 \to$. We transform the proof tree in the following way: let $\forall x_1 \ldots \forall x_m \exists y\, \varphi \in \Phi$ and let f be the skolem function symbol corresponding to y. For $i = 1, \ldots, m$, let t_i be the term substituted for x_i by an application of the rule ($\forall$-left) in T. We construct a derivation tree T' in which we replace all occurrences of y in T by $f(t_1 \ldots t_m)$. We apply this process repeatedly to the tree T' until there are no existential quantifiers appearing in the tree at all. We obtain in this way a modified central sequent $\Psi \to$ containing no free variables.

It is easy to see that the formulae in Ψ are precisely of the form $\sigma(\psi_i)$ where $\psi_i \in \widehat{\Phi}$ and σ is a substitution whose codomain comprises ground terms over the signature obtained by extending the original one by the skolem function symbols in $\widehat{\Phi}$. Moreover, the sequent $\Psi \to$ is provable by construction, and is as in the statement of the theorem.

We must now show conversely that the provability of a sequent $\varphi_1, \ldots, \varphi_n \to$ as in the statement of the theorem implies the provability of the original sequent $\Phi \to$. If $\varphi_1, \ldots, \varphi_n \to$ is provable, then it is also valid, and so there exists no interpretation falsifying $\varphi_1, \ldots, \varphi_n \to$. Thus if $\mathcal{I}$ is any interpretation, there must exist an i, $0 \le i \le n$ such that

$\mathcal{I} \not\models \varphi_i$. Since φ_i is precisely $\sigma(\psi_i)$ for some $\psi_i \in \widehat{\Phi}$, and since without loss of generality we may assume that $Dom(\sigma) = FV(\psi_i)$, we must have that $\mathcal{I} \not\models \forall x_i^1 \dots \forall x_i^{k_i} \psi_i$, where $\{x_i^1, \dots, x_i^{k_i}\} = FV(\psi_i)$. Thus if $\{\psi_1, \dots, \psi_m\} = \widehat{\Phi}$ and $\{x_i^1, \dots, x_i^{k_i}\} = FV(\psi_i)$ for $i = 1, \dots, m$, then the sequent

$$\forall x_1^1 \dots \forall x_1^{k_1} \psi_1, \ \dots, \ \forall x_m^1 \dots \forall x_m^{k_m} \psi_m \to$$

is valid. But then since $\{\psi_1, \dots, \psi_m\} = \widehat{\Phi}$ and $\{x_i^1, \dots, x_i^{k_i}\} = FV(\psi_i)$ for $i = 1, \dots, m$, we have $\{\forall x_1^1 \dots \forall x_1^{k_1} \psi_1, \dots, \forall x_n^1 \dots \forall x_n^{k_n} \psi_n\} = F(\Phi)$, and so $F(\Phi) \to$ is valid. By Theorem 6.3.1, the validity, and therefore the provability in G', of the sequent $\Phi \to$ follows.

It should be mentioned that it is also possible to prove the second part of the theorem directly using proof transformations, but this requires considerably more effort. The interested reader can find such a proof on pages 345–349 of [Gal86]. □

Herbrand's Theorem for prenex normal forms can be broken into two distinct parts. The first part says that skolemization offers a means of constructing from a prenex normal form a formula with no existential quantifiers which is satisfiable iff the formula from which it was constructed is. The second part of the theorem entails that for every prenex formula φ with matrix ψ there exists a set of instances of ψ which is unsatisfiable iff φ is. Herbrand's Theorem *cannot* in general indicate how these substitution instances are to be constructed, however, since that would imply decidability of the validity of predicate logic formulae.

To find this set of provable instances of ψ we can enumerate all of its ground instances over the extended Herbrand universe of ψ. Eventually we will necessarily have enumerated an unsatisfiable set of instances of ψ, but this is clearly not a very efficient way to find the instances we seek. We will see later in Section 7.2 how *unification* can be used to determine which instances of ψ are relevant to a particular proof search. Unification provides a means of capitalizing on the fact, implicit in the statement of Herbrand's Theorem, that the ground terms by which variables of ψ are replaced during the course of proving φ are very closely related to the subterms of ψ itself.

For the completeness proof of resolution in the next chapter we will use the following, equivalent, version of Herbrand's Theorem. It says that every formula in prenex normal form has a corresponding set of clauses which is ground satisfiable over the extended Herbrand universe iff the original formula is satisfiable.

For any clause $C = \varphi_1, \ldots, \varphi_n \rightarrow \psi_1, \ldots, \psi_m$, write $\sigma(C)$ for the instance $\sigma(\varphi_1), \ldots, \sigma(\varphi_n) \rightarrow \sigma(\psi_1), \ldots, \sigma(\psi_m)$ of C.

Theorem 6.3.3   *(Herbrand's Theorem) Let Φ be a set of formulae in prenex normal form and let S be the clausal form of $\widehat{\Phi}$. The set Φ of formulae is unsatisfiable iff there exists a set $\{C_1, \ldots, C_n\}$ of ground instances of clauses from S which is unsatisfiable. Moreover, for $i = 1, \ldots, n$, if $C_i = \sigma(C')$ for some $C' \in S$, then the terms in $Cod(\sigma)$ are ground terms over the signature obtained by extending the original signature by the skolem function symbols in $\widehat{\Phi}$.*

For any set S of clauses, write $\overline{S}$ for the (infinite) set of all ground instances of clauses in S. Then since for any (finite) set of clauses S there exists a formula φ in prenex normal form such that S is the clausal form of $\widehat{\varphi}$, Herbrand's Theorem implies that S is satisfiable iff every (finite) set of ground instances of clauses from S is satisfiable. The same result therefore holds for $\overline{S}$ itself.

Corollary 6.3.1   *If S is any (finite) set of clauses, then S is satisfiable iff $\overline{S}$ is.*

Proof. Suppose $\overline{S}$ is satisfiable. Then every finite subset of $\overline{S}$ is also satisfiable, and so every finite set of ground instances of clauses from S is satisfiable. Thus S is itself satisfiable.

Conversely, suppose S is satisfiable, and let S' be any finite set of (ground instances of) clauses from $\overline{S}$. Then since this set is also a finite set of ground instances of clauses from S, it must be satisfiable since S is. That is, every finite set of ground instances of clauses from $\overline{S}$ is satisfiable. Thus $\overline{S}$ is itself satisfiable. □

We end this chapter by observing that the given method for skolemization can yield skolem function symbols of unnecessarily large arity. To control the proliferation of symbols introduced by skolemization, it is advisable to first use the equivalence

$$\forall x\, \varphi \simeq \exists x\, \varphi \simeq \varphi \quad \text{if} \quad x \notin FV(\varphi)$$

to remove all superfluous quantifiers from the given formula. It is furthermore advisable to decrease the scopes of the quantified variables using the equivalence

$$Qx\,(\varphi * \psi) \quad \simeq \quad (Qx\,\varphi) * \psi$$

if $x \notin FV(\psi)$ for $Q \in \{\exists, \forall\}$ and $* \in \{\wedge, \vee\}$, together with the equivalences

$$\exists x\,(\varphi \vee \psi) \quad \simeq \quad (\exists x\,\varphi) \vee \exists y\,(\psi\{x \leftarrow y\})$$

and

$$\forall x\, (\varphi \wedge \psi) \quad \simeq \quad (\forall x\, \varphi) \wedge \forall y\, (\psi\{x \leftarrow y\}).$$

The following example illustrates the diversity among various skolemization possibilities.

Example 6.3.3   Let

$$\varphi = \forall x \forall y \forall z \exists u\, (P(z,u) \wedge P(y,y)).$$

Skolemization as in Definition 6.3.1 produces the formula

$$\forall x \forall y \forall z\, (P(z, f(x,y,z)) \wedge P(y,y)).$$

But the formula φ is semantically equivalent to the formula

$$\psi = (\forall z \exists u\, P(z,u)) \wedge (\forall y\, P(y,y)).$$

Thus φ also admits the simpler skolemization $(\forall z\, P(z, g(z))) \wedge (\forall y\, P(y,y))$.

7

Resolution and Unification

7.1 Ground Resolution

Our results from Chapter 6 suggest that an arbitrary formula φ can be proved—and hence $\neg\varphi$ can be refuted—by first converting $\neg\varphi$ to a satisfiability-equivalent formula ψ in prenex normal form, and then refuting a set of instantiated clauses—derived from the clausal form of the matrix of $F(\psi)$—which is ground satisfiable over the extended Herbrand universe of φ iff $\neg\varphi$ is satisfiable. The existence of such a set of instantiated clauses is guaranteed by Herbrand's Theorem, whose proof, unfortunately, provides no insight into how to actually find one. A rather straightforward method for generating a set of clauses with the required property is simply to enumerate, in turn, all ground instances of the clauses in the matrix of $F(\psi)$ until such a set is found; in practice, however, this kind of uncontrolled enumeration emerges as considerably less than efficient. In the next section we will learn of unification, a technique for eliminating brute-force enumeration of ground clauses from our refutation method for arbitrary formulae by enabling the systematic recognition of ground instances of nonground clauses which are relevant to refutations. The remainder of this section is dedicated to describing a refutation method for ground clauses that can be used in conjunction with precisely such a brute-force enumeration; in Section 7.4 we see how to combine unification with a generalization of this method for ground clauses to arrive at an efficient refutation technique for arbitrary clauses.

Recall from Chapter 6 that a clause is an ordered pair $\langle \Phi, \Psi \rangle$ of finite sets of atomic formulae, usually written in the form $\Phi \rightarrow \Psi$, as in Definition 5.1.1. We denote the *empty clause* $\emptyset \rightarrow \emptyset$ by $\square$.

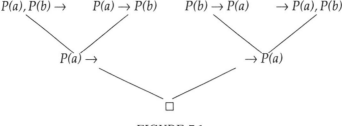

$$P(a), P(b) \rightarrow \qquad P(a) \rightarrow P(b) \qquad P(b) \rightarrow P(a) \qquad \rightarrow P(a), P(b)$$

$$P(a) \rightarrow \qquad\qquad\qquad \rightarrow P(a)$$

$$\square$$

FIGURE 7.1.

The following rule forms the basis of our refutation method for ground clauses.

Definition 7.1.1   The *resolution rule for ground clauses* is

$$\frac{\Phi \rightarrow \Psi, A \qquad \Phi', A \rightarrow \Psi'}{\Phi, \Phi' \rightarrow \Psi, \Psi'}.$$

Here Φ, Φ', Ψ, and Ψ' are sets of ground atoms and A is a single such atom. The conclusion of the resolution rule is called the *resolvent* of the two clauses in its premise.

The resolution rule for ground clauses "cuts" an atom A appearing in the antecedent of one of the premise clauses and in the succedent of the other, and combines the remainders of these two clauses. A *ground resolution derivation* out of S_0 is a sequence $S_0, S_1, S_2, \ldots$ of sets of ground clauses such that, for each k, S_{k+1} is obtained by an application of the resolution rule for ground clauses to some pair of clauses in S_k. A *ground resolution refutation* of a set S of clauses is a ground resolution derivation out of S with $\square \in S_k$ for some $k \geq 0$.

Example 7.1.1   Let

$$S = \{P(a), P(b) \rightarrow, \ P(a) \rightarrow P(b), \ P(b) \rightarrow P(a), \ \rightarrow P(a), P(b)\}.$$

From the clauses $P(a), P(b) \rightarrow$ and $P(a) \rightarrow P(b)$ the resolvent $P(a) \rightarrow$ can be derived. (Note that the two occurrences of the atom $P(a)$ in the antecedent of the resolvent are collapsed into one, since clauses are pairs of *sets* of atoms.) Moreover, from $P(b) \rightarrow P(a)$ and $\rightarrow P(a), P(b)$ the resolvent $\rightarrow P(a)$ can be obtained. The two clauses $P(a) \rightarrow$ and $\rightarrow P(a)$ can then be resolved to produce the empty clause $\square$. This resolution derivation is represented graphically as in Figure 7.1.

The resolution rule for ground clauses will be seen in Section 7.4 to be a particular instance of a more general resolution rule accommodating sets of clauses which are not necessarily ground clauses. This more general resolution rule forms the basis of the promised refutation method for arbitrary clauses, which is more efficient than the straightforward method of enumerating ground instances of certain clauses described in the discussion preceding Definition 7.1.1. The refutation method for arbitrary clauses (and therefore that for ground clauses as well) will be proved sound and complete later in this chapter; for now we motivate the need for such a method by considering the problem of refuting a set of nonground clauses.

Example 7.1.2   Consider the set $S = \{(\to P(x,b)), (P(a,y) \to)\}$ of nonground clauses. The atoms $P(x,b)$ and $P(a,y)$ are different, and so the ground resolution rule does not apply. But since the set S is unsatisfiable, by Corollary 6.3.1 there must exist an unsatisfiable set of ground instances of clauses from S. An obvious candidate for an appropriate ground substitution σ giving rise to such a set of ground instances is $\sigma = \{x \leftarrow a, y \leftarrow b\}$; indeed the two atoms $P(x,b)$ and $P(a,y)$ become identical under application of σ, the ground resolution rule is then applicable, and the empty clause can immediately be derived from $\to P(a,b)$ and $P(a,b) \to$.

The substitution σ in Example 7.1.2 is said to be a *unifier* of $P(x,b)$ and $P(a,y)$. *Unification*—the process of computing unifiers of atoms—will provide a systematic means of finding substitutions which give rise to the sets of ground instances of clauses whose existence is guaranteed by Herbrand's Theorem. Since unification is a key component of our resolution-based refutation method for arbitrary clauses, the next two sections are devoted to gaining an understanding of that process and its complexity before using it to develop our general refutation method in Section 7.4.

7.2   Unification

In this section and the next we define more formally the notion of a unifier of two terms and investigate more thoroughly the process of unification.

Definition 7.2.1   Let s and t be terms (or atoms[1]).

1. A *unifier* of s and t is a substitution σ such that $\sigma(s) = \sigma(s)$ holds. If σ is a unifier of s and t, then we say that σ *unifies* s and t. The set of all unifiers of s and t is denoted $u(s,t)$. The terms s and t are said to be *unifiable* provided $u(s,t) \neq \emptyset$.

---

[1]We formulate unification here only for terms since this suffices for our purposes; the results are analogous for atoms.

2. A *matching substitution* of s to t is a substitution σ such that $\sigma(s) = t$ holds. The set of all matching substitutions of s to t is denoted $m(s,t)$.

Although $u(s,t) = u(t,s)$ for all terms s and t, $m(s,t)$ will not necessarily be the same as $m(t,s)$ for an arbitrary pair of terms s and t.

Example 7.2.1

1. Let $s = f(x,b)$ and $t = f(a,y)$. Then $\sigma = \{x \leftarrow a, y \leftarrow b\}$ is a unifier of s and t. Moreover, σ is the only unifier of s and t with $Dom(\sigma) = \{x,y\}$. Note that there exists neither a matching substitution of s to t nor a matching substitution of t to s.

2. Let $s = f(x,y)$ and $t = f(y,x)$. Then every substitution mapping x and y to the same term is a unifier of s and t, and so s and t have infinitely many unifiers. The "simplest" unifiers are $\sigma = \{x \leftarrow y\}$ and $\tau = \{y \leftarrow x\}$. The substitution $\nu = \{x \leftarrow y, y \leftarrow x\}$ is in $m(s,t)$ and also in $m(t,s)$, and since it is the only substitution in either, we have $m(s,t) = m(t,s)$ for the given terms s and t.

3. Let $s = a$ and $t = b$. Then there exists no unifier of s and t, no matching substitution of s to t, and no matching substitution of t to s.

4. Let $s = x$ and $t = f(x)$. Then s and t are not unifiable, since the terms $\sigma(x)$ and $\sigma(f(x)) = f(\sigma(x))$ are different for every substitution σ. For the same reason, there is no matching substitution of t to s; the substitution $\tau = \{x \leftarrow f(x)\}$, on the other hand, is a matching substitution of s to t.

Although Part 2 of Example 7.2.1 establishes that it is possible for two terms to have infinitely many unifiers, in the context of automated deduction we will always be interested only in finding the "simplest" unifiers of a given pair of terms. Searching for unifiers of a pair of terms s and t can be interpreted as solving the equational constraint $s \approx t$,[2] i.e., as searching for instantiation terms for the variables in s and t so that the instantiated versions of the constraint terms s and t are identical. The substitution σ in Part 1 of Example 7.2.1, for instance, corresponds to instantiating x with a and y with b in the equational constraint $s \approx t$. Below we will give an inference system for unification which is based on exactly this interpretation of the unification problem. First, however, we make precise the notions we will require in that enterprise.

---

[2]Although we have restricted our attention to first-order languages which do not contain the connective $\approx$, the use of this symbol here is not unrelated to its use as a connective in first-order languages. Indeed, determining solvability of the equational constraint $s \approx t$ can be regarded as determining the satisfiability of the atomic formula $s \approx t$ in a first-order language with equality.

Definition 7.2.2

1. An *equational constraint*, or simply an *equation*, is an ordered pair $\langle s, t \rangle$ of terms, usually written in the form $s \approx t$. A *system of equations*, or simply a *system*, is a set of equations. The substitution σ *unifies* the equation $s \approx t$ if σ unifies the terms s and t; if σ unifies $s \approx t$ then we say that σ is a *unifier* of $s \approx t$. The substitution σ *unifies* a system E of equations if it simultaneously unifies every equation in E. We denote the set of unifiers of E by $u(E)$, and the set of variables occurring in terms in E by $Var(E)$. If $u(E) \neq \emptyset$, we say that E is *unifiable*.

2. The system E is *more general* than the system E', denoted $E \leq E'$, provided $u(E') \subseteq u(E)$. The systems E and E' are *equivalent*, denoted $E \sim E'$, if $u(E) = u(E')$.

3. An equation $x_i \approx t_i$ in a system of equations $E = \{x_1 \approx t_1, \ldots, x_n \approx t_n\}$ is *solved in* E if x_i occurs in E exactly once, i.e., if

   - $x_i \neq x_j$ for $i \neq j$, and
   - $x_i \notin Var(t_j)$ for $i, j \in \{1, \ldots, n\}$.

   A system E of equations is said to be *solved* if every equation in E is solved in E.

4. If the system E is solved, then E is a *solution* for E' if $E' \leq E$ holds, and E is a *most general solution* for E' if $E \leq E'$ also holds, i.e., if $E' \sim E$ holds. A system E' of equations is said to be *solvable* if there exists some solution E for E', and is said to be *unsolvable* otherwise.

According to Part 3 of Definition 7.2.2, every idempotent substitution $\sigma = \{x_1 \leftarrow t_1, \ldots, x_n \leftarrow t_n\}$ can be represented as a solved system $[\sigma] = \{x_1 \approx t_1, \ldots, x_n \approx t_n\}$, and every solved system $E = \{x_1 \approx t_1, \ldots, x_n \approx t_n\}$ determines a unique idempotent substitution $\sigma_E = \{x_1 \leftarrow t_1, \ldots, x_n \leftarrow t_n\}$. Indeed, there is an obvious bijection between the set of idempotent substitutions and the set of solved systems of equations. The next lemma indicates a deeper relationship between solved systems and idempotent substitutions.

Lemma 7.2.1

1. *If E is a solved system of equations, then the function σ_E is a well-defined idempotent substitution and $\sigma_E \in u(E)$. Thus if E is a solution of E', then σ_E is also a unifier of E'.*

2. *If σ is an idempotent unifier of E', then $[\sigma]$ is a solution of E'.*

Proof. 1. The function σ_E is well-defined, i.e., every variable x_i is mapped to precisely one term, since $x_i \neq x_j$ holds if $i \neq j$. The idempotence of σ_E follows directly from the definition of σ_E. Finally, $\sigma_E(x_i) = t_i = \sigma_E(t_i)$ holds for $i = 1, \ldots, n$ and so $\sigma_E \in u(E)$.

2. Suppose that $\sigma \in u(E')$ and $\tau \in u([\sigma])$. We want to show that $\tau \in u(E')$, which we do by first showing that $\tau\sigma = \tau$ holds. If $x \notin Dom(\sigma)$ then clearly $\tau(\sigma(x)) = \tau(x)$; if $x \in Dom(\sigma)$ then $x = x_i$ for some $i \in \{1, \ldots, n\}$ and so $\tau(\sigma(x)) = \tau(\sigma(x_i)) = \tau(t_i) = \tau(x_i)$. Thus $\tau\sigma = \tau$. Now let $s \approx t \in E'$. Then $\tau(s) = \tau(\sigma(s)) = \tau(\sigma(t)) = \tau(t)$, and so $\tau \in u(E')$. Thus $u([\sigma]) \subseteq u(E')$ and therefore $E' \leq [\sigma]$. Moreover, $[\sigma]$ is solved, and so $[\sigma]$ is a solution for E'. $\square$

Thus solutions of systems and their idempotent unifiers are merely different representations of the same objects, and so a system is unifiable iff it is solvable. Because of the bijection between solutions of systems and their idempotent unifiers we say that σ_E is a *most general unifier* of E' whenever E is a most general solution for E'. As indicated in the second part of Example 7.2.1, a given system can have more than one most general solution (both σ and τ there determine most general solutions for the system $\{s \approx t\}$), but of course the various most general solutions of a system are all idempotent, as well as identical up to variable renaming. Note that if σ is a most general unifier of a system E then the variables in the domain and codomain of σ may, without loss of generality, be taken to be among those appearing in E, and that if E is a solution for E' then the variables in E may likewise be taken to be among those appearing in E'. In addition, by the argument of the proof of the second part of Lemma 7.2.1, we have that if σ is a most general unifier of a system E of equations and if τ is any unifier of E, then $\tau\sigma = \tau$. Indeed,

Lemma 7.2.2   *Let σ be a substitution, and let E be an equational system. The following statements are equivalent:*

1. *The substitution σ is a most general unifier of E.*

2. *The substitution σ is a unifier of E and, for all $\tau \in u(E)$, $\tau\sigma = \tau$ holds.*

3. *The substitution σ is a unifier of E and, for all $\tau \in u(E)$, there exists a substitution λ such that $\lambda\sigma = \tau$ holds.*

Proof. This lemma follows from the proof of Lemma 7.2.1. $\square$

We sometimes write $s \succeq t$ for the problem of matching s to t. Since it is easy to see that the matching problem $s \succeq t$ is solvable iff the unification problem $\{s \approx \theta(t)\}$ is—where $\theta = \{x \leftarrow c_x \mid x \in Var(t)\}$ is a substitution which maps every variable x occurring in t to a new constant c_x—we may consider matching problems to be special cases of unification problems.

We now give an inference system serving as the foundation of an algorithm which calculates from every system of equations a most general solution of that system in case one exists, and which halts with the information that the system is unsolvable otherwise. If $E = \{s_1 \approx t_1, \ldots, s_n \approx t_n\}$ is a system of equations and σ is a substitution, we write $\sigma(E)$ for the system of equations $\{\sigma(s_1) \approx \sigma(t_1), \ldots, \sigma(s_n) \approx \sigma(t_n)\}$. We write $E\{x \leftarrow t\}$ for $\sigma(E)$ when σ comprises the single substitution component $\{x \leftarrow t\}$.

Definition 7.2.3   The inference system $\mathcal{U}$ for unification of ordered pairs $\langle S, E \rangle$ of systems of equations is given by the following rules:

- *Trivial*

$$\frac{\langle S, E \cup \{t \approx t\} \rangle}{\langle S, E \rangle}$$

- *Decomposition*

$$\frac{\langle S, E \cup \{ft_1 \ldots t_n \approx fs_1 \ldots s_n\} \rangle}{\langle S, E \cup \{t_1 \approx s_1, \ldots, t_n \approx s_n\} \rangle}$$

- *Orientation*

$$\frac{\langle S, E \cup \{t \approx x\} \rangle}{\langle S, E \cup \{x \approx t\} \rangle}$$

provided $t \notin \mathcal{V}$.

- *Substitution*

$$\frac{\langle S, E \cup \{x \approx t\} \rangle}{\langle S\{x \leftarrow t\} \cup \{x \leftarrow t\}, E\{x \leftarrow t\} \rangle}$$

provided $x \notin Var(t)$.

- *Occur-check*

$$\frac{\langle S, E \cup \{x \approx t\} \rangle}{\bot}$$

provided $x \in Var(t)$.

- *Clash*

$$\frac{\langle S, E \cup \{ft_1 \ldots t_n \approx gs_1 \ldots s_m\} \rangle}{\bot}$$

provided $f \neq g$.

The intuition here is that S represents part of the system $S \cup E$ of equations which is solved in $S \cup E$, while E represents the part which still needs to be solved. In Definition 7.2.3, the symbol $\bot$ stands for any pair $\langle S, E \rangle$ such that $S \cup E$ is unsolvable. It is worth remarking that the last two rules are not strictly necessary—they merely provide a mechanism for early termination of unsuccessful computations via sequences of applications of rules from $\mathcal{U}$. We write $\langle S, E \rangle \Rightarrow_{\mathcal{U}} \langle S', E' \rangle$ in case $\langle S', E' \rangle$ is obtainable from $\langle S, E \rangle$ via an application of a rule from $\mathcal{U}$; a $\mathcal{U}$-derivation out of $\langle S_0, E_0 \rangle$ is a sequence $\langle S_0, E_0 \rangle \Rightarrow_{\mathcal{U}} \langle S_1, E_1 \rangle \Rightarrow_{\mathcal{U}} \cdots$.

The set $\mathcal{U}$ is merely a set of inference rules, and since the order of their application to pairs of systems is not prescribed, these give rise to the nondeterministic unification algorithm which simply selects inference rules and equations at random and applies the inference rules to the equations. A concrete unification algorithm requires, in addition to the set $\mathcal{U}$ of inference rules on which it is based, a control structure which specifies the order of the applications of the rules from $\mathcal{U}$ together with some criteria for choosing the equations to which these rules are applied. Such a control structure might take the form of a precedence among the rules in $\mathcal{U}$, for example; in this case we would probably assign to the failure rules *Occur-check* and *Clash* and the rule *Trivial* a higher priority than that assigned to the other rules in order to avoid unnecessary deduction steps. Indeed, if a failure rule is applicable in a derivation, then the derivation can be terminated immediately and the remaining equations need not be considered further.

We now establish that, on input of the form $\langle \emptyset, E \rangle$, the inference system $\mathcal{U}$ always terminates either with a solution for E or with the information that E is unsolvable. We first show that every $\mathcal{U}$-derivation terminates.

Lemma 7.2.3 *The inference system $\mathcal{U}$ is terminating, i.e., there exists no infinite $\mathcal{U}$-derivation $\langle S_0, E_0 \rangle \Rightarrow_{\mathcal{U}} \langle S_1, E_1 \rangle \Rightarrow_{\mathcal{U}} \cdots$.*

Proof. Since the failure rules halt computation (and induce immediate notification that the input system is unsolvable), when establishing the termination of $\mathcal{U}$ we need only consider the system $\mathcal{U}'$ obtained from $\mathcal{U}$ by removing the failure rules. For any system $E = \{s_1 \approx t_1, \ldots, s_n \approx t_n\}$, let $|E|$ be the number of occurrences of function symbols and variables in E, i.e., let

$$|E| = \sum_{i=1}^{n} (|s_i| + |t_i|),$$

and let $v(E)$ be the number of variables which occur in E. Let $un(E)$ be the number of equations in E of the form $t \approx x$ where t is not a variable. We define a termination function μ which assigns to each pair $\langle S, E \rangle$ the ordered triple $\langle v(E), |E|, un(E) \rangle$ of natural numbers and then show that $\mathcal{U}'$ is terminating by establishing that if $\langle S, E \rangle \Rightarrow_{\mathcal{U}'} \langle S', E' \rangle$ then $\mu(\langle S, E \rangle) >_{lex} \mu(\langle S', E' \rangle)$, where $>_{lex}$ is the lexicographic extension of the ordering $>$ on the natural numbers.

An application of the rule *Trivial* to $\langle S, E \rangle$ clearly decreases $|E|$ and does not increase $v(E)$; similarly for the rule *Decomposition*. An application of the rule *Substitution* to $\langle S, E \rangle$ decreases $v(E)$, and an application of the rule *Orientation* to $\langle S, E \rangle$ changes neither $|E|$ nor $v(E)$, but does decrease $un(E)$. Thus each application of a rule in $\mathcal{U}$ decreases the size, as measured by μ, of a pair of systems.

Now observe that the ordering $>_{lex}$ is noetherian, i.e., there exists no infinite decreasing sequence $t_0 >_{lex} t_1 >_{lex} \ldots$. Since the existence of an infinite derivation $\langle S_0, E_0 \rangle \Rightarrow_{\mathcal{U}'} \langle S_1, E_1 \rangle \Rightarrow_{\mathcal{U}'} \ldots$ would imply the existence of an infinite sequence $\mu(\langle S_0, E_0 \rangle) >_{lex} \mu(\langle S_1, E_1 \rangle) >_{lex} \ldots$, the system $\mathcal{U}'$, and hence the system $\mathcal{U}$, must indeed be terminating. □

Lemma 7.2.4 *Let $\langle S_0, E_0 \rangle \Rightarrow_{\mathcal{U}} \langle S_1, E_1 \rangle \Rightarrow_{\mathcal{U}} \ldots \Rightarrow_{\mathcal{U}} \langle S_n, E_n \rangle$ with $S_0 = \emptyset$ be a $\mathcal{U}$-derivation such that $\langle S_n, E_n \rangle$ is $\mathcal{U}$-irreducible, i.e., such that there exists no pair $\langle S', E' \rangle$ of systems of equations such that $\langle S_n, E_n \rangle \Rightarrow_{\mathcal{U}} \langle S', E' \rangle$.*

1. *If E_0 is solvable, then $E_n = \emptyset$ and S_n is a most general solution for E_0.*

2. *If E_0 is not solvable, then $E_n = \bot$.*

Proof. We first show that applications of rules from the inference system $\mathcal{U}'$ preserve solutions of systems, i.e., that if $\langle S, E \rangle \Rightarrow_{\mathcal{U}'} \langle S', E' \rangle$ then $(S \cup E) \sim (S' \cup E')$.

Let $\langle S', E' \rangle$ be obtained from $\langle S, E \rangle$ by an application of *Trivial* to the equation $t \approx t$ from $\langle S, E \rangle$. Since every substitution solves the equation $t \approx t$, $u(S \cup E) = u(S' \cup E')$.

Next, suppose that $\langle S, E \rangle \Rightarrow_{\mathcal{U}'} \langle S', E' \rangle$ by an application of the rule *Decomposition*. Then since $\sigma(ft_1 \ldots t_n) = f(\sigma(t_1), \ldots, \sigma(t_n))$, we have $\sigma \in u(ft_1 \ldots t_n \approx fs_1 \ldots s_n)$ iff $\sigma \in u(t_1 \approx s_1, \ldots, t_n \approx s_n)$. It thus follows that $u(S \cup E) = u(S' \cup E')$.

Now suppose that $\langle S, E \rangle \Rightarrow_{\mathcal{U}'} \langle S', E' \rangle$ by an application of the rule *Orientation*. Since $u(x, t) = u(t, x)$ we have $u(S \cup E) = u(S' \cup E')$.

Finally, suppose $\langle S, E \rangle \Rightarrow_{\mathcal{U}'} \langle S', E' \rangle$ by an application of the rule *Substitution*, and let $\sigma \in u(x \approx t)$. Then $\sigma(x) = \sigma(t)$ and so for $l \approx r \in S \cup E$ we have

$$\sigma(l\{x \leftarrow t\}) = \sigma(l) = \sigma(r) = \sigma(r\{x \leftarrow t\}).$$

Thus $\sigma \in u(S \cup E \cup \{x \approx t\})$ iff $\sigma \in u(S\{x \leftarrow t\} \cup E\{x \leftarrow t\} \cup \{x \approx t\})$, and therefore $u(S \cup E) = u(S' \cup E')$ holds.

TABLE 7.1.

S_i	E_i	Rule
$\emptyset$	$\{f(x, g(a, y)) \approx f(h(y), g(a, a)),$ $\quad g(x, h(a)) \approx g(z, z)\}$	
$\emptyset$	$\{x \approx h(y), g(a, y) \approx g(a, a),$ $\quad x \approx z, h(a) \approx z\}$	Decomposition (twice)
$\{x \approx h(y)\}$	$\{g(a, y) \approx g(a, a), h(y) \approx z, h(a), \approx z\}$	Substitution
$\{x \approx h(y)\}$	$\{a \approx a, y \approx a, h(y) \approx z, h(a) \approx z\}$	Decomposition
$\{x \approx h(y)\}$	$\{y \approx a, h(y) \approx z, h(a) \approx z\}$	Trivial
$\{x \approx h(a), y \approx a\}$	$\{h(a) \approx z\}$	Substitution
$\{x \approx h(a), y \approx a\}$	$\{z \approx h(a)\}$	Orientation
$\{x \approx h(a), y \approx a,$ $\quad z \approx h(a)\}$	$\emptyset$	Substitution

Now observe that if E_0 is solvable, then, since $(S_0 \cup E_0) \sim (S_n \cup E_n)$, it must be the case that $(S_n \cup E_n)$ is solvable as well. Thus $E_n \neq \perp$. Since $S_n \cup E_n$ is solvable and no rule from $\mathcal{U}$ applies to $\langle S_n, E_n \rangle$, we must have $E_n = \emptyset$, so that in fact $E_0 = (S_0 \cup E_0) \sim (S_n \cup E_n) = S_n$. By construction, S_n is solved, and so S_n is in fact a most general solution for E_0.

If E_0 is unsolvable, then $S_n \cup E_n$ is also unsolvable. Since $S_0 = \emptyset$, and since each pair in S_n is solved in $S_n \cup E_n$ by construction, it must be the case that E_n is unsolvable, i.e., that E_n is precisely $\perp$. □

Thus the inference system $\mathcal{U}$ provides a means of determining solvability of systems of equations and of computing most general solutions of systems which are unifiable.

Example 7.2.2   Let $E = \{f(x, g(a, y)) \approx f(h(y), g(y, a)), g(x, h(y)) \approx g(z, z)\}$. The $\mathcal{U}$-derivation in Table 7.1 computes a most general solution of E:

7.3   Improving Unification Algorithms

A simple analysis of the inference system $\mathcal{U}$ for solving equational constraints introduced in the previous section shows that it is, in the worst case, of exponential time complexity. But note that the efficiency of an algorithm based on this inference system actually depends on the underlying data structure chosen to represent terms, as the following example makes clear.

Example 7.3.1   Let n be an arbitrary natural number, let $s = f(g(x_1, x_1), g(x_2, x_2), \dots, g(x_{n-1}, x_{n-1}))$, and let $t = f(x_2, x_3, \dots, x_n)$. Then the system $\{s \approx t\}$ has the following most general solution:

$$\{x_2 \approx g(x_1, x_1),$$
$$x_3 \approx g(g(x_1, x_1), g(x_1, x_1)),$$
$$\vdots$$
$$x_n \approx g(g(\ldots, g(x_1, x_1) \ldots), g(\ldots, g(x_1, x_1) \ldots))\},$$

where the term on the right side of the equality for each x_n contains $2^n - 1$ symbol occurrences.

It must therefore be the case that no unification algorithm which uses the usual tree representations of terms as its underlying data structure can improve on this unfavorable complexity, since a term with $2^n - 1$ symbol occurrences must be given as part of the solution to this particular unification problem. It can be argued that in practical applications a particular solution to a unification problem is not required, and that it is only the solvability or unsolvability of a given system which is of interest (See Section 8.1). Unfortunately, however, the time complexity of a tree-based unification decision algorithm is also exponential, since any such algorithm must still work internally (as a consequence of the rule *Substitution*) with exponentially growing terms like those of Example 7.3.1.

Nevertheless, there exist methods for solving equational constraints which are of polynomial time complexity ([MM82]), and among these there is in fact one which is of linear time complexity ([PW78]). Such methods do not operate on the usual tree representations of terms, but rather work on representations of terms as certain kinds of *directed acyclic graphs*, or *DAGs*, for short (see below). In this section we present an improved equational constraint solving technique which operates on precisely such DAG representations of terms. The technique is based on that of Corbin and Bidoit ([CB83]), and the resulting algorithm is of quadratic time complexity. Although the time complexity of this algorithm is worse theoretically than the linear algorithm of Patterson and Wegman, in practice it exhibits better performance, in part because it is possible to implement it in a far simpler and more direct manner than its theoretically more efficient counterpart.

The essential advantage of DAGs over tree representations of terms lies in the possibility of representing different occurrences of the same subterm in a given term by the same part of its corresponding graph, i.e., the advantage lies in the possibility of *subterm sharing*. The solution of the system $\{s \approx t\}$ of Example 7.3.1 example can be represented, for instance, as in Figure 7.2. Here the size of the solution is clearly linear in n.

More specifically, the theoretical foundation for the unification algorithm of Corbin and Bidoit is the notion of a directed, acyclic, labeled, oriented

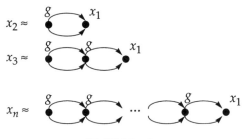

FIGURE 7.2.

multigraph. The fundamental ideas of graph theory which are relevant
for the purposes of its development are only sketched here; a more
comprehensive treatment can be found in any of the excellent books on
graph theory available (e.g., [BM76]).

A *directed labeled multigraph* is a quadruple $G = \langle N, A, L, \lambda \rangle$, where

- N is a set of *nodes*,

- A is a multiset of ordered pairs of distinct nodes, called *arcs*,

- L is a set of *labels*, and

- λ is a function assigning a label to each node.

In discussing the unification algorithm of Corbin and Bidoit we will always
take L to be the set $\mathcal{F} \cup \mathcal{V}$ comprising the function symbols and variables
over which terms are built; by suppressing explicit mention of the set of
labels we may therefore always represent a directed labeled multigraph as
a triple rather than as a quadruple. A node k in $G = \langle N, A, \lambda \rangle$ such that
$\lambda(k) \in \mathcal{V}$ is called a *variable node*. The node k' is *adjacent* to the node k
if $\langle k, k' \rangle \in A$, and k' is *connected* to k if there exists a sequence of nodes
$k = k_0, k_1, \ldots, k_n = k'$ such that k_i is adjacent to k_{i-1} for $i = 1, \ldots, n$.
That is, k' is connected to k if there exists a path from k to k'. For each
node k we define $succ_G(k)$ to be the multiset of nodes adjacent to k, i.e.,
the multiset of *children* of k.

A directed labeled multigraph G must also satisfy the following three
conditions:

- If $\lambda(k) \in \mathcal{V}$, then $succ_G(k) = \emptyset$.

- If $\lambda(k) \in \mathcal{F}_n$, then $|succ_G(k)| = n$.

- The function λ is injective on the set of variable nodes.

The final condition here states that each variable appears as the label of
at most one node in a directed labeled multigraph. A given variable node
may nevertheless be adjacent to more than one other node.

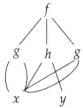

FIGURE 7.3.

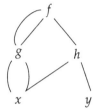

FIGURE 7.4.

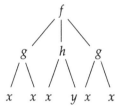

FIGURE 7.5.

Although every term t can be represented by a directed labeled multigraph in an "obvious" way, a given term may have more than one representation as a directed labeled multigraph. There are two principal reasons for this. The first is that a directed labeled multigraph may feature "subterm sharing." The term $f(gxx, hxy, gxx)$, for example, can be represented by the directed labeled multigraph in Figure 7.3 or by that in Figure 7.4. Of course, in either representation any variable node whose label appears in t more than once will necessarily be adjacent to more than one node.

The second reason that representations of terms as directed labeled multigraphs are not unique is a familiar one, namely that the children of the nodes in such graphs are not necessarily ordered. This means that even if we restrict attention to directed labeled graphs without any subterm sharing whatsoever, for instance, there need not be a "canonical" representation of a given term; again $f(gxx, hxy, gxx)$ provides an example of a term which has two such representations (see Figures 7.5 and 7.6).

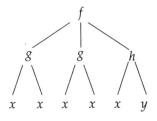

FIGURE 7.6.

On the other hand, if we insist that directed labeled multigraphs representing terms have their natural left-to-right order—so that, for each node k in G, $succ_G(k)$ is ordered—and identify those directed labeled multigraphs which differ only in orientation, and if we further insist that directed labeled multigraphs share no subterms other than variables, then in fact each term has a *unique* representation as a directed labeled multigraph. Every graph obtained in this manner is *acyclic*—i.e., contains no sequence of nodes of the form $k_1, k_2, \ldots, k_n$ such that k_{i+1} is adjacent to k_i for $i \in 0, \ldots, n-1$ and k_0 is adjacent to k_n—and so such graphs are called *directed acyclic (labeled) (multi)graphs*, or *DAGs*, for short. If G is the unique DAG representing the term t, then G is said to be the *DAG-representation* of t, and is denoted $DAG(t)$. Note that each graph $DAG(t)$ has exactly one *isolated node*, i.e., each graph $DAG(t)$ has exactly one node which is not adjacent to any other nodes. If k is the unique isolated node in a DAG G, then we identify G with the ordered pair $\langle G, k \rangle$. This will be convenient later.

It is not hard to see that the DAG-representation for a term t can be obtained from the usual tree representation for t by identifying all variable nodes of t's tree representation which correspond to the same variable of t.

From DAG-representations for terms we may obtain DAG-representations for systems of equations of the form $E = \{s_1 \approx t_1, \ldots, s_n \approx t_n\}$ by first generating the $2n$ DAG-representations $DAG(s_i)$ and $DAG(t_i)$, $i \in \{1, \ldots n\}$, and then identifying all variable nodes in these graphs having the same label. The resulting set G of graphs has nodes $k_1, \ldots, k_n$ and $k'_1, \ldots, k'_n$ "representing" the terms s_i and t_i for $i = 1, \ldots, n$ (more formally, such that $s_i = \tau(\langle G, k_i \rangle)$ and $t_i = \tau(\langle G, k'_i \rangle)$ holds for $i = 1, \ldots, n$ and the mapping τ defined below). The nodes $k_1, \ldots, k_n, k'_1, \ldots, k'_n$ need not be distinct. By $DAG(E)$ we denote the pair $\langle G, \{k_1 \approx k'_1, \ldots, k_n \approx k'_n\}\rangle$. Figure 7.7, for example, depicts the DAG-representation G of the system $E = \{s \approx t\}$ from Example 7.3.1. The topmost node k labeled with f represents s, while the lower node k' labeled with f represents t. That $s \approx t$ is in E is represented by the dotted line from node k to node k'. Here, $DAG(E) = \langle G, \{k \approx k'\}\rangle$.

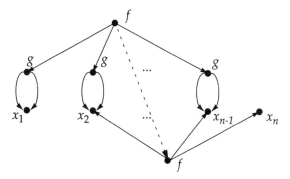

FIGURE 7.7.

Having seen that we may construct a DAG-representation for any term, we now see that from each DAG with a unique isolated node we may generate a term in a uniform manner. Let G be any DAG and suppose k is any node in G. We define the *term of G at k*, denoted $\tau(\langle G, k \rangle)$, by:

- $\tau(\langle G, k \rangle) = \lambda(k)$ if k is a variable node of G, and

- $\tau(\langle G, k \rangle) = f(\tau(\langle G, k_1 \rangle), \ldots, \tau(\langle G, k_n \rangle))$ if $\lambda(k) = f \in \mathcal{F}^n$ and $\{k_1, \ldots, k_n\} = succ_G(k)$.

Note that τ is defined for all directed acyclic labeled multigraphs, including those which feature subterm sharing, and also that τ actually defines a function. Writing $\tau(G)$ for $\tau(\langle G, k \rangle)$ when k is the unique isolated node in G, we see that every directed acyclic labeled multigraph G with a unique isolated node represents the term $t = \tau(G)$. Moreover, it is not hard to see that, for any term t and any DAG G with a unique isolated node, $DAG(\tau(G)) = G$ and $\tau(DAG(t)) = t$ holds. Thus there is actually a bijection between terms t and DAGs of the form $DAG(t)$.

In our discussion of the unification algorithm of Corbin and Bidoit, it will be useful to have extended the function τ to accommodate triples of the form $\langle G, F, U \rangle$, where G is a DAG and F and U are sets of ordered pairs of nodes in G; indeed, these are the kinds of triples on which the algorithm actually acts. We effect such an extension by defining

$$\tau(\langle G, F, U \rangle) = \{\tau(\langle G, k \rangle) \approx \tau(\langle G, k' \rangle) \mid \langle k, k' \rangle \in F \cup U\},$$

so that the extended function τ transforms a triple $\langle G, F, U \rangle$ into an ordinary system of equations.

The most critical aspect of any unification algorithm is the subprocedure which effects substitution. Since our unification algorithm must capture term-substitution by means of triples of the form $\langle G, F, U \rangle$ whose first

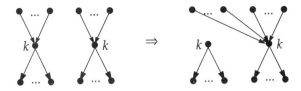

FIGURE 7.8.

component is a DAG, we will need to have at our disposal a notion of DAG-substitution. We define this as follows. If k and k' are nodes of $G = \langle N, A, \lambda \rangle$, then let $G[k \leftarrow k']$ be the graph $G' = \langle N, A', \lambda \rangle$ where the set A' of arcs is given by

$$A' = (A - \{\langle l, k \rangle \mid l \in N\}) \cup \{\langle l, k' \rangle \mid \langle l, k \rangle \in A\}.$$

DAG-substitution is illustrated in Figure 7.8. If U is a set of pairs of nodes in a graph G, and k and k' are nodes in G, then $U[k \leftarrow k']$ denotes the set of pairs of nodes obtained by replacing all occurrences of k in U by k'.

Any graph G resulting from an application of DAG-substitution is again a DAG (with subterm-sharing, in general), and if $G = \langle N, A, \lambda \rangle$, then

$$\tau(\langle G[k \leftarrow k'], l \rangle) = \tau(\langle G, l \rangle)\{x \leftarrow \tau(G, k')\}$$

holds for all vertices $l \in N$ provided $x = \lambda(k)$. By virtue of the function τ we see that such DAG-substitutions can be thought of as graphically representing term-substitutions. We can further use our notion of DAG-substitution to define a similar notion for *sets* of DAGs in the obvious way. Since substitution for sets of DAGs corresponds to substitution for *systems* of equations, we abuse notation and denote by $E[k \leftarrow k']$ the system of equations given by

$$\{\tau(\langle G[k \leftarrow k'], k_i \rangle) \approx \tau(\langle G[k \leftarrow k'], l_i \rangle)\},$$

where $DAG(E) = \langle G, \{k_1 \approx l_1, \ldots, k_n \approx l_n\} \rangle$. We will make considerable use of substitution for sets of DAGs, as well as for sets of pairs of nodes, in describing the unification algorithm of Corbin and Bidoit. This algorithm arises from the nondeterministic application of rules from the following inference system.

Definition 7.3.1   The inference system $\mathcal{CB}$ is given by the following:

- *Trivial*

$$\frac{\langle G, F, U \cup \{\langle k, k \rangle\} \rangle}{\langle G, F, U \rangle}$$

- *Decomposition*

$$\frac{\langle G, F, U \cup \{\langle k, k' \rangle\}\rangle}{\langle G[k \leftarrow k'], F, U[k \leftarrow k'] \cup \{\langle k_1, k'_1 \rangle, \ldots, \langle k_n, k'_n \rangle\}\rangle}$$

provided $\lambda(k) = \lambda(k') \in \mathcal{F}$, $succ(k) = \{k_1, \ldots, k_n\}$, and $succ(k') = \{k'_1, \ldots, k'_n\}$.

- *Orientation*

$$\frac{\langle G, F, U \cup \{\langle k, k' \rangle\}\rangle}{\langle G, F, U \cup \{\langle k', k \rangle\}\rangle}$$

provided k is not a variable node and k' is.

- *Substitution*

$$\frac{\langle G, F, U \cup \{\langle k, k' \rangle\}\rangle}{\langle G[k \leftarrow k'], F \cup \{\langle k, k' \rangle\}, U[k \leftarrow k']\rangle}$$

provided k is a variable node and k is not connected to k'.

- *Occur-check*

$$\frac{\langle G, F, U \cup \{\langle k, k' \rangle\}\rangle}{\bot}$$

provided k is a variable node and k' is connected to u.

- *Clash*

$$\frac{\langle G, F, U \cup \{\langle k, k' \rangle\}\rangle}{\bot}$$

provided $\lambda(k), \lambda(k') \in \mathcal{F}$ and $\lambda(k) \neq \lambda(k')$.

Here, $\bot$ stands for any triple $\langle G, F, U \rangle$ such that $F \cup U$ is unsolvable. As noted above, if G is a DAG and if G' is obtained from G by an application of a rule in $\mathcal{CB}$, then G' is also a DAG, although G' may feature subterm sharing, even if G itself does not. We write $\langle G, F, U \rangle \Rightarrow_{\mathcal{CB}} \langle G', F', U' \rangle$ in case $\langle G', F', U' \rangle$ is obtained from $\langle G, F, U \rangle$ via an application of a rule in $\mathcal{CB}$; a $\mathcal{CB}$-*derivation* is a sequence $\langle G_0, F_0, U_0 \rangle \Rightarrow_{\mathcal{CB}} \langle G_1, F_1, U_1 \rangle \Rightarrow_{\mathcal{CB}} \ldots$.

In a manner analogous to that of the previous section, it can be shown that $\mathcal{CB}$ preserves solution sets, i.e., that if $\langle G, F, U \rangle \Rightarrow_{\mathcal{CB}} \langle G', F', U' \rangle$, then $\tau(\langle G, F, U \rangle) \sim \tau(\langle G', F', U' \rangle)$. The soundness and completeness of the inference system $\mathcal{CB}$ are then formulated and proved as in Lemmas 7.2.3

and 7.2.4. We state these results below, referring the reader to [CB83] for their proofs.

Lemma 7.3.1 *The inference system $\mathcal{CB}$ is terminating, i.e., there exists no infinite $\mathcal{CB}$-derivation $\langle G_0, F_0, U_0 \rangle \Rightarrow_{\mathcal{CB}} \langle G_1, F_1, U_1 \rangle \Rightarrow_{\mathcal{CB}} \dots$.*

Lemma 7.3.2 *Let $\langle G_0, F_0, U_0 \rangle \Rightarrow_{\mathcal{CB}} \dots \Rightarrow_{\mathcal{CB}} \langle G_n, F_n, U_n \rangle$ with $F_0 = \emptyset$ be a $\mathcal{CB}$-derivation such that $\langle G_n, F_n, U_n \rangle$ is $\mathcal{CB}$-irreducible.*

> *1. If $E = \{\tau(\langle G, k \rangle) \approx \tau(\langle G, k' \rangle) \mid \langle k, k' \rangle \in U_0\}$ is solvable, then $U_n = \emptyset$ and $\{\tau(\langle G, k \rangle) \approx \tau(\langle G, k' \rangle) \mid \langle k, k' \rangle \in F_n\}$ is a most general solution for E.*
>
> *2. If E is not solvable, then $U_n = \perp$.*

By contrast with the inference system $\mathcal{U}$, the system $\mathcal{CB}$ gives rise to unification algorithms which are of polynomial complexity. More precisely,

Lemma 7.3.3 *Any unification algorithm based on the inference system $\mathcal{CB}$ is of time complexity $O(n^2)$, where n is the total number of symbol occurrences appearing in the input system.*

Proof. Let E be a system of equations to be solved, let $\langle G, E' \rangle = DAG(E)$, and let e be the number of edges of G. Clearly $n = e + 2|E|$ holds (note carefully that n is the number of *occurrences* of symbols in the input system, rather than the number of symbols which occur in E). Finally, let $v = |Var(E)|$. Applications of rules in $\mathcal{CB}$ do not change v. Moreover, since n and $|E|$ do not change via applications of rules in $\mathcal{CB}$, neither does e. That is, e and v are constant throughout any $\mathcal{CB}$-derivation.

By applying the rule *Substitution*, all edges leading to a certain variable node are reconnected. Since there are at most e such edges, the rule *Substitution* is of complexity $O(e)$. The rule itself can be applied at most v times, since every application eliminates a variable from further consideration for substitution. The rule *Substitution* thus contributes a factor of at most $O(ve)$ to the overall complexity of any algorithm based on $\mathcal{CB}$.

In applying the rule *Occur-check* it is essential to check whether or not given pairs of nodes are connected to one another. Testing adjacency of a given pair of nodes can be accomplished in such a way that every edge of G is considered at most once, i.e., such that the adjacency test is of time complexity $O(e)$ (see [AHU74], for example). The adjacency test need be applied at most $O(v)$ times, and so the rule *Occur-check* contributes a factor of at most $O(ve)$ to the overall complexity of any algorithm based on $\mathcal{CB}$.

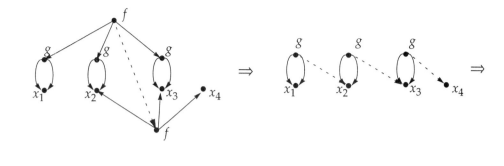

FIGURE 7.9.

The rule *Orientation* can be applied at most $\frac{n(n+1)}{2}$ times, since there are at most $\frac{n(n+1)}{2}$ node pairs available for orientation in G or any DAG derived from G by the application of rules in $\mathcal{CB}$, and since each application of the rule *Orientation* changes the orientation of exactly one such pair (which cannot subsequently be returned to its original state). This rule therefore contributes a factor of at most $O(n^2)$ to the overall time complexity of an algorithm based on $\mathcal{CB}$.

The application of the rule *Decomposition* to an equation $k \approx k'$ involves at most e edges. Such an application isolates the node k from G. Since, after the application of the rule, k no longer appears in the third component of the given triple, *Decomposition* can be applied at most e times, and so in general this rule contributes a factor of at most $O(e^2)$ to the overall time complexity of any algorithm based on $\mathcal{CB}$.

In applying the rule *Clash*, the condition on k and k' can be checked in constant time. Thus *Clash* does not contribute to the overall complexity of any algorithm based on $\mathcal{CB}$.

Since $e < n$ and $v \leq n$, we have an overall time complexity of $O(n^2)$ for the algorithm. □

Application of the inference system $\mathcal{CB}$ is illustrated for the system of equations in Example 7.3.1 (with $n = 4$); the results are shown in Figure 7.9. Equations are denoted by dotted lines, and isolated nodes are not shown.

7.4   Resolution and Subsumption

This section introduces an inference system $\mathcal{R}$ for refuting unsatisfiable sets of arbitrary clauses. The central component of $\mathcal{R}$ is an extension of the ground resolution rule which is capable of resolving nonground, as well as ground, clauses. The fundamental insight giving rise to this more general resolution rule is that *all* ground instances of a set of clauses to be refuted need not be enumerated before ground resolution can be applied to even a *single* pair of clauses; instead, unification can be used to instantiate nonground clauses "as needed," and ground resolution can then be applied eagerly to their instantiated versions. This alternative approach to discovering an unsatisfiable set of ground instances of an unsatisfiable set of clauses boasts the obvious advantage for efficiency of circumventing a thorough enumeration of the set of ground instances of its clauses. But the fact that substitutions unifying pairs of atoms in sets of clauses to be resolved are actually applied to both clauses in their entirety means that, in addition, the instantiations made at one general resolution step will typically constrain the instantiations possible at later such steps. This has the effect of increasing the efficiency of the resulting refutation method for clauses in a second significant way, as instantiations which might otherwise be undertaken can be discovered early on to contribute nothing to refutations being constructed and so can be eliminated from further consideration.

The inference system $\mathcal{R}$ operates on sets of clauses. It follows from the remark immediately preceding Herbrand's Theorem for prenex normal forms that, without loss of generality, we may assume that the clauses in any set of clauses to be refuted are variable disjoint. In addition to the resolution rule for arbitrary clauses, $\mathcal{R}$ possesses failure rules and other rules allowing certain unnecessary clauses to be eliminated in derivations; these rules enable further decreases in the size of refutation search spaces. We begin our description of $\mathcal{R}$ by singling out for special attention certain kinds of clauses which can be removed from sets of clauses without affecting their unsatisfiability.

Recall that if $\Phi \to \Psi = \varphi_1, \ldots, \varphi_m \to \psi_1, \ldots \psi_n$ is a clause and σ is a substitution, then we write $\sigma(\Phi \to \Psi)$ for the clause $\sigma(\varphi_1), \ldots, \sigma(\varphi_m) \to \sigma(\psi_1), \ldots \sigma(\psi_n)$. We have

Definition 7.4.1   1. A ground clause $\Phi \to \Psi$ is a *tautology* if $\Phi \cap \Psi \neq \emptyset$.

2. An arbitrary clause C is a *tautology* if every ground instance $\sigma(C)$ of C is a tautology.

Thus the problem of determining whether or not a given nonground clause is a tautology reduces to that of determining whether or not every ground instance of that clause is a tautology. A similar statement holds for the following notion of subsumption for clauses.

Definition 7.4.2   1. Let $C = \Phi \to \Psi$ and $D = \Phi' \to \Psi'$ be distinct ground clauses. The clause D is said to *subsume* the clause C provided $\Phi' \subseteq \Phi$ and $\Psi' \subseteq \Psi$ both hold.

2. Let $C = \Phi \to \Psi$ and $D = \Phi' \to \Psi'$ be arbitrary but distinct clauses. The clause D is said to *subsume* the clause C provided every ground instance of C is subsumed by a ground instance of D.

It follows from Definition 7.4.2 that, for ground clauses C and D, if $\mathcal{I} \models D$ and D subsumes C, then $\mathcal{I} \models C$. That is, $D \models C$ whenever D subsumes C and C and D are ground.

Note that, according to Definition 7.4.2, no clause subsumes itself, and a clause C can actually be subsumed by another clause D which is larger than C, i.e., which is such that $|D| > |C|$. Of particular interest for our purposes, however, will be clauses which are subsumed by smaller clauses. This restriction is embodied in the next definition; the requirement there that $|D| < |C|$ will be discussed in detail after the inference system $\mathcal{R}$ has been defined, and will be critical in proving the refutation completeness of the inference system $\mathcal{R}$ (see Lemma 7.4.7 in particular).

It is sometimes useful to have the following alternative characterizations of *tautology* and *subsumption* at our disposal.

Lemma 7.4.1   1. *A clause $\Phi \to \Psi$ is a tautology iff $\Phi \cap \Psi \neq \emptyset$.*

2. *The clause $\Phi \to \Psi$ subsumes the clause $\Phi' \to \Psi'$ iff there exists a substitution σ such that $\sigma(\Phi) \subseteq \Phi'$ and $\sigma(\Psi) \subseteq \Psi'$.*

Proof. Given a clause C, we define a substitution $\theta_C = \{x \to c_x | x \in Var(C)\}$, where the c_x are "new" constants, and a function $\theta_C^{-1} = \{c_x \to x | x \in Var(C)\}$. Although θ_C^{-1} is not a substitution, it is easy to see that $\theta_C^{-1}\theta_C = id$.

1. If $C = \Phi \to \Psi$ and $\Phi \cap \Psi \neq \emptyset$, then clearly C is a tautology in the sense of Definition 7.4.1. Conversely, if C is a tautology, i.e., if every ground instance of C is a tautology, then in particular $\theta_C(\Phi) \cap \theta_C(\Psi) \neq \emptyset$, so that

$$\Phi \cap \Psi = \theta_C^{-1}(\theta_C(\Phi)) \cap \theta_C^{-1}(\theta_C(\Psi)) \neq \emptyset.$$

2. Let $C = \Phi \to \Psi$ and $D = \Phi' \to \Psi'$. If there exists a substitution σ such that $\sigma(\Phi) \subseteq \Phi'$ and $\sigma(\Psi) \subseteq \Psi'$, then clearly C subsumes D.

Conversely, if C subsumes D, i.e., if every ground instance of D is subsumed by some ground instance of C, then in particular $\theta_D(D)$ is subsumed by some ground instance $\tau(C)$ of C. That is, for some ground substitution τ, $\tau(\Phi) \subseteq \theta_D(\Phi')$ and $\tau(\Psi) \subseteq \theta_D(\Psi')$. Then $\theta_D^{-1}(\tau(\Phi)) \subseteq \theta_D^{-1}(\theta_D(\Phi')) = \Phi'$, and, in addition, $\theta_D^{-1}(\tau(\Psi)) \subseteq \theta_D^{-1}(\theta_D(\Psi')) = \Psi'$. We may therefore take σ to be $\theta_D^{-1}\tau$. □

Definition 7.4.3   A clause C is *redundant (with respect to S)* if either $C \in S$, C is a tautology, or C is subsumed by some clause D in S such that $|D| < |C|$.

The rules of the next two definitions comprise the ingredients essential for describing $\mathcal{R}$. The inference system itself is given in Definition 7.4.6.

Definition 7.4.4   The *(classical) resolution rule* is given by

$$\frac{\Phi \to \Psi, A \qquad \Phi', B \to \Psi'}{\sigma(\Phi), \sigma(\Phi') \to \sigma(\Psi), \sigma(\Psi')}$$

provided σ is a most general unifier of A and B.

The conclusion of an application of the resolution rule is called a *resolvent* of its two premises.

Definition 7.4.5   The *(positive) factorization rule* is given by

$$\frac{\Phi \to \Psi, A, B}{\sigma(\Phi) \to \sigma(\Psi), \sigma(A)}$$

provided σ is a most general unifier of A and B.

The conclusion of an application of the factorization rule is called a *factor* of its premise. There is also a *negative factorization rule*—namely,

$$\frac{\Phi, A, B \to \Psi}{\sigma(\Phi), \sigma(A) \to \sigma(\Psi)}$$

provided σ is a most general unifier of A and B—in which the atoms A and B appear in the antecedent, rather than in the succedent, of the premise. Note that a ground clause has neither positive nor negative factors since A and B will have no unifiers at all in this case: recall that the antecedents and succedents of clauses are *sets*, and so the ground atoms A and B in the factorization rule are necessarily distinct.

It is easy to see that the resolution rule for ground clauses is obtained as the special case of the classical resolution rule in which σ is the identity substitution. Indeed, the classical resolution rule can be thought of as generalizing the resolution rule for ground clauses to account for two clauses being "potentially identical." The factorization rule can likewise be thought of as allowing deletion of "potential duplicates," although the fact that clauses are pairs of *sets* of atoms implies that removal of duplicate atoms from clauses, which would clearly not affect the unsatisfiability of sets of clauses, is never required in the ground case.

The inference system $\mathcal{R}$ is based on these various inference rules for transforming sets of clauses.

Definition 7.4.6 The inference system $\mathcal{R}$ for refutation of clauses comprises the following inference rules:

- *Deduction*

$$\frac{S}{S \cup \{C\}}$$

provided C is a resolvent or a positive factor of clauses in S.

- *Reduction*

$$\frac{S \cup \{C\}}{S}$$

provided C is redundant with respect to $S - \{C\}$.

Note that since C cannot appear in $S - \{C\}$ (because "$-$" here denotes set-theoretic difference) we actually require, in applying the rule *Reduction*, either that C is a tautology or else that C is subsumed by some clause $D \in (S - \{C\})$ such that $|D| < |C|$. Allowing the possibility that $C \in S$ in Definition 7.4.3 will be convenient later (see the proof of Lemma 7.4.9).

We write $S \Rightarrow_{\mathcal{R}} S'$ to indicate that S' is obtained from S by an application of a rule in $\mathcal{R}$. A *(classical resolution) derivation* out of S_0 is a sequence $S_0, S_1, S_2, \ldots$ of sets of clauses, where for each natural number n, $S_n \Rightarrow_{\mathcal{R}} S_{n+1}$ holds. A *(classical resolution) refutation* of a set S of clauses is a resolution derivation out of S with $\square \in S_n$ for some $n \geq 0$. The choice of the positive factorization rule is, incidentally, arbitrary; we could equally well have taken the negative factorization rule in place of the positive version in the definition of $\mathcal{R}$.

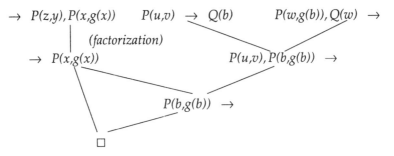

FIGURE 7.10.

Example 7.4.1   Let S be the set of clauses

$$\{\to P(z,y), P(x,g(x)),$$
$$P(u,v) \to Q(b),$$
$$P(w,g(b)), Q(w) \to\}.$$

A resolution refutation for S is represented in Figure 7.10. In depicting resolution derivations, it is customary not to propagate the set S in applications of the rule *Deduction* even though, strictly speaking, this should be done. We will adopt this convention throughout the book.

Because Definition 7.4.6 in no way specifies the order in which the rules of $\mathcal{R}$ are to be applied, the inference system $\mathcal{R}$ for refutation of unsatisfiable sets of clauses—like the inference systems $\mathcal{U}$ and $\mathcal{CB}$ for unification of sets of terms—gives rise to the nondeterministic algorithm which simply applies inference rules from $\mathcal{R}$ at random. A concrete algorithm for refuting sets of clauses is thus obtained by also specifying a control structure detailing the order in which rules from $\mathcal{R}$ are to be applied, as well as some criteria for selecting the clauses to which they are to be applied.

Observe that the rule *Reduction* provides a means by which redundant clauses can be removed from resolution derivations. Although the condition that $|D| < |C|$ in the rule *Reduction* (inherited from Definition 7.4.3) seems inexplicable at first glance, we observe that if it were omitted, then *Reduction* could be applied immediately to remove every newly derived factor C of clauses in the set S, since C would be redundant in S (clauses necessarily render their own factors redundant). That is, the rules *Deduction* and *Reduction* could be applied one after the other indefinitely, leading to nonterminating resolution derivations. This, of course, is not intended, and explains our need to incorporate some restriction into our definition of redundancy.

Although it has no analogue in the ground setting, the factorization rule is critical to the refutation completeness of the negative calculus based on $\mathcal{R}$, as illustrated by the following simple example.

Example 7.4.2   If S is the unsatisfiable set of clauses

$$\{(Px, Py \rightarrow),\ (\rightarrow Pu, Pv)\},$$

then it is easy to see that each clause that can be derived from S by resolution must be built from *two* atoms (remember that the clauses in any set of clauses to be refuted can be taken to be variable disjoint). Thus the empty clause can never be derived without the use of the factorization rule, and so that rule is necessary if $\mathcal{R}$ is to be refutation complete.

This example also indicates that without the proviso that $|D| < |C|$ in Definition 7.4.3 and hence in the rule *Reduction*, no concrete refutation algorithm based on $\mathcal{R}$ in which the rule *Reduction* is applied eagerly can possibly be complete. This is because eager application of the rule *Reduction* would amount to "undoing," as soon as they were performed, all applications of the rule *Deduction* in which the newly derived clause is a factor of a clause in the original set. Thus any resolution derivation in which *Reduction* is performed eagerly in the absence of the proviso would be equivalent to a resolution derivation in the inference system obtained from $\mathcal{R}$ by removing the factorization rule. Example 7.4.2 implies that no such algorithm can be complete.

It is interesting to observe that the unification of clauses described in the resolution and factorization rules need not be performed eagerly. In fact, by altering the set $\mathcal{R}$ of inference rules to operate on (and produce) ordered pairs of the form $\langle C, E \rangle$—where C is a set of clauses and E is a *solvable* system of equations representing a partially constructed most general unifier of the atoms in C—unifiers of atoms to be resolved or factored can be recorded without being applied. It can be shown that the new, modified inference system has at least the deductive power of $\mathcal{R}$, whose soundness and refutation completeness we now prove. We discuss this modification of $\mathcal{R}$ in detail in Section 8.1.

To establish the soundness of $\mathcal{R}$ we must show that any set of clauses which is refutable by $\mathcal{R}$ is also unsatisfiable; to establish its refutation completeness we must show that every unsatisfiable set of clauses actually has a refutation in $\mathcal{R}$.

In discussing the soundness and refutation completeness of $\mathcal{R}$, it will be convenient to identify an interpretation $\mathcal{I}$ with the set $\mathcal{I}^*$ of ground atoms which it satisfies. We may then regard a ground atom as being either *in $\mathcal{I}$* or not according as it is satisfied by $\mathcal{I}$ or not.

Lemma 7.4.2   *If $\mathcal{I}$ is an interpretation, then $\mathcal{I}$ satisfies the ground clause $\Phi \rightarrow \Psi$ provided*

$$\Phi \nsubseteq \mathcal{I} \quad or \quad \Psi \cap \mathcal{I} \neq \emptyset.$$

The interpretation $\mathcal{I}$ satisfies the set S of ground clauses if it satisfies every clause in S.

The shift in point-of-view embodied in Lemma 7.4.2 simplifies the terminology in the proof of the next lemma, which is key in establishing the soundness of $\mathcal{R}$.

Lemma 7.4.3   *If R is a resolvent of ground clauses C and D, then $\{C, D\} \models R$.*

Proof. Let $\mathcal{I}$ be any interpretation such that $\mathcal{I} \models \{C, D\}$. Further, let $C = \Phi, A \rightarrow \Psi$, let $D = \Phi' \rightarrow \Psi', A$, and let $R = \Phi, \Phi' \rightarrow \Psi, \Psi'$ be a resolvent of C and D. Since $\mathcal{I} \models C$, we have that either $\Phi \cup \{A\} \not\subseteq \mathcal{I}$ or else $\Psi \cap \mathcal{I} \neq \emptyset$, and since $\mathcal{I} \models D$, we have that either $\Phi' \not\subseteq \mathcal{I}$ or else $(\Psi' \cup \{A\}) \cap \mathcal{I} \neq \emptyset$. We want to show that $\mathcal{I} \models R$, i.e., that either $\Phi, \Phi' \not\subseteq \mathcal{I}$ or else $(\Psi \cup \Psi') \cap \mathcal{I} \neq \emptyset$. Suppose, therefore, that $\Phi, \Phi' \subseteq \mathcal{I}$. If $A \in \mathcal{I}$, then $\Phi \subseteq \mathcal{I}$ implies $\Psi \cap \mathcal{I} \neq \emptyset$, so that $(\Psi \cup \Psi') \cap \mathcal{I} \neq \emptyset$. If $A \notin \mathcal{I}$, then $\Phi' \subseteq \mathcal{I}$ implies $(\Psi' \cup \{A\}) \cap \mathcal{I} \neq \emptyset$, so that $\Psi' \cap \mathcal{I} \neq \emptyset$, and therefore $(\Psi \cup \Psi') \cap \mathcal{I} \neq \emptyset$. In either case, we conclude that $\mathcal{I} \models R$. □

This lemma can be used to show that each inference rule in $\mathcal{R}$ preserves satisfiability of sets of clauses, a fact from which the soundness of $\mathcal{R}$ will immediately follow. As in Section 6.3, for any given set S of clauses we write $\overline{S}$ for the set of all ground instances of clauses in S, and write, for simplicity, $\overline{C}$ instead of $\overline{\{C\}}$. Then

Lemma 7.4.4   *Let S and S' be sets of clauses such that $S \Rightarrow_{\mathcal{R}} S'$. Then S' is satisfiable iff S is. Equivalently, S is unsatisfiable if S' is.*

Proof. We show that if S is satisfiable then S' is satisfiable. Suppose, therefore, that S is satisfiable.

If S' is obtained by an application of the rule *Reduction* to S, then $S' \subseteq S$ and therefore S' is satisfiable since S is.

To show that S' is satisfiable if it is obtained from S by an application of the rule *Deduction*, we first observe that, by Corollary 6.3.1, $\overline{S}$ is satisfiable since S is.

If the clause introduced by the application of the rule *Deduction* is a resolvent R of the clauses C and D in S, then $S' = S \cup \{R\}$. Every ground instance of R is a resolvent of corresponding ground instances of C and D. According to the previous lemma, $\overline{S} \models R'$ must hold for every ground instance R' of R. Therefore $\overline{S \cup \{R\}} = \overline{S} \cup \overline{R}$ is satisfiable since $\overline{S}$ is satisfiable and since $\overline{S} \models R'$ for all $R' \in \overline{R}$. By Corollary 6.3.1, then, $S \cup \{R\}$ is satisfiable.

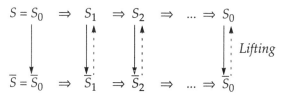

$$S = S_0 \;\Rightarrow\; S_1 \;\Rightarrow\; S_2 \;\Rightarrow\; \dots \;\Rightarrow\; S_0$$

Lifting

$$\overline{S} = \overline{S}_0 \;\Rightarrow\; \overline{S}_1 \;\Rightarrow\; \overline{S}_2 \;\Rightarrow\; \dots \;\Rightarrow\; \overline{S}_0$$

ground resolution refutation

FIGURE 7.11.

If the clause introduced by the application of the rule *Deduction* is a factor R of a clause in S, then $S' = S \cup \{R\}$. Then $R = \sigma(\Phi) \to \sigma(\Psi), \sigma(A)$ for some clause $\Phi \to \Psi, A, B$ in S, where σ is a most general unifier of A and B. Although $S' \subseteq S$ does not hold in general, $\overline{S'} \subseteq \overline{S}$ does, and so $\overline{S'}$ is satisfiable since $\overline{S}$ is. By Corollary 6.3.1, S' must itself be satisfiable.

Theorem 7.4.1   *(Soundness of $\mathcal{R}$) If $S_0, S_1, \dots, S_n$ is a resolution derivation with $\square \in S_n$, then S_0 is unsatisfiable.*

Proof. Since $\square$, and hence S_n, is unsatisfiable, repeated application of the previous lemma guarantees that each of the sets of clause S_i is also unsatisfiable. In particular, then, S_0 is unsatisfiable. $\square$

Having established the soundness of the inference system $\mathcal{R}$, we now turn our attention to its refutation completeness, which we show in two stages. In the first stage we show that $\mathcal{R}$ is complete for ground clauses, in the sense that every unsatisfiable set of ground clauses has a resolution refutation. In the second stage we observe that, by Corollary 6.3.1, every unsatisfiable set of clauses S has an unsatisfiable set of ground instances S', and so the set $\overline{S}$ of all ground instances of S is unsatisfiable. By the result of the first stage of the completeness proof, $\overline{S}$ must have a resolution refutation in $\mathcal{R}$, and we may apply a "lifting lemma," together with a "redundancy preservation lemma" to see that this resolution refutation of $\overline{S}$ induces a corresponding resolution refutation of S itself. This principle is depicted in Figure 7.11.

The refutation completeness of resolution calculi is one of the most important classes of results in automated deduction. There are many versions of the theorem, but nearly all are proved using this two-step process. The Lifting Lemma (Lemma 7.4.8) is a purely technical result, the true content of the completeness result being derived from the first part of the construction, i.e., from the completeness result for ground clauses. The following proof of the completeness of $\mathcal{R}$ is a modified version of that in [Bez90]. We begin with

Definition 7.4.7   A set S of clauses is said to be *closed under* $\mathcal{R}$ if every factor and every resolvent of clauses in S is redundant with respect to S.

We have

Lemma 7.4.5   *Let S be a set of ground clauses. If S is closed under $\mathcal{R}$ and if $\square \notin S$, then S is satisfiable.*

Proof. We construct a model for S. The set $S^+ = \{\Phi \to \Psi \in S \mid \Phi = \emptyset\}$ is defined to be the set of *positive* clauses of S. If $S^+ = \emptyset$, then $\mathcal{I} = \emptyset$ constitutes a model for S, since $\Phi \neq \emptyset$, and therefore $\Phi \not\subseteq \mathcal{I}$, holds for each clause $\Phi \to \Psi \in S$. We therefore assume in what follows that $S^+ \neq \emptyset$, and let

$$X = \bigcup \{\Psi \mid \to \Psi \in S^+\}$$

be the set of all atoms appearing in clauses in S^+. The set X *covers* S^+, in the sense that for every clause in S^+ some atom from S^+ appears in X. (Note that since $\square \notin S$, every clause in S^+ has a nonempty succedent.) We construct a minimal—with respect to the inclusion ordering on sets—subset of X which covers S^+, and then show that this minimal such subset constitutes a model for S.

Let Z be the set of all subsets of X which cover S^+. Then $X \in Z$, and so Z is nonempty. If we show that every decreasing sequence in Z has a lower bound in Z, then by Zorn's Lemma it follows that Z has a minimal element (with respect to the inclusion ordering). In other words, we need only apply Zorn's Lemma to construct the desired $\subseteq$-minimal subset of X which covers S^+.

To establish that every decreasing sequence of sets in Z has a lower bound in Z, let Z' be a decreasing sequence of sets in Z. Then the set $\cap Z'$ is a lower bound for Z'. To see that $\cap Z'$ is in Z, assume that it is not, i.e., assume that $\cap Z'$ does not cover S^+. Then there must exist a clause $\to A_1, \ldots, A_n \in S^+$ such that $\{A_1, \ldots, A_n\} \cap (\cap Z') = \emptyset$, and, therefore for each $i \in \{1, \ldots, n\}$, there must exist a $Y_i \in Z'$ such that $A_i \notin Y_i$. Since Z' is a decreasing sequence, the Y_i are totally ordered by the inclusion ordering, and so there must also exist a Y_k which is a subset of every Y_i and which therefore contains no A_i. This Y_k does not cover S^+, contradicting the fact that $Y_k \in Z' \subseteq Z$. We have therefore shown that $\cap Z' \in Z$ holds.

Since the hypotheses of Zorn's Lemma are satisfied, there must exist a minimal element $\mathcal{I}$ of Z which covers S^+. We now show that $\mathcal{I}$ is a model for S. By the construction of $\mathcal{I}$ it is clear that $\mathcal{I}$ satisfies all clauses in S^+. To see that $\mathcal{I}$ satisfies $S - S^+$ it will be important to note that for every atom $A \in \mathcal{I}$ there is a clause in S^+ containing no atom from $\mathcal{I}$ other than A (otherwise the set $\mathcal{I} - \{A\}$ would be a smaller cover of S^+).

Suppose there is a clause $C = \Phi \to \Psi \in S - S^+$ which is not satisfied by $\mathcal{I}$. Then $\emptyset \neq \Phi \subseteq \mathcal{I}$ and $\Psi \cap \mathcal{I} = \emptyset$. We may assume without loss of generality that among all clauses not satisfied by $\mathcal{I}$, C has the smallest (with respect to the inclusion ordering) antecedent, i.e., we may assume that C is such that every clause $\Phi' \to \Psi' \in S$ with Φ' a proper subset of Φ is satisfied by $\mathcal{I}$. Let $A \in \Phi$. Since $\Phi \subseteq \mathcal{I}$ we also have $A \in \mathcal{I}$. We can therefore find a clause D in S^+ such that A is the only element of $\mathcal{I}$ appearing in D. Then for some Φ' and Ψ',

$$C = \Phi', A \to \Psi \quad \text{and} \quad D = \to \Psi', A$$

with $\Phi = \Phi' \cup \{A\}$. For this Φ' and Ψ', we have $\Psi' \cap \mathcal{I} = \emptyset$ and therefore also $\Psi' \cap \Phi' = \emptyset$. The resolvent $R = \Phi' \to \Psi, \Psi'$ of C and D is thus not a tautology. Because S is closed under $\mathcal{R}$, either R or some smaller clause R' which subsumes R is in S. Let $R' = \Phi'' \to \Psi'' \in S$ be such that $\Phi'' \subseteq \Phi'$ and $\Psi'' \subseteq \Psi \cup \Psi'$. Then

$$\Phi'' \subseteq \Phi' \subset \Phi \subseteq \mathcal{I} \quad \text{and} \quad \Psi'' \cap \mathcal{I} \subseteq (\Psi \cup \Psi') \cap \mathcal{I} = \emptyset.$$

Thus R' is also not satisfied by $\mathcal{I}$, and yet the antecedent of R' is a proper subset of that of C. This contradicts the choice of C. Thus $\mathcal{I} \not\models C$ for every clause C in $S - S^+$, as well as for every clause in S^+, and therefore $\mathcal{I}$ is a model of S. $\square$

The model construction outlined in the proof of Lemma 7.4.5 is illustrated in the next example.

Example 7.4.3   Let S be the satisfiable set of clauses

$$S = \{(\to P, Q), (\to Q, R), (\to P, R), (P \to Q, R),$$
$$(Q \to P, R), (R \to P, Q), (P, Q, R \to)\}.$$

Then the set of positive clauses in S is

$$S^+ = \{(\to P, Q), (\to Q, R), (\to P, R)\}$$

and the set $X = \{P, Q, R\}$ covers S^+. From this set we can choose different smallest covering sets, for example, $\mathcal{I} = \{P, Q\}$. It is not hard to see that for each of P and Q there are indeed clauses in S^+ containing no atoms from $\mathcal{I}$ other than P (resp., Q), and that the interpretation $\mathcal{I}$ is indeed a model for S.

Note that in Example 7.4.3 the nonminimal cover $X = \{P, Q, R\}$ for S is *not* a model for S since it fails to satisfy the clause $P, Q, R, \to$. This observation demonstrates that minimality of the interpretation $\mathcal{I}$ is indeed necessary.

Completeness of $\mathcal{R}$ for ground clauses, as well as for nonground clauses is proved only with respect to certain kinds of resolution derivations, called *fair* derivations; we will see at the end of this chapter that fair derivations for arbitrary sets of clauses do indeed exist, and this will be sufficient to establish the refutation completeness of the inference system $\mathcal{R}$. Loosely speaking, a fair derivation is one in which every rule in $\mathcal{R}$ that can be applied to clauses in the derivation is eventually applied. That is, in a fair derivation, every rule in $\mathcal{R}$ eventually fails to add new clauses to the set of clauses being constructed. More formally,

Definition 7.4.8   An $\mathcal{R}$-derivation $S_0, S_1, S_2, \ldots$ is said to be *fair* if the set

$$S^\infty = \bigcup_{k \geq 0} \bigcap_{j \geq k} S_j$$

is closed under $\mathcal{R}$. The set S^∞ is called the set of *persistent clauses* of S.

In proving the refutation completeness of $\mathcal{R}$ for ground clauses we will require a technical result about fair derivations, which itself relies on the following lemma:

Lemma 7.4.6   *If S and U are sets of clauses, and if every clause in U is subsumed by some clauses in S, then S is satisfiable iff $S \cup U$ is.*

Proof. We need only show that if S is satisfiable then $S \cup U$ is satisfiable, since the converse clearly holds.

Suppose S is satisfiable. Then Corollary 6.3.1 implies that $\overline{S}$ is also satisfiable by some interpretation $\mathcal{I}$. Let $C \in U$ and $X \in \overline{C}$ be arbitrary. Since C is subsumed by some clause D in S, there must exist a $Y \in \overline{D}$ such that Y subsumes X. Since X and Y are ground clauses, and since $\mathcal{I} \models \overline{S}$ implies $\mathcal{I} \models \overline{D}$ and hence $\mathcal{I} \models Y$, we have $\mathcal{I} \models X$ as well. Since X was arbitrary in $\overline{C}$, this implies that $\mathcal{I} \models \overline{C}$, and since C was arbitrary in U, it follows that $\mathcal{I} \models \overline{U}$. Finally, since $\mathcal{I} \models \overline{S}$ and $\mathcal{I} \models \overline{U}$, we have $\mathcal{I} \models \overline{S} \cup \overline{U}$, i.e., $\mathcal{I} \models \overline{S \cup U}$. But then since $\overline{S \cup U}$ is satisfiable, by Corollary 6.3.1, $S \cup U$ must also be satisfiable. $\square$

Corollary 7.4.1   *If S and U are sets of clauses, and if every clause in U is redundant with respect to S, then S is satisfiable iff $S \cup U$ is.*

We can now prove

Lemma 7.4.7   *If the set S of clauses is unsatisfiable, and if $S_0, S_1, S_2, \ldots$ is a fair resolution derivation with $S_0 = S$, then S^∞ is unsatisfiable.*

Proof. Suppose that S is unsatisfiable. Then the superset $U = \bigcup_{j \geq 0} S_j$ of S must also be unsatisfiable. We will show that if S^∞ is satisfiable, then so is U, and this contradiction will establish the lemma.

Suppose that S^∞ is satisfiable. We first observe that, for every i, every clause C in $S_i - S^\infty$ is either a tautology or else is subsumed by some clause $D \in S_k$ with $|D| < |C|$, for some $k \geq i$. This is because if C is a clause in $S_i - S^\infty$, then for every $k \geq 0$, $C \notin \bigcap_{j \geq k} S_j$. But then for each $k \geq 0$ there exists a smallest $l > k$ such that $C \notin S_l$. In particular there exists a (smallest) $l > i$ such that $C \in S_{l-1}$ but $C \notin S_l$. Since the only way for a clause to be in S_{l-1} but not in S_l is for it to be either a tautology or to be subsumed by some smaller clause in S_{l-1}, each clause $C \in S_i - S^\infty$ must either be a tautology or else must be subsumed by some smaller clause in S_k for some $k \geq i$.

Now, if C is subsumed by some smaller clause in S_k for some $k \geq 0$, then C must be redundant with respect to S^∞. This can be seen by observing, first, that if $C \in S^\infty$ or if C is a tautology then there is nothing to prove, so we need only consider the possibility that C is not a tautology, C is not in S^∞, and C is subsumed by some clause D_0 in S_k which is smaller than C. Now D_0 cannot be a tautology because C is not, but if $D_0 \in S^\infty$, then we are done. The only other possibility is that $D_0 \notin S^\infty$, but since then $D_0 \in (S_k - S^\infty)$, this implies that D_0 must be subsumed by some clause $D_1 \in S_l$, for some $l \geq k$, which is smaller than D_0 and which itself is either a tautology, is in S^∞, or is subsumed by some clause $D_2 \in S_n$, for some $n \geq l$, which is smaller than D_1, and so on. The resulting "subsumption chain" $D_0, D_1, D_2, \ldots$ must, however, be finite, since for each natural number i, $|D_{i+1}| < |D_i|$ must hold. Because the final clause D_n in this chain cannot be subsumed and cannot be a tautology, it necessarily belongs to S^∞. Since $D_n \in S^\infty$ subsumes C and $|D_n| < |C|$, the claim is established.

Since every clause C in $U - S^\infty$ is in $S_i - S^\infty$ for some $i \geq 0$ and is therefore redundant with respect to S^∞, and since S^∞ is satisfiable, Corollary 7.4.1 implies that $U = S^\infty \cup (U - S^\infty)$ is satisfiable. But this contradicts our observation above that U is unsatisfiable, and thus the proof is complete. □

With the next theorem, the first stage of the proof of the refutation completeness of $\mathcal{R}$ is completed.

Theorem 7.4.2   *(Completeness of $\mathcal{R}$ for ground clauses) If S is an unsatisfiable set of ground clauses and if $S_0, S_1, S_2, \ldots$ is a fair resolution derivation such that $S_0 = S$, then there exists an $n \geq 0$ such that S_n contains the empty clause.*

Proof. Let $S_0, S_1, S_2, \ldots$ be a fair resolution derivation such that $S_0 = S$. Then S^∞ is closed under $\mathcal{R}$, and is unsatisfiable by the previous lemma, and so $\square \in S^\infty$ by Lemma 7.4.5. Thus there exists an $n \geq 0$ such that $\square \in \cap_{j \geq n} S_j$, and therefore such that $\square \in S_n$. $\square$

We have now established the resolution completeness of $\mathcal{R}$ for ground clauses and fair derivations, and come to the second stage in our completeness proof. We want to show that Theorem 7.4.2 holds even if we delete from its hypotheses the assumption that the clauses in S are ground clauses, i.e., we want to show that if S is any unsatisfiable set of clauses and if $S_0, S_1, S_2, \ldots$ is a fair resolution derivation such that $S_0 = S$, then there is an $n \geq 0$ such that S_n contains the empty clause. The idea is to use the completeness of $\mathcal{R}$ for unsatisfiable sets of ground clauses to infer its completeness for unsatisfiable sets of arbitrary clauses.

By Corollary 6.3.1 we know that, for any unsatisfiable set of clauses S, $\overline{S}$ is an unsatisfiable set of ground clauses. If we also knew that every fair resolution derivation $S_0, S_1, S_2, \ldots$ out of S induced a fair ground resolution derivation $\overline{S_0}, \overline{S_1}, \overline{S_2}, \ldots$ out of $\overline{S}$, then we could conclude that there must exist some $n \geq 0$ such that $\overline{S_n}$ contains the empty clause. Then since every clause in $\overline{S_n}$ is an instance of some clause in S_n, it would follow that S_n must contain the empty clause, and the proof of the refutation completeness of $\mathcal{R}$ would thus be complete. We want to establish, therefore, that if $S_0, S_1, S_2, \ldots$ is fair—i.e., if S^∞ is closed under $\mathcal{R}$—then $\overline{S_0}, \overline{S_1}, \overline{S_2}, \ldots$ is also fair, i.e, $\overline{S}^\infty$ is closed under $\mathcal{R}$. Our proof of this fact relies on the following lifting and redundancy preservation lemmas.

Lemma 7.4.8   *(Lifting Lemma for $\mathcal{R}$) Let C and D be clauses and let C' and D' be ground instances of C and D, respectively. If R' is a resolvent of C' and D', then there is a clause R derivable in $\mathcal{R}$ from C and D with the property that R' is a ground instance of R.*

Proof. Let $C = \Phi \to \Psi$ and $D = \Phi' \to \Psi'$. The clauses C and D may, without loss of generality, be assumed to have no variables in common. Thus there exists a ground substitution σ such that $C' = \sigma(\Phi) \to \sigma(\Psi)$

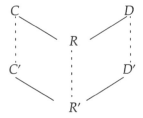

FIGURE 7.12.

and $D' = \sigma(\Phi') \to \sigma(\Psi')$. Moreover, for any resolvent R' of C' and D', there exist atoms $B_1, \ldots, B_n \in \Psi$ and $A_1, \ldots, A_m \in \Phi'$ such that

$$\sigma(B_1) = \ldots = \sigma(B_n) = \sigma(A_1) = \ldots = \sigma(A_m)$$

and

$$R' = \sigma(\Phi), (\sigma(\Phi') - \{\sigma(A_1)\}) \to (\sigma(\Psi) - \{\sigma(B_1)\}), \sigma(\Psi').$$

For simplicity of exposition we consider the case when $m = n = 2$; the proof in the more general case proceeds in a similar manner.

Because σ is a unifier of B_1 and B_2, there exists a factor

$$C_1 = \tau(\Phi) \to \tau(\Psi - \{B_2\})$$

of C, where τ is a most general unifier of B_1 and B_2. Note that since τ is a most general unifier of B_1 and B_2, and since σ is also a unifier of B_1 and B_2, we must have $\sigma\tau = \sigma$. In addition, since A_1 and $\tau(B_1)$ are unifiable by σ, there exists a resolvent

$$R_1 = \theta(\tau(\Phi)), \theta(\Phi' - \{A_1\}) \to \theta(\Psi'), \theta(\tau(\Psi - \{B_2\}) - \{\tau(B_1)\})$$

of C_1 and D, where θ is a most general unifier of A_1 and $\tau(B_1)$. Since σ is also a unifier of A_1 and $\tau(B_1)$, we must have $\sigma\theta = \sigma$.

Unfortunately, however, R_1 is not quite the clause we are seeking: it is still possible, for example, that $\theta(A_2)$ appears in the set of atoms $\theta(\Phi' - \{A_1\})$, so that instantiating R_1 by σ would not actually yield a clause whose antecedent is $\sigma(\Phi), (\sigma(\Phi') - \{\sigma(A_1)\})$. In fact, this instantiation will not yield the desired antecedent unless $\theta(A_2) = \theta(A_1)$. Similarly, $\theta(\tau(B_1))$ could still appear in $\theta(\tau(\Psi - \{B_2\}))$, $\tau(B_2)$ could still appear in Ψ, and $\theta(\tau(B_2))$ could still appear in $\theta(\tau(\Psi))$. Thus instantiation of R_1 by σ will not necessarily yield a clause with succedent $(\sigma(\Psi) - \{\sigma(B_1)\}), \sigma(\Psi')$, either. But we can eliminate these atoms—all of which are unifiable by σ—from R_1 by resolving the clauses R_1 and C_1 to arrive at

$$\sigma(R) = \nu(\tau(\Phi)), \nu(\theta(\tau(\Phi)) \cup \theta(\Phi' - \{A_1\}) - \{\theta(A_2)\}) \to$$
$$\nu(\theta(\tau(\Psi - \{B_2\}) - \tau(B_1))), \nu(\theta(\Psi')), \nu(\tau(\Psi - \{B_2\}) - \theta(\tau(B_2)))$$

where ν is a most general unifier of A_2 and $\theta(\tau(B_2))$. In this case, we must have $\sigma\nu = \sigma$.

We now show that R is the desired resolvent of C and D by verifying that $R' = \sigma(R)$. Since A_1 and A_2 are the only atoms in Φ' whose instantiations by σ are precisely $\sigma(A_1)$, and since B_1 and B_2 are the only atoms in Ψ

whose instantiations by σ are identically $\sigma(B_1)$, it follows that

$$
\begin{aligned}
\sigma(R) \;=\;& \sigma(\nu(\tau(\Phi))), \sigma(\nu(\theta(\tau(\Phi)))), \sigma(\nu(\theta(\Phi') - \{\theta(A_1)\}) - \{\nu(\theta(A_2))\}) \\
& \to \sigma(\nu(\theta(\Psi'))), \sigma(\nu(\tau(\Psi) - \{\tau(B_2)\})), \\
& \sigma[\nu(\theta(\tau(\Psi) - \{\tau(B_2)\}) - \{\theta(\tau(B_1))\}) - \{\nu(\theta(\tau(B_2)))\}] \\
\;=\;& \sigma(\Phi), (\sigma(\Phi') - \{\sigma(A_1)\}) \to (\sigma(\Psi) - \{\sigma(B_1)\}), \sigma(\Psi'),
\end{aligned}
$$

as desired. $\square$

We illustrate this lifting process with the set of clauses from Example 7.4.1.

Example 7.4.4   Consider the ground instance

$$
S' = \{ \to P(b, g(b)), \; P(b, g(b)) \to Q(b), \; P(b, g(b)), Q(b) \to \}
$$

of

$$
S = \{ \to P(z, y), P(x, g(x)), \; P(u, v) \to Q(b), \; P(w, g(b)), Q(w) \to \}.
$$

In Figure 7.13, a ground resolution refutation for S' is represented. Lifting the steps in this refutation gives precisely the derivation of Figure 7.10. Repeated lifting of ground resolution steps as described in Lemma 7.4.8 thus provides a means of lifting resolution refutations for unsatisfiable sets of ground instances of unsatisfiable sets of clauses to resolution refutations out of those sets of clauses themselves.

The Lifting Lemma says that resolution steps can be lifted from the ground level to the more general level. By contrast, the Redundancy Preservation Lemma, which we will state and prove momentarily, says that if the clause C is redundant with respect to the set S, then every ground instance of C is redundant with respect to the set $\overline{S}$ of all ground instances of S. This means that redundancy in lifted resolution derivations must be inherited from the corresponding ground resolution derivations. Together, the Lifting Lemma and the Redundancy Preservation Lemma provide precisely the knowledge we need in order to show that $\overline{S}^\infty$ is closed under $\mathcal{R}$ if S^∞ is.

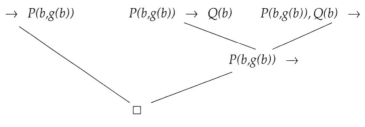

FIGURE 7.13.

The Redundancy Preservation Lemma is as follows:

Lemma 7.4.9   *(Redundancy Preservation Lemma) If C is redundant with respect to the set S of clauses, then every ground instance of C is redundant with respect to $\overline{S}$.*

Proof. Suppose that C is redundant with respect to the set S of clauses. If $C \in S$, then every ground instance of C is in $\overline{S}$, and is therefore redundant with respect to $\overline{S}$. If C is a tautology, then every ground instance of C is also a tautology, and is therefore redundant with respect to $\overline{S}$. If C is subsumed by some smaller clause D in S, then every ground instance C' of C is either subsumed by some ground instance of D, or else some collapsing of literals takes place and C' is equal to some ground instance of D, and hence is in $\overline{S}$. In either case, however, C' is redundant with respect to $\overline{S}$. ▫

Applying the next lemma to the set S^∞ of clauses demonstrates that if S^∞ is closed under $\mathcal{R}$, then so is $\overline{S^\infty} = \overline{S}^\infty$.

Lemma 7.4.10   *Let S be a set of clauses. If S is closed under $\mathcal{R}$, then $\overline{S}$ is also closed under $\mathcal{R}$.*

Proof. Since ground clauses have no factors, that $\overline{S}$ is closed under $\mathcal{R}$ can be seen by letting R' be a resolvent of two clauses C' and D' in $\overline{S}$. Then there must exist clauses C and D in S such that C' and D' are ground instances of C and D, respectively. The Lifting Lemma implies the existence of a resolvent R of C and D such that R' is a ground instance of R. Then R must be redundant with respect to S since S is closed under $\mathcal{R}$, and from the Redundancy Preservation Lemma it follows that R' is redundant with respect to $\overline{S}$. Thus $\overline{S}$ is closed under $\mathcal{R}$. ▫

The refutation completeness of $\mathcal{R}$ now follows directly.

Theorem 7.4.3   *(Completeness of $\mathcal{R}$) If S is an unsatisfiable set of clauses and if $S_0, S_1, S_2, \ldots$ is a fair $\mathcal{R}$-derivation with $S = S_0$, then there exists an $n \geq 0$ such that S_n contains the empty clause.*

Proof. First note that since S is unsatisfiable, by Corollary 6.3.1 $\overline{S}$ is unsatisfiable as well. Moreover, if $S_0, S_1, S_2, \ldots$ is a fair resolution derivation such that $S_0 = S$, then S^∞ is closed under $\mathcal{R}$, and so by Lemma 7.4.10, $\overline{S^\infty} = \overline{S}^\infty$ is also closed under $\mathcal{R}$. This means that the resolution derivation $\overline{S_0}, \overline{S_1}, \overline{S_2}, \ldots$ is fair, and thus Theorem 7.4.2 implies the existence of some $n \geq 0$ such that $\overline{S_n}$ contains the empty clause. But since every clause in $\overline{S_n}$ is an instance of a clause in S_n, it must be the case that S_n itself contains the empty clause. ▫

7.5   Fair Derivation Strategies

Having established the refutation completeness of the inference system $\mathcal{R}$ for arbitrary clauses and fair resolution derivations, it remains only to verify that fair derivations actually do exist in order to see that $\mathcal{R}$ is refutation complete for sets of arbitrary clauses. A classic—and perhaps the most obvious—example of a fair derivation strategy (i.e., of a strategy for producing fair derivations) is the method of level saturation, which we now describe. For each given set S of clauses, let $\mathcal{R}^n(S)$ denote the set of all resolvents or factors which are reachable from S by at most n applications of rules in $\mathcal{R}$. We can think of each set $\mathcal{R}^n(S) - \mathcal{R}^{n-1}(S)$ as comprising the clauses appearing in a "level" in the tree representation of the resolution search space out of S for the nondeterministic algorithm based on $\mathcal{R}$. The method of level saturation uses the sets $\mathcal{R}^{n-1}(S)$ to generate each of the sets $\mathcal{R}^n(S)$ in turn. The set $\mathcal{R}^\infty(S)$ of all clauses reachable from S via any number of applications of the resolution or factorization rules is precisely the set of all clauses appearing in the search space out of S for the nondeterministic algorithm based on $\mathcal{R}$. The method of level saturation corresponds to a breadth-first search of $\mathcal{R}^\infty(S)$, which is well-known to be fair.

More precisely, let M_1 and M_2 be two sets of clauses, and denote by $R(M_1, M_2)$ the set of all clauses obtained by applying the resolution rule with one premise from the set of clauses M_1 and the other premise from the set of clauses M_2. Further, for any set M of clauses, let $F(M)$ stand for the set of all clauses obtained by applying the factorization rule to some clause in M. We have

Definition 7.5.1   Let S be a set of clauses and define the set S_n for $n \geq 0$ inductively by:

$$
\begin{aligned}
S_0 &= \emptyset \\
S_1 &= S \\
S_{n+2} &= S_{n+1} \cup R(S_{n+1} - S_n, S_{n+1}) \cup F(S_{n+1} - S_n)
\end{aligned}
$$

The method of *level saturation* constructs from S the derivation $S_1, S_2, \ldots$.

Note that the derivations constructed by the method of level saturation are not true resolution derivations since each set S_j in such a derivation actually comprises clauses obtained via several applications of rules in $\mathcal{R}$. That is, derivations constructed by the method of level saturation regard many applications of rules in $\mathcal{R}$ as a single step. Similar remarks will apply at several places below, and we will abuse terminology in each instance, treating derivations obtained from such derivation strategies as resolution derivations even though they are not resolution derivations in the strictest sense. It follows from the proof of Lemma 7.4.4 that each step in such a derivation preserves satisfiability.

It is easy to see that the method of level saturation is a fair derivation strategy, since every possible resolvent and every possible factor of every initial set of clauses is eventually obtained in the derivation the method induces. But, unfortunately, the method of level saturation has no provision for removal of clauses which are redundant in derivations and which therefore unnecessarily explode search spaces without actually contributing to possible refutations. A more efficient version of the method of level saturation might thus apply the rule *Reduction* "eagerly by levels" to remove certain such clauses from derivations.

Definition 7.5.2 Let S be a set of clauses, and define the set S_n for $n \geq 0$ inductively by:

$$
\begin{aligned}
S_0 &= \emptyset \\
S_1 &= S \\
S_2 &= S_1 - \{C \in S_1 \mid C \text{ is redundant with respect to } S_0\} \\
S_{2n+1} &= S_{2n} \cup R(S_{2n} - S_{2n-2}, S_{2n}) \cup F(S_{2n} - S_{2n-2}) \\
S_{2n+2} &= S_{2n+1} - \{C \in S_{2n+1} \mid C \text{ is redundant with respect to } S_{2n}\}
\end{aligned}
$$

The method of *level saturation with solution* constructs from S the derivation $S_1, S_2, \ldots$.

The name "level saturation with solution" comes from the standard terminology in which a clause is said to be *solved* when it is removed from a derivation by an application of the rule *Reduction*.

The method of level saturation with solution provides an example of a second, more efficient, fair derivation strategy. To verify fairness we show that every resolvent and every factor of clauses in S^∞ (for the sets $S_0, S_1, S_2, \ldots$ given in Definition 7.5.2) is redundant with respect to S^∞. Let R be a resolvent of the clauses C and D in S^∞. Because $C \in S^\infty$ and $D \in S^\infty$, there exists an $n \geq 0$ such that $C \in \cap_{i \geq n} S_i$ and $D \in \cap_{j \geq n} S_j$. Without loss of generality, n may be taken to be odd. The clauses C and D are therefore neither tautologies nor subsumed by smaller clauses in S_n, since otherwise they would become solved, and so would not appear in S_{n+1}. Their resolvent R must therefore be in S_{n+2}. If R is not in S^∞, then it must necessarily either be a tautology or else be subsumed by some smaller clause in S_j for some $j > n$. But then by the argument of Lemma 7.4.7, R is redundant with respect to S^∞ as desired. It can be shown in a similar manner that every factor of a clause in S^∞ must be redundant with respect to S^∞, and thus that the method of level saturation with solution is fair.

Even more efficient fair derivation strategies are, of course, conceivable. In building the set of clauses S_{2n+2} in level saturation, for example, it is not necessary first to saturate S_{2n} to get S_{2n+1} and then to solve the resulting redundant clauses in S_{2n+1} to get S_{2n+2}. Instead, refutation search spaces associated with level saturation with solution can be reduced significantly simply by solving all redundant clauses immediately after each application of a rule in $\mathcal{R}$. This leads to a derivation strategy known as the method of *level saturation with immediate solution*, which we illustrate in the next example. As discussed after Example 7.4.2, the method of level saturation with immediate solution gives rise to a complete refutation algorithm based on $\mathcal{R}$ only by virtue of the proviso that $|D| < |C|$ in Definition 7.4.3; as above we can verify in a straightforward manner that it is indeed a complete derivation strategy.

Example 7.5.1   Let

$$S = \{(\to P, Q), (P \to Q), (Q \to P), (P, Q \to)\}.$$

After constructing the resolvent $\to Q$ from $\to P, Q$ and $P \to Q$, these two clauses are immediately solvable. Solving them directly spares us the construction of the resolvents $\to P$ and $P \to$ which is required by the method of level saturation and the method of level saturation with solution. Note that although a shortest refutation of S requires the same number of *resolution* steps under level saturation, level saturation with solution, or level saturation with immediate solution, the sets from which the resolvents are drawn are smaller under level saturation with solution than under level saturation, and these sets are smaller still under level saturation with immediate solution.

We see, then, that whether or not a derivation strategy is fair depends on the manner in which it causes resolution search spaces to be traversed. Level saturation, for example, corresponds to breadth-first search, which is well-known to exhaust search spaces. Breadth-first search is, however, one of the least efficient such strategies, since it moves completely blindly through search spaces. On the other hand, depth-first search can, with luck, relatively quickly find the empty clause in the resolution search space for a refutable set of clauses. Of course, the possibility of traversing an infinite branch in the search space using this method is far greater than with breadth-first search, and depth-first search is not fair. A search method which more cleverly traverses entire resolution search spaces, and which can therefore exhibit greater efficiency than either breadth-first or depth-first search, is a heuristic search based on an evaluation function. Using this search method, the nodes of the search tree (in this case, sets of clauses) are evaluated based on some criteria, and the node which is "best" according to these criteria is used to generate the next derivation step. Perhaps the simplest example of an evaluation function for clauses is that which assigns to each clause a natural number related to size and which favors, in the corresponding heuristic search, those to which the smallest such number is assigned. Many evaluation functions are possible: we might, for example, evaluate clauses based on their length, on the number of symbols appearing in them, or with respect to the particular user-defined weighting function on symbols appearing in clauses.

Suppose that an evaluation function γ has been given, and that γ assigns to each clause C a number $\gamma(C) > 0$. Such a function induces an ordering $>_\gamma$ on the set of clauses—namely, that defined by $C >_\gamma D$ iff $\gamma(C) > \gamma(D)$ holds—and this ordering in turn induces a search method as described in the preceding paragraph. In light of the hypotheses of Theorem 7.4.3, we would like to know the conditions under which such derivations determined by an induced search strategy are fair. To investigate this concern, let

$$min_\gamma(S) = \{C \in S \mid C \text{ is } >_\gamma\text{-minimal in } S\}.$$

In order to make clearer our analysis of the preference strategy, we apply a reduction strategy simpler than that given by Definition 7.5.2. If M_1 and M_2 are sets of clauses, then let $R'(M_1, M_2)$ be the set of resolvents of clauses in M_1 with clauses in M_2 that are not redundant with respect to M_1, and let $F'(M_1, M_2)$ be the set of factors of clauses in M_2 which are not redundant with respect to M_1. These two sets of clauses can be used to define a notion of *forward reduction*, in which only newly generated clauses which are redundant with respect to the set of existing clauses are immediately solved. There is also the related notion of *backward reduction*, in which only existing clauses which are redundant with respect to the newly generated clauses and factors are immediately solved. Forward reduction is used in the following, more precise definition of the preference strategy.

Definition 7.5.3   Let γ be an evaluation function and let S be a set of clauses. Define the sets S_k, M_k, and N_k for $n \geq 0$ inductively by:

$$
\begin{aligned}
S_0 &= \emptyset \\
N_0 &= S \\
M_0 &= min_\gamma(N_0) \\
S_{n+1} &= S_n \cup M_n \\
N_{n+1} &= (N_n - M_n) \cup R'(S_{n+1}, M_n) \cup F'(S_{n+1}, M_n) \\
M_{n+1} &= min_\gamma(N_{n+1})
\end{aligned}
$$

The *preference strategy with evaluation function* γ constructs from S the derivation $S_1, S_2, \ldots$.

The following examples clarify the method. Notice that under the evaluation functions in Examples 7.5.3 and 7.5.4, entire search spaces are traversed.

Example 7.5.2   Consider the evaluation function defined by $\gamma(C) = |C|$ which assigns to each clause its length, i.e, which assigns to each clause the number of atoms appearing in that clause. The preference strategy with this evaluation function γ is *not* fair because the number of clauses of a certain length (over a given signature) is unlimited. Consider, for example, the set of clauses $S = \{C_1, C_2, C_3, C_4\}$, where

$$
\begin{aligned}
C_1 &= \ \to P(a), \\
C_2 &= \ P(x) \to P(f(x)), \\
C_3 &= \ Q(x), Q(y) \to, \\
C_4 &= \ \to Q(z), Q(w), Q(u).
\end{aligned}
$$

Here $\gamma(C_1) = 1$, $\gamma(C_2) = \gamma(C_3) = 2$, and $\gamma(C_4) = 3$. According to the preference strategy, we must therefore first construct all resolvents of C_1 with other clauses. The only possibility for a resolution partner with C_1 is C_2, from which we derive the clause $D_1 = \ \to P(f(a))$. But since $\gamma(D_1)$ is again 1, resolvents in whose derivation D_1 participates must be generated before those in whose derivations D_1 does not participate. From D_1 and C_2 we generate the clause $D_2 = \ \to P(f(f(a)))$, which, in turn, is such that $\gamma(D_2) = 1$. It is easy to see that continuing in the mandated fashion produces at the kth step the clause $D_k = \ \to P(f^k(a))$. Thus the factorization step deriving from the clause C_4 the factor $C_5 = \ \to Q(z)$, which is necessary to refute S, is pushed ever farther down the preference list, since there exist in the search space for S infinitely many clauses D_k of length 1.

Example 7.5.3   Consider the evaluation function γ which assigns to each clause the total number of symbols appearing in that clause. That is, consider the function γ defined by

$$
\begin{aligned}
\gamma(Pt_1 \ldots t_n) &= 1 + |t_1| + \ldots + |t_n| \\
\gamma(\Phi \to \Psi) &= \Sigma_{A \in \Phi} \gamma(A) + \Sigma_{B \in \Psi} \gamma(B).
\end{aligned}
$$

Let k be fixed but arbitrary, let C be any (finite) set of clauses, and let $\mathcal{C}_k$ be the set of clauses D over alphabet elements appearing in C with $\gamma(D) = k$. Since only finitely many alphabet elements appear in C, for each k the set $\mathcal{C}_k$ contains only finitely many clauses which are not variants of one another. For the clauses D_k from the previous example we have $\gamma(D_k) = k + 2$, and so the clauses D_k are not simply generated one after another. As an exercise, the reader should establish that with this evaluation function γ, a resolution refutation of S will indeed be found.

Example 7.5.4   If γ is taken to be the evaluation function assigning to each clause the depth of a (shortest) derivation of it, then the preference strategy based on γ is precisely the method of level saturation.

Theoretically speaking, we have completely solved the problem of automatically proving theorems in first-order logic since we have seen that the inference system $\mathcal{R}$ is sound and complete for arbitrary unsatisfiable sets of clauses, and we have also established the existence of (several) fair derivation strategies. But although the inference system $\mathcal{R}$ is both sound and refutation complete, it is not quite suitable as the basis for refutation algorithms for practical applications without further modification. Even for small examples, the sizes of search spaces associated with algorithms based on $\mathcal{R}$ can contain on the order of ten to a hundred thousand clauses.

Example 7.5.5   Consider the set $U_n = \{C_1, C_2(n)\}$ of clauses, where n is any natural number,

$$
\begin{aligned}
C_1 &= \ \rightarrow P(x), P(f(x)), \text{ and} \\
C_2(n) &= \ P(y), P(f^n(y)) \rightarrow .
\end{aligned}
$$

The set U_n is unsatisfiable. The refutation search space for U_n grows in size very, very rapidly as n increases. For $n = 2$, the empty clause can be found only after ten steps of level saturation with immediate solution. For $n = 4$ this number is already in the hundreds, and for $n = 6$ the number of clauses which must be considered reaches into the tens of thousands. For $n = 8$, it is no longer practical to search for a solution without the aid of special strategies for somehow reducing the search space.

Fortunately, as inference systems based on the resolution rule have made the transition from serving as mere theoretical tools for establishing the unsatisfiability of sets of clauses to becoming practical tools for incorporation into resolution theorem provers and other automated deduction systems, many techniques have evolved for coping with the large search spaces associated with the nondeterministic algorithms they induce. In the next chapter we will see how some of the most important and most promising of these techniques can be applied to develop more efficient refutation methods based on the inference system $\mathcal{R}$.

8

Improving Deduction Efficiency

Generalizing Theorem 7.4.3, we may infer that an arbitrary resolution calculus is refutation complete if, for every unsatisfiable set S of clauses and every fair derivation out of S, the empty clause lies in the resolution search space generated from S by that calculus. In particular, since fair derivation strategies provide means of traversing entire resolution search spaces, in proving the refutation completeness of a given resolution calculus it suffices to consider only completeness with respect to fair derivations. Completeness of the calculus in question then follows by demonstrating the existence of at least one fair derivation strategy for it.

In Section 7.5 we learned of some derivation strategies for the resolution calculus determined by $\mathcal{R}$. Indeed, we considered strategies based on general search methods, such as breadth-first and depth-first search, and we also considered particular preference strategies for clauses which take into account their utility in constructing resolution refutations. Each of the derivation strategies discussed in that section leads to the—perhaps clever—traversal of entire resolution search spaces, and is therefore easily seen to be fair.

We now observe that in addition to providing means by which resolution derivations can be proved fair—and, therefore, that resolution methods can be proved refutation complete—such clever traversals of entire resolution search spaces can also be seen as inducing techniques for improving the efficiency of resolution-based refutation algorithms. From this perspective, each of the derivation strategies of the last chapter can be regarded as describing an efficiency improvement over the nondeterministic refutation algorithm induced by the inference system $\mathcal{R}$; most significantly, each of these strategies preserves completeness.

In this chapter we will consider some additional methods for improving the deduction efficiency of refutation algorithms based on $\mathcal{R}$, as well as the circumstances under which each of these methods is complete. But each of the techniques discussed here will be concerned with actually shrinking resolution search spaces generated from unsatisfiable sets of clauses, rather than merely with traversing them, in their entirety, a bit more cleverly. Of course, in order to establish the refutation completeness of such resolution methods, it must be verified that in spite of any pruning undertaken, the empty clause may still be found in the generated resolution search spaces. This can sometimes be quite a difficult task.

Most of the resolution search space reduction methods we will see in this chapter effect prunings of resolution search spaces by limiting applications of the underlying inference rules themselves: applications of inference rules (especially of the resolution and factorization rules) are restricted to apply only when atoms in their premises possess certain properties. The efficacy of the resulting derivation strategies depends on the observation that there are, in general, many different refutations of a given clause, and that, of these many refutation possibilities, only one need be found. Of course, limiting the application of inference rules can increase the minimum length of available refutations, even while simultaneously decreasing the sizes of resolution search spaces generally. That is, it is entirely possible that, despite smaller overall search spaces, shorter derivations will not be permitted under a given derivation strategy and that only longer, less favorable ones will be obtainable. This situation is illustrated in the following example.

Example 8.1   Consider the set of clauses $S = \{C_1, \ldots, C_8\}$ where

$$
\begin{aligned}
C_1 &= \ \rightarrow P, Q, R \\
C_2 &= \ P \rightarrow Q, R \\
C_3 &= \ Q \rightarrow P, R \\
C_4 &= \ R \rightarrow P, Q \\
C_5 &= \ P, Q \rightarrow R \\
C_6 &= \ P, R \rightarrow Q \\
C_7 &= \ Q, R \rightarrow P \\
C_8 &= \ P, Q, R \rightarrow
\end{aligned}
$$

A resolution refutation of S which takes exactly seven derivation steps exists. There also exists a restriction of the resolution method, called *positive resolution*, which permits applications of the resolution and factorization rules only between pairs consisting of one arbitrary clause and one positive clause (recall from the proof of Lemma 7.4.5 that positive clauses are those which have empty antecedents). Although overall resolution search spaces are pruned considerably when applications of the resolution and factorization rules are restricted to positive instances, the lengths of shortest refutations can, unfortunately, increase. No positive resolution refutation of the clause set S, for example, requires fewer than twelve derivation steps.

Thus in devising efficiency-improving strategies, the benefits of restricting applications of the underlying inference rules on which refutation calculi are based must be balanced against the losses entailed by increasing the lengths of the shortest derivations available.

The inference system presented in the last section of this chapter illustrates a second technique by means of which derivation strategies can be made more efficient. Efficiency-improving strategies which make use of this second technique rely on solving certain clauses—which are generalizations of the redundant clauses of Definition 7.4.3—in much the same manner as tautologies and subsumed clauses can be solved in $\mathcal{R}$-derivations. In general, such strategies neither impede proof searches nor increase the minimum lengths of derivable proofs, and so their application is essentially unproblematic. It must be observed, however, that tests for solvability must typically be applied very often, and that although the test for tautology does not critically affect the time complexity of the search for refutations of clause sets, the test for subsumption has NP-complete time complexity ([KN86]). Fortunately, in practical applications the cost of testing for solvability can often be contained, since the reduction of search spaces it induces can more than compensate for any time spent on it.

Since the conception of resolution as a deduction tool, a number of strategies have been developed for increasing the efficiency of resolution-based refutation methods while maintaining their completeness. Nevertheless, there currently exists no method which satisfactorily improves efficiency in all practical applications—these are far too many and too varied for that to be the case. In fact, the majority of existing efficiency-increasing strategies are very well-suited for certain classes of problems but are of limited use for others. Readers intending to implement systems capable of handling very general classes of deduction problems are thus advised to provide users with the means to employ a considerable range of resolution strategies.

We conclude this introductory discussion by observing that each of the fair derivation strategies we have seen thus far is compatible with each of the various methods to be presented for reducing refutation search spaces. Indeed, fair derivation strategies can always be combined with complete calculi without sacrificing completeness. We caution, however, that different methods of pruning search spaces cannot always be combined: the combination of two inference systems, each of which is complete, is not necessarily again complete, and neither need be the combination of a complete inference system and an arbitrary notion of redundancy.

8.1 Delaying Unification

All of the efficiency-improving refutation methods described in this chapter
are based on an inference system $\mathcal{R}'$ which is a slight modification of the
inference system $\mathcal{R}$ of Chapter 7, and which is also sound and refutation
complete. The inference system $\mathcal{R}'$ takes advantage of the fact that in
applications of the resolution and factorization rules, atoms in the premise
clauses need not actually be unified. That is, $\mathcal{R}'$ embodies the observation
that only *unifiability* of atoms need be established in order to determine the
applicability of an inference rule from $\mathcal{R}$, and that the actual computation
of (most general) unifiers is therefore not required in deriving resolution
refutations. This observation is encoded in $\mathcal{R}'$ by recording information
about atoms to be unified as equational constraints whose solvability must
be demonstrated in order for the resolution or factorization step from which
they arise to be permissible.

The advantages of the inference system $\mathcal{R}'$ over $\mathcal{R}$ are primarily two. First,
trading resolution refutations obtained via $\mathcal{R}$ for those obtained via $\mathcal{R}'$
facilitates a fundamental shift from a point of view in which syntactic
unification of atoms is of primary concern to one in which syntactic
unifiability of atoms is seen as just one of many conceivable criteria which
must be met in order for applications of inference rules to be allowed.
This shift in viewpoint provides a framework for discussing refutation
algorithms based on resolution calculi requiring that constraints other than
mere syntactic unifiability of atoms be met in order for applications of
inference rules to be permitted. The refutation algorithm for sorted first-
order clauses given in Chapter 9, for example, is based on precisely such
a calculus, and the inference system $\mathcal{R}'$ is easily generalized to the sorted
setting as discussed in Section 9.5.

Secondly, as mentioned above, $\mathcal{R}'$ exemplifies a computational paradigm
in which solutions to various constraint problems are no longer actually
computed, but rather in which only the *solvability* of these constraints
is determined. In some settings—like that of sorted deduction—it is
significantly easier to determine solvability of the relevant constraints than
it is actually to compute their solutions, and in such settings, delaying
the solution of constraints can dramatically improve the efficiency of
refutation algorithms. On the other hand, in settings in which only the
simple equational constraints imposed by the requirements of syntactic
unification need to be solved, delaying solution is not especially prudent
computationally since the cost of syntactically unifying a system is typically
no larger than the cost of verifying its unifiability. Nevertheless, inference
systems in which constraint solving is delayed often serve as important
tools for reasoning about resolution under such equational constraints.

We begin our discussion of delayed unification by defining the inference system $\mathcal{R}'$ and then showing that the soundness and completeness of $\mathcal{R}$ imply the soundness and completeness of $\mathcal{R}'$.

The inference system $\mathcal{R}'$ operates on ordered pairs of the form $\langle C, E \rangle$, where C is a clause and E is a *solvable* equational system. Such a pair is called a *clause closure*, or, more simply, just a *clause*, and is usually denoted by $C.E$. Any clause closure of the form $C.\emptyset$ can be identified with the ordinary clause C; we henceforth refer to clauses of the form $C.\emptyset$—and therefore of the form C—as *pure* clauses. Similarly, any clause closure of the form $\square.E$ can be identified with the pure clause $\square$, since E is a *solvable* equational system. As with pure clauses, we may always assume that any two clause closures $C.E$ and $D.E'$ are variable disjoint.

The following notions will be especially useful in defining $\mathcal{R}'$.

Definition 8.1.1   1. If $C.E$ is a clause and σ is a substitution, then the pure clause $\sigma(C)$ is said to be a *(ground) instance* of $C.E$ if $\sigma \in u(E)$ holds (and $Var(\sigma(C)) = \emptyset$).

2. A clause $C.E$ is a *tautology* if every ground instance $\sigma(C)$ of $C.E$ is a tautology (cf. Definition 7.4.1).

3. Let $C = \Phi \to \Psi . E$ and $D = \Phi' \to \Psi' . E'$ be arbitrary but distinct clauses. The clause D is said to *subsume* the clause C provided every ground instance of C is subsumed by a ground instance of D (cf. Definition 7.4.2).

4. A clause C is *redundant (with respect to S)* if either $C \in S$, C is a tautology, or C is subsumed by some clause D such that $|D| < |C|$ (cf. Definition 7.4.3).

5. An interpretation *satisfies* the clause closure $C.E$ iff it satisfies every instance of $C.E$.

We may use Definition 8.1.1 to extend resolution and factorization rules of the last chapter to clause closures.

Definition 8.1.2   The *resolution rule* for clause closures is given by

$$\frac{\Phi \to \Psi, A . E \qquad \Phi', B \to \Psi' . E'}{\Phi, \Phi' \to \Psi, \Psi' . E \cup E' \cup \{A \approx B\}}$$

provided $E \cup E' \cup \{A \approx B\}$ is solvable.

Definition 8.1.3 The *(positive) factorization rule* for clause closures is given by

$$\frac{\Phi \rightarrow \Psi, A, B \, . \, E}{\Phi \rightarrow \Psi, A \, . \, E \cup \{A \approx B\}}$$

provided $E \cup \{A \approx B\}$ is solvable.

As in the corresponding definitions for pure clauses, the conclusion of an application of the resolution rule for clause closures is called a *resolvent* of its two premises, and the conclusion of an application of the factorization rule for clause closures is called a *factor* of its premise. There is also a negative factorization rule for clause closures, defined symmetrically to the positive factorization rule, in which the atoms A and B appear in the antecedent of the premise of the rule.

Definition 8.1.4 The inference system $\mathcal{R}'$ for refutation of clause closures comprises the following inference rules:

- *Deduction*

$$\frac{S}{S \cup \{C\}}$$

  provided C is a resolvent or a positive factor of clauses in S.

- *Reduction*

$$\frac{S \cup \{C\}}{S}$$

  provided C is redundant with respect to $S - \{C\}$.

We write $S \Rightarrow_{\mathcal{R}'} S'$ to indicate that S' is obtained from S by an application of a rule in $\mathcal{R}'$. An $\mathcal{R}'$-*derivation* out of S_0 is a sequence $S_0, S_1, S_2, \ldots$ of sets of clauses, where S_0 is a set of *pure* clauses, and, for each natural number n, $S_n \Rightarrow_{\mathcal{R}'} S_{n+1}$ holds. An $\mathcal{R}'$-*refutation* of a pure clause S is an $\mathcal{R}'$-derivation out of S, with $\square \in S_n$ for some $n \geq 0$; note that there is no notion of an $\mathcal{R}'$-derivation out of a set of clauses which are not pure. As in the definition of the inference system $\mathcal{R}$ for pure clauses, the decision to include in $\mathcal{R}'$ the positive factorization rule is arbitrary, and we could just as well have chosen to use the negative factorization rule in its definition.

The inference system $\mathcal{R}'$ induces a nondeterministic algorithm for refuting unsatisfiable sets of (pure) clauses which simply applies inference rules from $\mathcal{R}'$ to sets of clause closures randomly. Concrete algorithms for refuting sets of (pure) clauses can be obtained by specifying a control structure detailing the order in which rules from $\mathcal{R}'$ are to be applied, together with criteria for selecting the clauses to which they are to be applied.

The inference system $\mathcal{R}'$ is sound and complete and its rules clearly lie in a one-to-one correspondence with those of $\mathcal{R}$. Moreover, any rule in $\mathcal{R}'$ has the same effect on ground clauses as its corresponding rule from $\mathcal{R}$. In particular, corresponding applications of the resolution rule for clause closures and the classical resolution rule have exactly the same effect on ground clauses, and both actually coincide with the resolution rule for ground clauses when restricted to such clauses (see Definition 7.1.1).

Below we prove that, in addition to comprising rules which lie in a one-to-one corresondence with those of $\mathcal{R}$, the soundness and completeness of $\mathcal{R}$ implies that of $\mathcal{R}'$. As previously discussed, this fact, together with the observation that $\mathcal{R}'$ does not prescribe the explicit solution of unification problems, implies that in refuting clauses it is not at all necessary to solve explicitly the equational systems which are the second components of clause closures. Indeed, it suffices merely to establish that these equational systems are solvable. Interestingly, however, it is even possible to omit the requirement "provided $E \cup E' \cup \{A \approx B\}$ is solvable" and "provided $E \cup \{A \approx B\}$ is solvable" in Definitions 8.1.2 and 8.1.3 so that verification of solvability is longer required at all. Of course, it then becomes necessary to traverse very large search spaces in constructing resolution refutations since many more resolvents can be produced in the absence of the solvability requirement than in its presence, even though most will actually contribute nothing toward the discovery of any particular refutation.

Theorem 8.1.1 *(Completeness of $\mathcal{R}'$) If S is an unsatisfiable set of clauses and if $S_0, S_1, S_2, \ldots$ is a fair $\mathcal{R}'$-derivation with $S = S_0$, then there exists an $n \geq 0$ such that S_n contains the empty clause.*

Proof. To establish the assertion of the theorem, we begin by showing that to each application of the rules *Deduction* and *Reduction* in Definition 8.1.4 there corresponds an application of a rule *Deduction* or *Reduction* from Definition 7.4.6, as appropriate. More precisely, consider the mapping α from clause closures to pure clauses given by

$$\alpha(\Phi \to \Psi \,.\, E) = \sigma(\Phi) \to \sigma(\Psi),$$

where σ is a most general unifier of E. We show that for any set S of clause closures, if $S \Rightarrow_{\mathcal{R}'} S'$ then $\alpha(S) \Rightarrow_{\mathcal{R}} \alpha(S')$.

Let S be an arbitrary set of clause closures, and consider a single application to S of the resolution rule in the notation of Definition 8.1.2. Let σ and σ' be most general unifiers of E and E', respectively. We construct an application of classical resolution which corresponds to the given application of resolution for clause closures as follows. By assumption, the system $E \cup E' \cup \{A \approx B\}$ is unifiable. Moreover, since E and E' may be taken to be variable disjoint, σ and σ' have a common extension θ which is a most general unifier of both E and E'. Now, α maps the two clause closures in the premise of the given application of the resolution rule for clause closures to the pure clauses

$$\theta(\Phi) \to \theta(\Psi), \theta(A) \quad \text{and} \quad \theta(\Phi'), \theta(B) \to \theta(\Psi'),$$

respectively. If τ is a most general unifier of $\{\theta(A) \approx \theta(B)\}$, then the classical resolvent of these two clauses is

$$\tau(\theta(\Phi)), \tau(\theta(\Phi')) \to \tau(\theta(\Psi)), \tau(\theta(\Psi')).$$

We show that $\tau\theta$ is a most general unifier of the system $E \cup E' \cup \{A \approx B\}$, and so conclude that α maps the $\mathcal{R}'$-resolvent of the original premises exactly to the classical resolvent of the corresponding pure premises.

It easy to see that $\tau\theta$ is a unifier of $E \cup E' \cup \{A \approx B\}$: from $\theta \in u(E \cup E')$ it follows that $\tau\theta \in u(E \cup E')$, and from $\tau \in u(\{\theta(A) \approx \theta(B)\})$ it follows that $\tau\theta \in u(\{A \approx B\})$. But $\tau\theta$ is in fact a most general unifier of $E \cup E' \cup \{A \approx B\}$. This can be seen by observing that if φ is any unifier of $E \cup E' \cup \{A \approx B\}$), then $\varphi \in u(E \cup E')$ implies $\varphi = \lambda\theta$ for some λ. Then $\varphi \in u(\{A \approx B\})$ implies $\lambda \in u(\{\theta(A) \approx \theta(B)\})$, which in turn implies that $\lambda = \psi\tau$ for some ψ, since τ is a most general unifier of $\{\theta(A) \approx \theta(B)\}$. Thus $\varphi = \psi\tau\theta$, and so $\tau\theta$ is indeed a most general unifier of $E \cup E' \cup \{A \approx B\}$.

In a similar manner we may show that, for any set S of clause closures, if $S \Rightarrow_{\mathcal{R}'} S'$ by an application of the factorization rule for clause closures, then $\alpha(S) \Rightarrow_{\mathcal{R}} \alpha(S')$ by an application of the classical factorization rule. To see that $S \Rightarrow_{\mathcal{R}'} S'$ by an application of the rule *Reduction* in the notation of Definition 8.1.4 implies that $\alpha(S) \Rightarrow_{\mathcal{R}} \alpha(S')$ by the corresponding rule in Definition 7.4.6, note that if σ is a most general unifier of E then every ground instance of $\Phi \to \Psi . E$ is a ground instance of $\sigma(\Phi) \to \sigma(\Psi)$, and conversely. Indeed, in this case $\tau(\Phi) \to \tau(\Psi)$ is a ground instance of $\Phi \to \Psi . E$ iff $\tau \in u(E)$ and τ is ground, and $\tau \in u(E)$ iff there exists a λ such that $\tau = \lambda\sigma$. But this is the case iff $\lambda(\sigma(\Phi)) \to \lambda(\sigma(\Psi))$ is a ground instance of $\sigma(\Phi) \to \sigma(\Psi)$, as desired. Using this observation it is a simple matter to see that if a clause C is redundant with respect to a clause set S as in Definition 8.1.1, then $\alpha(C)$ is in fact redundant with respect to $\alpha(S)$ as in Definition 7.4.3. This result provides the final piece of information necessary to establish that, for all sets S of clause closures, $S \Rightarrow_{\mathcal{R}'} S'$ implies $\alpha(S) \Rightarrow_{\mathcal{R}} \alpha(S')$.

We see that for every $\mathcal{R}'$-derivation $S_0, S_1, S_2, \dots$ there is an $\mathcal{R}$-derivation $\alpha(S_0), \alpha(S_1), \alpha(S_2), \dots$. Since the last part of Definition 8.1.1 guarantees that, for any set S of clauses, S is unsatisfiable iff $\alpha(S)$ is unsatisfiable, we need only show that if an $\mathcal{R}'$-derivation is fair, then so is the $\mathcal{R}$-derivation it induces. Together with the facts that $\alpha(\square) = \square$, and that $\square$ is the only clause whose image under α is $\square$, this will complete the proof of the theorem.

Consider an $\mathcal{R}'$-derivation and an $\mathcal{R}$-derivation as in the previous paragraph, and suppose that $\alpha(C)$ and $\alpha(D)$ are in $T = \bigcup_{k \geq 0} \bigcap_{j \geq k} \alpha(S_j) \supseteq \alpha(\bigcup_{k \geq 0} \bigcap_{j \geq k} S_j)$. We want to show that every resolvent of $\alpha(C)$ and $\alpha(D)$ is again in T, and that every factor of every clause $\alpha(C)$ in T is again in T. We prove the former here and leave the latter as an exercise for the reader. Note that C and D must necessarily be in $S^\infty = \bigcup_{k \geq 0} \bigcap_{j \geq k} S_j$.

If R is a resolvent of $\alpha(C) = \sigma(\Phi) \rightarrow \sigma(\Psi), \sigma(A)$ and $\alpha(D) = \sigma(\Phi'), \sigma(B) \rightarrow \sigma(\Psi')$, then we must have

$$R = \tau(\sigma(\Phi)), \tau(\sigma(\Phi')) \rightarrow \tau(\sigma(\Psi)), \tau(\sigma(\Psi')),$$

where τ is a most general unifier of $\sigma(A)$ and $\sigma(B)$, $C = \Phi \rightarrow \Psi, A \cdot E$, $D = \Phi', B \rightarrow \Psi' \cdot E$, and $[\sigma] \sim E$. If we could establish that there must exist a resolvent R' of C and D such that $\alpha(R') = R$, then the fact that S^∞ is closed under $\mathcal{R}'$ would imply that T is also closed under $\mathcal{R}$. We therefore need only show that such a resolvent R' exists.

Consider the resolvent

$$R' = \Phi, \Phi' \rightarrow \Psi, \Psi' \cdot E \cup \{A \approx B\}$$

of C and D. We would like to see that $\alpha(R') = R$ for the resolvent R of $\alpha(C)$ and $\alpha(D)$ above. To do this we need to see that $[\tau\sigma] \sim (E \cup \{A \approx B\})$, i.e., that $\lambda \in u([\tau\sigma])$ iff $\lambda \in u(E \cup \{A \approx B\})$. Let $\lambda \in u([\tau\sigma])$. Then $\lambda = \lambda\tau\sigma$ since $\tau\sigma$ is a most general unifier of $[\tau\sigma]$, so that

$$\lambda(A) = \lambda(\tau(\sigma(A))) = \lambda(\tau(\sigma(B))) = \lambda(B).$$

Moreover, σ is a (most general) unifier of E since $E \sim [\sigma]$ and σ is a most general unifier of $[\sigma]$. This fact and the observation that

$$\lambda\sigma = \lambda\tau\sigma\sigma = \lambda\tau\sigma = \lambda$$

imply that $\lambda \in u(E)$ as well. Thus if $\lambda \in u([\sigma\tau])$, then $\lambda \in u(E)$ and $\lambda \in u(\{A \approx B\})$. That is, $\lambda \in u(E \cup \{A \approx B\})$.

Conversely, if $\lambda \in u(E \cup \{A \approx B\})$, then $\lambda = \lambda\sigma$ (since $E \sim [\sigma]$) so σ is a most general unifier of E, and $\lambda(A) = \lambda(B)$. These imply that $\lambda(\sigma(A)) = \lambda(\sigma(B))$, and since τ is a most general unifier of $\{\sigma(A) \approx \sigma(B)\}$, we have $\lambda = \lambda\tau$. Thus,

$$\lambda\tau\sigma = \lambda\sigma = \lambda.$$

Since $\tau\sigma$ unifies $[\tau\sigma]$, $\lambda\tau\sigma = \lambda$ must as well. That is, $\lambda \in u([\sigma\tau])$, as desired, and the theorem is proved. $\square$

We may infer from Theorems 8.1.1 and 7.4.3 that the inference system $\mathcal{R}'$ is complete for refutation of pure clauses.

In the remainder of this chapter we will become acquainted with several refinements of the inference system $\mathcal{R}'$, each of which effects a pruning of deduction search spaces generated by $\mathcal{R}'$ and which—in light of Theorem 8.1.1—may be regarded as a means of increasing the deduction efficiency of classical refutation algorithms. While the majority of the refinements we will see give rise to refutation complete algorithms—i.e., for most, the empty clause will lie in the (reduced) search space generated by that algorithm from a given set S of pure clauses provided it lies in the search space generated from S by $\mathcal{R}'$, or, equivalently, $\mathcal{R}$—a few of the methods to be presented will be refutation complete only for restricted classes of sets of pure clauses. The soundness of each will follow immediately from that of $\mathcal{R}'$ and so will not be discussed further. The completeness of the various strategies is proved by first proving their completeness for ground clauses and then modifying the Lifting Lemma appropriately.

It is most common to approach the problem of restricting resolution search spaces from a purely syntactic point of view, determining applicability of inference rules according to the syntactic structure of clauses or according to the structure of derivations so far generated. Positive resolution (see Example 8.1), in which at least one of the resolution partners must be a positive clause, is an example of a syntax-based method for restricting resolution search spaces. It is also possible, however, to use semantic criteria to prune resolution search spaces. One example of a semantics-based reduction strategy is the method of *semantic resolution* (see Section 8.6). In semantic resolution an arbitrary interpretation $\mathcal{I}$ over the underlying signature over which terms are built is selected, and only applications of resolution at least one of whose premises is not satisfied by $\mathcal{I}$ are permitted. As discussed in Section 8.6, the semantic resolution strategy gives rise to a complete refutation method.

We begin by discussing some of the simplest syntactic techniques for reducing resolution search spaces; semantic methods are discussed in Sections 8.6 through 8.8. The inference system underlying each is the system $\mathcal{R}'$ of the previous section.

8.2   Unit Resolution

The method of unit resolution restricts applications of the resolution rule for clause closures by requiring that at least one of the resolution partners in any application of that rule be a unit clause. That is, at least one of the partners in any application of unit resolution must be a clause whose length is 1, but applications of the other rules from $\mathcal{R}'$ are unrestricted. Unit resolution derivations boast a very desirable property, namely, that

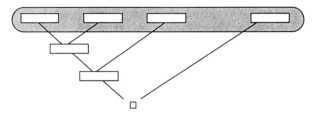

FIGURE 8.1.

the length of a resolvent is always one less than the length of the nonunit parent clause. Thus each unit resolution step trades one set of clauses to be refuted for another, simpler, one.

The fact that the set S of clauses in Example 7.5.1 is unsatisfiable shows that unit resolution cannot be complete in general (the set S of clauses there contains no unit clauses at all), but it turns out that unit resolution is always complete for sets of Horn clauses. In fact, unit resolution is complete for an even larger class of clauses, which, for lack of a better syntactic characterization, is called simply the class of "unit refutable clauses." A proof of the completeness of unit resolution for Horn clauses can be obtained by adapting the proof of Theorem 7.4.2 for ground clauses, and then modifying the Lifting Lemma appropriately; the details are left as an exercise for the reader.

8.3   Input Resolution

The method of input resolution disallows resolution steps between two derived clauses, but in no way restricts application of the other rules from $\mathcal{R}'$. That is, in any application of the resolution rule, at least one of the resolution partners must come from the original input set of clauses to be refuted. Input resolution thus induces linear derivations (see Figures 8.1 and 8.3). Like unit resolution, input resolution is not complete for arbitrary sets of clauses. In fact, it can be shown that input resolution and unit resolution are of equal deductive power, in the sense that a given set of clauses is input refutable iff it is unit refutable. This result is proved in the following for ground clauses and its analogue for nonground clauses, which is left as an exercise, follows from Theorem 8.3.1 and an appropriate adaptation of the Lifting Lemma.

Theorem 8.3.1   *If S is a set of ground clauses, then S is input refutable iff it is unit refutable.*

Proof. Suppose that S is input refutable, and let $\mathcal{A}(S)$ be the set of atoms appearing in S. We prove that S is unit refutable by induction on the cardinality of $\mathcal{A}(S)$.

If $|\mathcal{A}(S)| = 0$, then either $S = \emptyset$ or $S = \{\Box\}$. In either case, the conclusion holds.

If $|\mathcal{A}(S)| > 0$, then the set S must contain a unit clause since two unit clauses must have been resolved in the last step in the input refutation of S. We will assume that S contains a unit clause of the form $\to A$; the proof is similar if S contains only unit clauses of the form $A \to$. We proceed by constructing from S a set S' of clauses which contains fewer atoms than S, using the induction hypothesis to conclude that S' is unit refutable, and then using the unit refutability of S' to infer that of S.

We construct the set S' of clauses by deleting all clauses in S containing A in the succedent, and by removing A from the antecedents of the remaining clauses in S. That the set S' of clauses obtained in this manner is also input refutable can be seen by observing that (i) if A appears in both the antecedent and succedent of a clause in S, then that clause is a tautology and can be removed from S, (ii) if A appears in the succedent of a clause, then this clause is subsumed by the unit clause $\to A$, and so can be removed from S, and (iii) if A appears in the antecedent of a clause, then this clause can be resolved with $\to A$. Once this resolution step has taken place, the clause $\to A$ cannot be a partner in any other resolution step in the refutation of S, so it can be removed from S, and all clauses in S in which A appears in the antecedent can be replaced by the corresponding clauses obtained by removing A from their antecedents. This clearly gives a set S' of clauses which is input refutable iff S is (essentially, we may replace, in the input refutation of S, each clause in whose antecedent A appears by its corresponding clause in S' to arrive at an input refutation of S'). Moreover, the set S' obtained by following the above prescription contains strictly fewer atoms than the set S of clauses. By the induction hypothesis, then, S' must be unit refutable. But since every clause in S' is either in S or is the result of a unit resolution step with the clause $\to A$ from S, S must itself be unit refutable.

Conversely, suppose that S is unit refutable. Once again the proof proceeds by induction on the number $|\mathcal{A}(S)|$ of atoms appearing in S. If $|\mathcal{A}(S)| = 0$, then either $S = \emptyset$ or $S = \{\Box\}$ and, as before, in either case the conclusion holds.

If $|\mathcal{A}(S)| > 0$, then since S is unit refutable, S must contain a unit clause. As above, we will assume that S contains a unit clause of the form $\to A$; the proof is similar if S contains only unit clauses of the form $A \to$.

Let S' be as above. Then S' is a set of clauses containing strictly fewer atoms than S, and which is unit refutable iff S is (essentially, we may replace, in the unit refutation of S, each clause in whose antecedent A appears by its corresponding clause in S' to arrive at a unit refutation of S'). By the induction hypothesis, then, S' is input refutable. But since every clause in S' is either in S or is the result of an input resolution step with the clause $\rightarrow A$ from S, S itself must be input refutable. □

8.4   Linear Resolution

Linear resolution is another search space pruning technique which results in linear derivations, but by contrast with input resolution, it permits resolution between two previously derived clauses. The strategy of linear resolution was developed in 1970 by Loveland ([Lov70]).

For each given clause set S, let $\mathcal{R}'^n(S)$ denote the set of all resolvents and factors which are reachable from S by at most n applications of rules in $\mathcal{R}'$. Further, for any two sets M_1 and M_2 of clauses, denote by $R'(M_1, M_2)$ the set of all clauses obtained by applying the resolution rule for clause closures with one premise from the set of clauses M_1 and the other premise from the set of clauses M_2. Finally, for any set M of clauses, let $F'(M)$ stand for the set of all clauses obtained by applying the factorization rule for clause closures to some clause in M.

Definition 8.4.1   A *linear resolution derivation out of the clause set S with start clause C_0* is a sequence $S_0, S_1, S_2, \ldots$ where $C_0 \in S$ and

$$
\begin{aligned}
S_0 &= S \\
S_1 &= S_0 \cup \{C_1\}, \text{ where } C_1 \in R'(C_0, S_0) \cup F'(C_0) \\
&\vdots \\
S_n &= S_{n-1} \cup \{C_n\}, \text{ where } C_n \in R'(C_{n-1}, S_{n-1}) \cup F'(C_{n-1}).
\end{aligned}
$$

The clauses C_i are called *central clauses* of the derivation and the other clauses appearing in the derivation are called its *side clauses*.

According to Definition 8.4.1, at each stage in a linear resolution derivation, we may add to the current set of clauses either a factor of the most recently derived clause, or a resolvent of that clause with some clause in the current set of clauses. Although it is not specified there, in practice the partners in a linear resolution step will always be taken to be distinct. The method is illustrated in

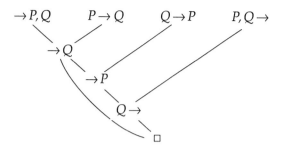

FIGURE 8.2.

Example 8.4.1   The clause set $S = \{C_1, C_2, C_3, C_4, C_5\}$ with

$$
\begin{aligned}
C_1 &= \ \to P, Q \\
C_2 &= \ P \to Q \\
C_3 &= \ Q \to P \\
C_4 &= \ P, Q \to \\
C_5 &= \ \to P, R
\end{aligned}
$$

is refutable by linear resolution if we choose C_1 as the start clause (see Figure 8.2).

Restricting $\mathcal{R}'$ to allow only linear resolution derivations preserves the refutation completeness of the resulting refutation method, but only under certain conditions on the start clause. This can be seen by considering the clause set S from Example 8.4.1. It is easy to see that there can be no linear refutation of S with start clause C_5, since every central clause in such a refutation would necessarily contain the atom R in the succedent. If, however, the start clause is chosen from a minimal unsatisfiable subset of S, then the refutation completeness of linear resolution with that start clause is ensured. In fact, to preserve refutation completeness, it suffices to require that start clauses satisfy only a weaker condition, namely, that they participate in some resolution refutation of S. In general we have

Theorem 8.4.1   *Let S be an unsatisfiable set of clauses and let $C \in S$. If there is an $\mathcal{R}'$-refutation of S in which C participates, then there is a linear resolution refutation of S with start clause C.*

Proof. We prove the result in the case when S contains only ground clauses; extending it to arbitrary sets of clauses requires an appropriate modification of the Lifting Lemma. Let S be an unsatisfiable set of clauses, and let $\mathcal{P}$ be a resolution refutation of S in which the clause C participates. Without loss of generality we may assume that $\mathcal{P}$ contains no tautologies, and we may identify $\mathcal{P}$ with the proof tree which represents it. Our goal is to transform $\mathcal{P}$ into a tree in linear form. Let $\mathcal{K}$ be the set of nodes of $\mathcal{P}$, and let $\mathcal{Q}$

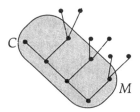

FIGURE 8.3.

be a maximal path from the root of $\mathcal{P}$ (which is labeled with the empty clause) to a leaf node labeled with C, i.e., suppose that $\mathcal{Q}$ is a path from the root of $\mathcal{P}$ to a leaf node labeled with C, and that $\mathcal{Q}$ is such that there is no longer such path in $\mathcal{P}$. Such a leaf node must necessarily exist since C participates in the refutation of S under consideration. Let $\mathcal{M}$ be the set of nodes defined by

$$\mathcal{M} = \{k \in \mathcal{K} \mid k \text{ is in } \mathcal{Q} \text{ or } k \text{ is a child of a node in } \mathcal{Q}\}.$$

(see Figure 8.3), and let $\mu(\mathcal{P}) = |\mathcal{K}| - |\mathcal{M}|$. Note carefully that if node q is a child of node p, then the clause with which q is labeled is a premise from which the clause labeling p is derived.

It is not hard to see that $\mu(\mathcal{P})$ does not depend on the particular choice of the maximal path $\mathcal{Q}$, i.e., that different choices of the maximal path $\mathcal{Q}$ give rise to the same number $\mu(\mathcal{P})$.

If $\mu(\mathcal{P}) = 0$, then $\mathcal{P}$ is clearly a linear refutation tree for S with start clause C. If $\mathcal{P}$ is a refutation of S with $\mu(\mathcal{P}) > 0$, then we will construct another refutation $\mathcal{P}'$ of S with start clause C such that $\mu(\mathcal{P}) > \mu(\mathcal{P}')$. Repeated application of this construction then shows that there must exist a linear refutation of S whose start clause is C.

If $\mu(\mathcal{P}) > 0$, then there must be a subtree of $\mathcal{P}$ of the form depicted in Figure 8.4, where

$$
\begin{aligned}
C_1 &= \Phi, A \to \Psi \\
C_2 &= \Phi' \to \Psi', A \\
C_3 &= \Phi, \Phi' \to \Psi, \Psi' \\
C_4 &= \Phi'', B \to \Psi'' \\
C_5 &= \Phi, \Phi', \Phi'' \to (\Psi \cup \Psi' \cup \Psi'') - \{B\}
\end{aligned}
$$

and $B \in \Psi \cup \Psi'$ (or one of the other symmetric possibilities which will not be handled explicitly here). In Figure 8.4, the path $\mathcal{P}$ includes C_4 and C_5, but not C_1, C_2, or C_3. Since tautologies are disallowed, $A \notin \Psi$. Together with $A \notin \Psi'$, this implies that $A \neq B$.

There are two cases to consider, according as $B \in \Psi$ or not. If $B \in \Psi$, then we must further consider two subcases, namely, the subcase in which $B \notin \Psi'$

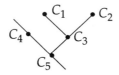

FIGURE 8.4.

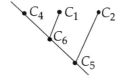

FIGURE 8.5.

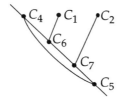

FIGURE 8.6.

and that in which $B \in \Psi'$. In the first subcase, there exists a proof $\mathcal{P}'$ of S with start clause C_4 and $C_6 = \Phi'', \Phi, A \to \Psi'', \Psi - \{B\}$ as in Figure 8.5, and in the second case there exists a proof $\mathcal{P}'$ of S with start clause C_4 and with $C_6 = \Phi'', \Phi, A \to \Psi'', \Psi - \{B\}$ and $C_7 = \Phi', \Phi'', \Phi \to \Psi', \Psi'', \Psi - \{B\}$ as in Figure 8.6. In either case, we see that $\mu(\mathcal{P}) > \mu(\mathcal{P}')$.

If $B \notin \Psi$, then $B \in \Psi'$. In this case it is also easy to construct a proof $\mathcal{P}'$ of S such that $\mu(\mathcal{P}) > \mu(\mathcal{P}')$. □

The completeness of linear resolution with (respect to fair derivation strategies) easily follows, and so we may always assume without loss of generality that derivations are linear.

Corollary 8.4.1 *Linear resolution is a complete refutation method.*

Proof. Let S be an arbitrary set of (pure) clauses. Certainly if there is a linear resolution refutation of S then S is $\mathcal{R}'$-refutable. Conversely, suppose that S is unsatisfiable. Then there must exist an $\mathcal{R}'$-refutation of S (in which some clause C from S participates). By Theorem 8.4.1, there must also exist a linear resolution refutation of S (with start clause C). □

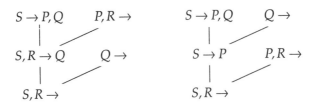

FIGURE 8.7.

8.5 Hyperresolution

Hyperresolution, developed in 1965 by J. A. Robinson, is based on the idea of combining many resolution steps into a single large resolution step. Combining resolution steps prunes resolution search spaces by considering as the same resolution derivation those which are identical up to reordering of applications of rules from the resolution calculus in question. That is, hyperresolution eliminates from resolution derivations redundancy resulting from the fact that the same clause is often derived many times over simply by interchanging the order in which rules from the calculus are applied.

Example 8.5.1   Let $S = \{C_1, C_2, C_3\}$ with

$$
\begin{array}{rcl}
C_1 & = & S \to P, Q \\
C_2 & = & P, R \to \\
C_3 & = & Q \to .
\end{array}
$$

The resolution derivations depicted in Figure 8.7 both result in the clause $S, R \to$. If the method of level saturation is used to find a refutation of a given clause, for example, then both derivations of $S, R \to$ will be generated, and so this same clause will be derived twice. This scheme is easily extended to derivations of length n, in which case there are $n!$ possible ways to derive exactly the same clause.

A hyperresolution step would combine the two individual resolution steps of Figure 8.7 into a single, large resolution step, and would therefore identify the two application sequences depicted there. The intermediate results (i.e., the clauses which appear in the corresponding interior nodes of the derivation tree) need no longer be mentioned explicitly. This leads to the representation in Figure 8.8 of the hyperresolution step corresponding to the derivations of Figure 8.7.

When developing the hyperresolution strategy, Robinson clearly had in mind the Bohr model of the atom. In the above hyperresolution derivation, the central clause $S \to P, Q$ is called the *nucleus*, and the satellite clauses

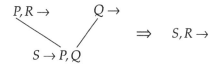

FIGURE 8.8.

$P, R \to$ and $Q \to$ are called the *electrons*, of the hyperresolution step. Just as in the atomic model, electrons have negative *polarity*, and the resulting hyperresolution method is called *negative hyperresolution*. By symmetry, we may consider instead the corresponding "mirror image" of this method, called *positive hyperresolution* (see Definition 8.5.1). Note carefully that in positive resolution, the electrons are positive clauses.

In negative (positive) hyperresolution, all atoms appearing in succedents (antecedents) of nuclei are resolved against appropriate electrons; as a result, such a resolution step has one nucleus and n electrons, where n is the number of atoms in the succedent (antecedent) of the nucleus. The clauses resulting from applications of hyperresolution are again electrons. Thus, in the course of a hyperresolution derivation new electrons are obtained, but new nuclei never are.

Example 8.5.2   Let

$$S = \{(x < y, \ y < z \ \to \ x < z), (\to a < b), (\to b < c), (\to c < d), (a < d \to)\},$$

where the predicate symbol $<$ is written infix for clarity. The set S of clauses is clearly unsatisfiable, as verified by the positive hyperresolution derivation in Figure 8.9.

More precisely, we have

Definition 8.5.1   1. Let $n \geq 1$. The *negative hyperresolution rule for n clauses* is given by

$$\frac{\Phi \to A_1, \ldots, A_n \,.\, E \quad \Phi_1, A'_1 \to \,.\, E_1 \quad \Phi_n, A'_n \to \,.\, E_n}{\Phi, \Phi_1, \ldots, \Phi_n \to \,.\, E'}$$

provided the system $E' = E \cup \bigcup_{i=1}^{n} (E_i \cup \{A_i \approx A'_i\})$ is solvable. The clause $\Phi \to A_1, \ldots, A_n \,.\, E$ is called the *nucleus*, and the clauses $A'_i, \Phi_i \to \,.\, E_i$ are called the *electrons*, of the negative hyperresolution step.

2. Let $n \geq 1$. The *positive hyperresolution rule for n clauses* is given by

$$\frac{A_1, \ldots, A_n \to \Psi \,.\, E \quad \to \Psi_1, A'_1 \,.\, E_1 \quad \to \Psi_n, A'_n \,.\, E_n}{\to \Psi, \Psi_1, \ldots, \Psi_n \,.\, E'}$$

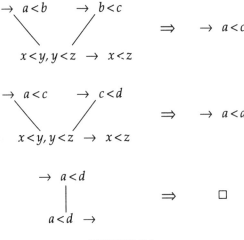

$$\begin{array}{l} \rightarrow a<b \qquad \rightarrow b<c \\ \qquad\qquad\qquad\qquad\qquad\qquad \Rightarrow \qquad \rightarrow a<c \\ x<y, y<z \rightarrow x<z \end{array}$$

$$\begin{array}{l} \rightarrow a<c \qquad \rightarrow c<d \\ \qquad\qquad\qquad\qquad\qquad\qquad \Rightarrow \qquad \rightarrow a<d \\ x<y, y<z \rightarrow x<z \end{array}$$

$$\begin{array}{l} \rightarrow a<d \\ \qquad\qquad\qquad\qquad\qquad \Rightarrow \qquad \square \\ a<d \rightarrow \end{array}$$

FIGURE 8.9.

provided the system $E' = E \cup \bigcup_{i=1}^{n}(E_i \cup \{A_i \approx A'_i\})$ is solvable. The clause $A_1, \ldots, A_n \rightarrow \Psi . E$ is called the *nucleus*, and the clauses $\rightarrow \Psi_i, A'_i . E_i$ are called the *electrons*, of the positive hyperresolution step.

As previously mentioned, the result of a negative (positive) hyperresolution step is again a negative (positive) clause, i.e., a clause which can be used as an electron of a new application of hyperresolution. In a hyperresolution derivation, factorization is accordingly adapted: in a negative hyperresolution derivation, the only applications of the factorization rule which are allowed are applications of the negative factorization rule, and similarly in positive hyperresolution derivations. Indeed, only electrons are ever permitted to be factored.

The soundness of hyperresolution follows directly from the corresponding result for resolution. The completeness of the method is not, however, immediately evident. Below we prove the completeness of positive hyperresolution for ground clauses; as usual, completeness of hyperresolution for nonground clauses follows directly from a suitable modification of the Lifting Lemma. Of course, a proof of the completeness of negative hyperresolution can be obtained in a manner similar to that used below to prove the completeness of positive hyperresolution.

Let $\mathcal{H}^+$ be the inference system comprising the inference rules for positive hyperresolution and positive factorization together with those for solving tautologies and subsumed clauses. We may define, for an arbitrary set of clauses, a notion of *closedness under $\mathcal{H}^+$* (and indeed under any set of inference rules) by analogy with Definition 7.4.7. Having done this, we obtain

Theorem 8.5.1   *Let S be a set of ground clauses. If S is closed under $\mathcal{H}^+$ and if $\square \notin S$, then S is satisfiable.*

Proof. As in the proof of Lemma 7.4.5, we need only construct a model for S in case S is closed under $\mathcal{H}^+$ and $\square \notin S$. Let S be such a set of ground clauses.

Let $S^+ = \{\Phi \to \Psi \in S \mid \Phi = \emptyset\}$ be the set of positive clauses of S. If $S^+ = \emptyset$ then $\mathcal{I} = \emptyset$ is a model for S. So suppose $S^+ \neq \emptyset$, i.e., suppose that some (positive) electrons always appear in S. Let X be the set of all atoms appearing in clauses of S^+, and let $\mathcal{I}$ be a $\subseteq$-minimal subset of X which covers S^+. Such a subset of X exists by an argument analogous to that in the proof of Lemma 7.4.5.

We show that $\mathcal{I}$ is a model for S. Clearly $\mathcal{I}$ is a model for S^+. Suppose that there were some clause $C = \Phi \to \Psi \in S$ which is not satisfied by $\mathcal{I}$. Then $\Phi \subseteq \mathcal{I}$ and $\Psi \cap \mathcal{I} = \emptyset$. If $\Phi = \emptyset$ then $C \in S^+$, and in this case we already know that C is satisfiable by $\mathcal{I}$. So let $\Phi = \{A_1, \ldots, A_n\}$, and let $i \in \{1, \ldots, n\}$ be fixed but arbitrary. Choose a clause D_i in S^+ such that A_i is the only element of $\mathcal{I}$ appearing in D_i (again, such a clause D_i exists by an argument analogous to that in the proof of Lemma 7.4.5). Then

$$C = A_1, \ldots, A_n \to \Psi \quad \text{and} \quad D_i = \to A_i, \Psi_i,$$

where $\Psi_i \cap \mathcal{I} = \emptyset$, and the hyperresolvent H of C with $D_1, \ldots, D_n$ is of the form

$$H = \to \Psi, \Psi_1, \ldots, \Psi_n.$$

In particular, H is not a tautology. Because S is closed under $\mathcal{H}^+$, S must contain either H itself or some clause H' which subsumes H. In either case, there exists an $H' = \to \Psi'' \in S$ and $\Psi'' \subseteq \Psi \cup \Psi_1 \cup \ldots \cup \Psi_n$ (if $H \in S$ then we may take $H' = H$). We must therefore have

$$\Psi'' \cap \mathcal{I} \subseteq (\Psi \cup \Psi_1 \cup \ldots \cup \Psi_n) \cap \mathcal{I} = \emptyset,$$

and so H' is not satisfied by $\mathcal{I}$. This contradicts the fact that all positive clauses are satisfied by $\mathcal{I}$, and so the hypothesis that there is some clause C in S which is not satisfied by $\mathcal{I}$ must be false. Thus $\mathcal{I} \models C$ for every clause $C \in S$, making $\mathcal{I}$ a model of S. $\square$

If we now define the clause set S^∞ and a notion of *fairness* for $\mathcal{H}^+$-derivations by analogy with Definition 7.4.8, then we may use the proof techniques of Lemma 7.4.7 and Theorem 7.4.2 to establish

Lemma 8.5.1   *If the set S of clauses is unsatisfiable, and if $S_0, S_1, S_2, \ldots$ is a fair $\mathcal{H}^+$-derivation with $S_0 = S$, then S^∞ is unsatisfiable.*

and, therefore,

Theorem 8.5.2 *(Completeness of positive hyperresolution for ground clauses) If S is an unsatisfiable set of ground clauses and if $S_0, S_1, S_2, \ldots$ is a fair $\mathcal{H}^+$-derivation out of S, then there exists an $n \geq 0$ such that S_n contains the empty clause.*

8.6   Semantic Resolution and the Set-of-Support Strategy

In the two closely related methods of semantic resolution and the set-of-support resolution strategy, an attempt is made to use semantic information to reduce resolution search spaces. In semantic resolution, loosely speaking, an arbitrary interpretation $\mathcal{I}$ over the underlying signature over which terms are built is chosen, and only applications of the resolution and factorization rules at least one of whose premises is not satisfied by $\mathcal{I}$ are permitted. In practice, $\mathcal{I}$ is typically taken to be a model for some arbitrarily chosen satisfiable subset of a given set S of clauses to be refuted, so that semantic resolution requires at least one of the partners in any application of the resolution rule to be from outside that subset. In the set-of-support strategy, on the other hand, one uses the fact that a set of clauses to be refuted is typically derived from a formula φ to be proved from a set Φ of axioms, and takes the satisfiable subset of S to be the set of all clauses derivable from the (satisfiable) set Φ of axioms. In the context of the set-of-support strategy, the satisfiable subset of S is called the *set of support*. The set-of-support strategy enables a goal-directed search for refutations, since at least one of the premises of each application of the resolution rule is derived from the goal φ (actually, from the negation of φ). The set-of-support strategy was developed in 1964 by Wos, Carson, and Robinson ([WCR65]).

Definition 8.6.1 (Semantic Resolution) Let $\mathcal{I}$ be an interpretation over the signature Σ. Semantic resolution with respect to $\mathcal{I}$ permits applications of the resolution and factorization rules only when at least one of their premises has a ground instance which is not satisfied by $\mathcal{I}$.

Let $S(\mathcal{I})$ denote the set of inference rules for semantic resolution and factorization with respect to $\mathcal{I}$, together with the rules for solving tautologies and subsumed clauses. In the special case when $\mathcal{I} = \emptyset$, the corresponding resolution strategy is exactly *positive resolution*; when $\mathcal{I}$ is the set $\mathcal{A}$ of all atoms, the resulting resolution strategy is precisely *negative resolution*, which requires that at least one of the premises in any application of the resolution or factorization rule must be a negative clause.

The key fact needed to prove the completess of semantic resolution is the completeness of positive resolution, which follows from the proof of Lemma 7.4.5 (the only resolution step referred to in that proof is a positive resolution step).

Theorem 8.6.1   *(Completeness of semantic resolution for ground clauses) Let $\mathcal{I}$ be any interpretation and let S be any set of ground clauses. If S is closed under $S(\mathcal{I})$ and if $\Box \notin S$, then S is satisfiable.*

Proof. Let S be a set of ground clauses which is closed under $S(\mathcal{I})$ and which does not contain the empty clause. As in the proof of Lemma 7.4.5, we need only construct a model for S.

Define a mapping α on S by

$$\alpha(\Phi \to \Psi) = (\Phi - \mathcal{I}) \cup (\Psi \cap \mathcal{I}) \to (\Psi - \mathcal{I}) \cup (\Phi \cap \mathcal{I}).$$

Note that the mapping α simply interchanges all atoms from $\mathcal{I}$ between the antecedent and the succedent of the clause $\Phi \to \Psi$, and is therefore bijective. If $\alpha(S) = \{\alpha(C) \mid C \in S\}$, then it is easy, if tedious, to see that S is satisfiable if $\alpha(S)$ is: if $\mathcal{I}'$ is a model of $\alpha(S)$, then $\mathcal{I}'' = (\mathcal{I}' - \mathcal{I}) \cup (\mathcal{I} - \mathcal{I}')$ is a model of S. Moreover, since $\Box \notin S$, we also have $\Box \notin \alpha(S)$.

It is clear that a clause C is not satisfiable by $\mathcal{I}$ iff $\alpha(C)$ is a positive clause. Since S is closed under $S(\mathcal{I})$, and since α is bijective, it follows that $\alpha(S)$ is closed under $S(\emptyset)$, i.e., it follows that $\alpha(S)$ is closed under positive resolution. Then $\alpha(S)$ is satisfiable, and by the argument of the previous paragraph we may therefore conclude that S itself is satisfiable. $\Box$

Definition 8.6.2   (Set-of-Support Strategy) Let S be a set of clauses, and let T be a subset of S such that $S - T$ is satisfiable. The set-of-support strategy for resolution with respect to T permits only applications of the resolution or factorization rules at least one of whose premises is not in $S - T$.

The system $SOS(T)$ comprises the inference rules for resolution and for positive and negative factorization, restricted as in Definition 8.6.2, as well as the rules for solving tautologies and subsumed clauses. The completeness of this strategy follows directly from the completeness of semantic resolution, since if $\mathcal{I}$ is any model of $S - T$, then any $S(\mathcal{I})$-refutation of S is also a $SOS(T)$-refutation of S.

8.7 Selection and Ordering Concepts

A very general concept for reducing the size of search spaces in automated deduction allows only applications of the resolution and factorization rules

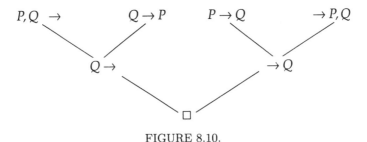

FIGURE 8.10.

in which the resolved atoms of both premises are maximal with respect to some previously chosen partial order on the set of all atoms. The induced resolution strategy is called *ordered resolution*.

A similar search space pruning method sorts the atoms of each clause into a certain fixed sequence, so that clauses are then pairs of *sequences* of atoms rather than pairs of *sets* of atoms. Then applications of the resolution rule are permitted only if, in at least one of the two premises, a maximal (in this case, leading) atom is resolved. This second resolution method is called the *selection method* because it can be considered to entail the selection of a subset of atoms with respect to which resolution is permitted to take place. In the literature, the selection method is often called *ordered resolution*, although it is not the same as ordered resolution as described above. The difference between ordered resolution and the selection method is clarified in the following example.

Example 8.7.1   Consider the set of clauses

$$S = \{(P, Q \to), (P \to Q), (Q \to P), (\to P, Q)\}.$$

In ordered resolution, an ordering $\succ$ is fixed on (at least) the set of atoms appearing in a set of clauses to be refuted; in this example, suppose $P \succ Q$. Then, for instance, the resolution step between the first and second clauses which resolves the atom Q is disallowed, and the only ordered resolution refutation of S which remains possible is shown in Figure 8.10.

Using the selection method, on the other hand, the atom P in the first and fourth clauses can be selected, and the atom Q can be selected in the second and third. If only inferences involving selected atoms in *both* premises were allowed, then the tautologies $P \to P$ and $Q \to Q$ would be the only clauses that could be derived from the unsatisfiable set S, and the selection method would fail to be refutation complete. But since applications of the resolution rule are permitted in which selection is applied to only one premise, then the refutation of Figure 8.11 is permitted (the selected atom in each resolution step appears in bold for clarity). The refutation completeness of the selection method for the set S is thus restored by admitting applications of the resolution rule which satisfy the less stringent selection requirement.

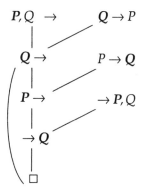

FIGURE 8.11.

It turns out that the selection method is best applied in conjunction with a linear strategy. In logic programming, *SLD resolution* ([KK71]) is precisely such a combination of selection and resolution methods.

In the next definition the selection of a set of atoms, rather than just the selection of individual atoms, is allowed. We restrict our attention to selected subsets of atoms in the antecedents of clauses.

Definition 8.7.1 A *selection function* ψ is a function mapping each clause $\Phi \rightarrow \Psi \,.\, E$ over a given signature to a set $\Phi' \subseteq \Phi$ such that $\Phi' = \emptyset$ iff $\Phi = \emptyset$.

Definition 8.7.2 The *resolution rule with selection function* ψ is given by

$$\frac{\Phi \rightarrow \Psi, A \,.\, E \qquad \Phi', B \rightarrow \Psi' \,.\, E'}{\Phi, \Phi' \rightarrow \Psi, \Psi' \,.\, E \cup E' \cup \{A \approx B\}}$$

provided $B \in \psi(\Phi', B \rightarrow \Psi' \,.\, E')$ and $E \cup E' \cup \{A \approx B\}$ is solvable.

For each selection function ψ, the inference system for *resolution with selection function* ψ (called ψ, S-*resolution*, or simply S-resolution when ψ is clear from context) comprises the appropriate S-resolution rule as in Definition 8.7.2, the correspondingly restricted negative factorization rule, and the usual rules for solving redundant clauses. The inference system for S-resolution can be shown to be refutation complete, although we do not do so here.

Recall that an ordering on a set M is an irreflexive and transitive binary relation, and that an ordering $\succ$ on the set M is noetherian iff there exists no infinite sequence of the form $m_1 \succ m_2 \succ m_3 \succ \dots$. An ordering $\succ$ on terms (atoms) is said to be *compatible with substitutions* if for every substitution σ and all terms (atoms) s and t, $s \succ t$ implies $\sigma(s) \succ \sigma(t)$. If $\succ$ is a noetherian ordering on M, then every subset of M must necessarily contain at least one minimal element.

Definition 8.7.3   An *ordering constraint* is a set

$$E = \{u_1 \approx v_1, \ldots, u_m \approx v_m, s_1 > t_1, \ldots, s_n > t_n\}$$

of term pairs. A *solution* of E is an ordered pair $\langle \sigma, \succ \rangle$ comprising a substitution σ and a noetherian ordering $\succ$ on the set of all atoms such that $u_i = v_i$ for $i = 1, \ldots, m$ and $\sigma(s_i) \succ \sigma(t_i)$ for $i = 1, \ldots, n$. An ordering constraint E is *solvable* if there exists a solution of E.

Definition 8.7.4   1. The *strict ordered resolution rule* is given by

$$\frac{\Phi \to \Psi, A \,.\, E \qquad \Phi', B \to \Psi' \,.\, E'}{\Phi, \Phi' \to \Psi, \Psi' \,.\, E''}$$

provided E'' is solvable, where

$$\begin{aligned} E'' = E \ &\cup\ E' \cup \{A \approx B\} \\ &\cup\ \{A > A' \mid A' \in \Phi \cup \Psi\} \\ &\cup\ \{B > B' \mid B' \in \Phi' \cup \Psi'\}. \end{aligned}$$

2. The *strict ordered factorization rule* is given by

$$\frac{\Phi \to \Psi, A, B \,.\, E}{\Phi \to \Psi, A \,.\, E'}$$

provided E' is solvable, where

$$E' = E \cup \{A \approx B\} \cup \{A > A' \mid A' \in \Phi \cup \Psi \cup \{B\}\}.$$

Strict ordered resolution requires a method for determining solvability of the relevant ordering constraints—such methods exist for determining solvability of constraints in the class of *lexicographic path orderings* ([Com90]) and *simplification orderings* ([Pla93], [JS94]), for example, but a description of these methods is beyond the scope of this book. Simpler rules for strict ordered resolution and factorization can be obtained by eliminating the requirements that the resulting systems E' and E'', respectively, be solvable, but of course this would represent a weakening of the method of ordered resolution.

In the following formulation of ordered resolution, strong conditions on an underlying ordering $\succ$ must be satisfied. Strict ordered resolution and ordered resolution differ in that an underlying ordering is assumed to be given in the latter, whereas demonstrating the existence of an ordering meeting the imposed constraints is part of the problem in the former. Let $\succ$ be a noetherian ordering on the set of all atoms which is compatible with substitutions and total on the set of all ground atoms. Such orderings—among them the Knuth-Bendix ordering ([KB70]) and the various path orderings (recursive, lexicographic, etc.)—are well-known in the area of term rewriting (see [Der87]).

Definition 8.7.5   1. The *ordered resolution rule for* $\succ$ is given by

$$\frac{\Phi \to \Psi, A . E \qquad \Phi', B \to \Psi' . E'}{\Phi, \Phi' \to \Psi, \Psi' . E''}$$

provided $E'' = E \cup E' \cup \{A \approx B\}$ is solvable with most general unifier σ, and where the following additional conditions are satisfied:

(a) $\sigma(A)$ is $\succ$-maximal in $\sigma(\Phi) \cup \sigma(\Psi) \cup \{\sigma(A)\}$, and

(b) $\sigma(B)$ is $\succ$-maximal in $\sigma(\Phi') \cup \sigma(\Psi') \cup \{\sigma(B)\}$.

2. The *ordered factorization rule for* $\succ$ is given by

$$\frac{\Phi \to \Psi, A, B . E}{\Phi \to \Psi, A . E}$$

provided $E' = E \cup \{A \approx B\}$ is solvable with most general unifier σ, and where $\sigma(A)$ is $\succ$-maximal in $\sigma(\Phi) \cup \sigma(\Psi) \cup \{\sigma(A)\} \cup \{\sigma(B)\}$.

It is easy to see that the strict ordered resolution (factorization) rule applies whenever the ordered resolution (resp., factorization) rule applies (for some $\succ$), and only slightly more difficult to see that the ordered resolution (factorization) rule (for some $\succ$) is applicable in all situations in which the strict ordered resolution rule is applicable. The latter assertion for resolution rules holds, for instance, since if the constraint E'' in Definition 8.7.5 is solvable, then there must exist a substitution τ and a noetherian ordering $\succ$ such that $\tau \in u(E \cup E' \cup \{A \approx B\})$, $\tau(A) \succ \tau(A')$ for all $A' \in \Phi \cup \Psi$, and $\tau(B) \succ \tau(B')$ for all $B' \in \Phi' \cup \Psi'$. If $\sigma(A)$ were not $\succ$-maximal in $\sigma(\Phi) \cup \sigma(\Psi) \cup \{\sigma(A)\}$, then there would necessarily exist an atom A' such that $\sigma \in \sigma(\Phi) \cup \sigma(\Psi)$ and $\sigma(A') \succ \sigma(A)$. But then since σ is a most general unifier of $E \cup E' \cup \{A \approx B\}$, there would exist a substitution μ such that $\tau = \sigma\mu$, from which $\tau(A') = \mu(\sigma(A')) \succ \mu(\sigma(A)) = \tau(A)$, a contradiction, follows. Similarly,

$\sigma(B)$ must be maximal in $\sigma(\Phi') \cup \sigma(\Psi') \cup \{\sigma(B)\}$. Of course strict ordered resolution and ordered resolution coincide for ground clauses.

Example 8.7.2 Let $\Sigma = \{P, f, a\}$ be a signature, where P is a unary predicate symbol, f is a unary function symbol, and a is a constant symbol. Consider once again the clause sets $S_n = \{C_1, C_2(n)\}$ from Example 7.5.5, where

$$
\begin{aligned}
C_1 &= \ \to P(x), P(f(x)) \\
C_2(n) &= \ P(y), P(f^n(y)) \to
\end{aligned}
$$

and n is a natural number. Ordered resolution is a particularly suitable method refuting these sets of clauses. For each term t and each atom A of the form $P(f^n(t))$, let $\nu(A) = n$ and consider the ordering $\succ$ on such atoms defined by

$$ A \succ B \quad \text{iff} \quad FV(A) = FV(B) \quad \text{and} \quad \nu(A) > \nu(B). $$

It is clear that the ordering is noetherian. The possible ground atoms over this signature are all of the form $P(f^n(a))$ for some $n \geq 0$, and from this it follows that the ordering $\succ$ is also total on the set of ground atoms. Finally, it is easy to see that $\succ$ is compatible with substitutions over this signature. In the following resolution refutation for S_6, ordered resolution is applied in its "classical" variant. In each clause, the maximal atom of the clause appears boxed for clarity, and, as usual, we do not carry forward all clauses from one step of the derivation to the next.

$$C_1:\qquad\qquad\qquad\qquad\qquad\qquad \rightarrow\ P(x), \boxed{P(f(x))}$$

$$C_2(6):\qquad\qquad P(y), \boxed{P(f^6(y))}\ \rightarrow$$

$$C_1, C_2(6) \Rightarrow C_3:\ \ P(y)\qquad\qquad \rightarrow\ \boxed{P(f^5(y))}$$

$$C_2(6), C_3 \Rightarrow C_4:\ \ P(y), \boxed{P(f(y))}\ \rightarrow$$
$$C_1, C_4 \Rightarrow C_5:\ \ P(x)\qquad\qquad \rightarrow\ P(x)$$

$$C_3, C_4 \Rightarrow C_6:\ \ P(y), \boxed{P(f^4(y))}\ \rightarrow$$

$$C_1, C_6 \Rightarrow C_7:\ \ P(y)\qquad\qquad \rightarrow\ \boxed{P(f^3(y))}$$

$$C_3, C_6 \Rightarrow C_8:\ \ P(y), \boxed{P(f(y))}\ \rightarrow$$

$$C_2(6), C_7 \Rightarrow C_9:\ \ P(y), \boxed{P(f^3(y))}\ \rightarrow$$

$$C_4, C_7 \Rightarrow C_{10}:\ \ P(y), \boxed{P(f^2(y))}\ \rightarrow$$

$$C_6, C_7 \Rightarrow C_{11}:\ \ P(y), \boxed{P(f(y))}\ \rightarrow$$

$$C_1, C_9 \Rightarrow C_{12}:\ \ P(y)\qquad\qquad \rightarrow\ \boxed{P(f^2(y))}$$

$$C_3, C_9 \Rightarrow C_{13}:\ \ P(y), \boxed{P(f^2(y))}\ \rightarrow$$
$$C_7, C_9 \Rightarrow C_{14}:\ \ P(y)\qquad\qquad \rightarrow$$
$$C_1, C_{14} \Rightarrow C_{15}:\qquad\qquad\qquad \rightarrow\ P(x)$$
$$C_{14}, C_{15} \Rightarrow C_{16}:\qquad\qquad\qquad \square$$

This refutation applies level saturation with immediate solution. All of the derivation steps are indicated, i.e., the search space comprises only 16 clauses.

The refutation completeness of the inference system for ordered resolution will be proved momentarily. First, however, we introduce a very general concept of redundancy based on the notion of a noetherian ordering.

8.8   A Notion of Redundancy

Embodied in the rule *Reduction* of $\mathcal{R}'$ are two methods—namely, subsumption and the removal of tautologies—for solving clauses which contribute nothing to resolution derivations. But there exist in addition other methods for simplifying clause sets without affecting their satisfiability. We might ask, therefore, whether or not there exists a general notion of redundancy which simultaneously abstracts the notions of redundancy corresponding to these various methods. How might such a notion be characterized?

Our first task in answering this question is to distinguish between *static* and *dynamic* redundancy. A notion of static redundancy is one which is defined independently of any particular inference system. Thus a clause C is statically redundant with respect to a set S if $S \cup \{C\}$ and $S - \{C\}$ are semantically equivalent, i.e., if $S \cup \{C\}$ and $S - \{C\}$ have exactly the same models. (Note that C need not necessarily be an element of S.) This is precisely the same as requiring that $S - \{C\} \models C$. Unfortunately, static redundancy is too strong a condition to serve as the basis of a solution rule in an inference system. Consider, for example, the clause set $\{C, D\}$, and let R be a resolvent of C and D. Then of course $\{C, D\} \models R$, and so R is statically redundant in $\{C, D, R\}$. If, in an effort to reduce resolution search spaces, one requires the eager solution of statically redundant clauses, then every resolvent will be solved again immediately following its introduction. A concept of redundancy must therefore refer to a particular inference system in order to guarantee the refutation completeness of eagerly solving redundant clauses. That is, a notion of dynamic redundancy is needed.

Ordered resolution makes use of precisely such a notion. In the remainder of this chapter, let $\succ$ denote an ordering on the set $\mathcal{A}$ of all atoms which is noetherian and compatible with substitutions. We extend such an ordering $\succ$ in the obvious way to ground clauses:

Definition 8.8.1 Let $C = \Phi \to \Psi$ and $D = \Phi' \to \Psi'$ be ground clauses. We define $C \succ\succ D$ to hold iff $\Phi \cup \Psi \succ_m \Phi' \cup \Psi'$ holds.

It is well-known that the multiset extension (and therefore also the set extension) of a noetherian ordering is again noetherian. The ordering $\succ\succ$ on clauses facilitates the definition of a concept of redundancy in ordered inference systems ([BG90]).

Definition 8.8.2 1. Let S be a set of ground clauses. The ground clause D is said to be *redundant with respect to S and $\succ$* if there exists some subset S' of S satisfying the conditions:

   (a) $S' \models D$, and

   (b) $D \succ\succ C$ for all $C \in S'$.

2. Let S be a set of clauses. The clause $D.E$ is said to be *redundant with respect to S and $\succ$* provided every ground instance of $D.E$ is redundant with respect to $\overline{S}$ and $\succ$.

3. The clause $D.E$ is said to be *redundant with respect to* S if, for every noetherian ordering on $\mathcal{A}$ which is compatible with substitutions, $D.E$ is redundant with respect to S and $\succ$.

From this definition the monotonicity property of redundancy follows immediately: if C is a clause which is redundant with respect to a set S, then C is also redundant with respect to every superset of S. We now show that the notions of redundancy in Definition 8.8.2 generalize that of Definition 7.4.3 to accommodate orderings more general than the one assigning to each clause its length.

Lemma 8.8.1   1. *If $C.E$ is a tautology then $C.E$ is redundant with respect to every set of clauses.*

2. *If the clause $D.E'$ is subsumed by the clause $C.E$, then $D.E'$ is redundant with respect to $\{C.E\}$.*

Proof. 1. Let $C.E$ be a tautology. We show that $C.E$ is redundant with respect to the empty set and any ordering $\succ$, and from this the conclusion of the lemma follows immediately by monotonicity of redundancy. If $C.E$ is a ground tautology, then $\emptyset \models C.E$ since every such tautology is satisfied by every interpretation. We may therefore take $S' = \emptyset$ in Definition 8.8.2. Moreover, the second clause of the first part of Definition 8.8.2 is trivially satisfied, so that $C.E$ is redundant with respect to $\succ$ and $\emptyset$, and hence with respect to $\emptyset$. If $C.E$ is an arbitrary tautology, then every ground instance $\overline{C}$ of $C.E$ is also a tautology, and therefore redundant with respect to $\emptyset$ and any ordering $\succ$. Thus by the second part of Defintion 8.8.2, $C.E$ is also redundant with respect to $\emptyset$ and $\succ$, and hence with respect to $\emptyset$.

2. Suppose $D.E'$ is subsumed by $C.E$. If $C.E$ and $D.E'$ are ground clauses, then $E = E' = \emptyset$, so that $C = \Phi \to \Psi$, $D = \Phi' \to \Psi'$, $\Phi \subseteq \Phi'$, and $\Psi \subseteq \Psi'$. Let $\mathcal{I}$ be a model for C. Then either $\Phi \not\subseteq \mathcal{I}$ or else $\Psi \cap \mathcal{I} \neq \emptyset$, and, therefore, either $\Phi' \not\subseteq \mathcal{I}$ or else $\Psi' \cap \mathcal{I} \neq \emptyset$, i.e., $\mathcal{I}$ is also a model for D. Thus we must have $\{C\} \models D$. Moreover, since C and D cannot be identical according to Definition 7.4.2, we must have that either $\Phi \subset \Phi'$ or $\Psi \subset \Psi'$. This implies that $D = \Phi' \to \Psi' \succ\succ \Phi \to \Psi = C$ for every ordering $\succ$ on atoms. Thus D is redundant with respect to $\{C.E\}$ and this ordering $\succ$, and therefore is redundant with respect to $\{C.E\}$.

Now let $C.E$ and $D.E'$ be arbitrary clauses such that $C.E$ subsumes $D.E'$. Then every ground instance of $D.E'$ is subsumed by a clause C' in the set $\overline{C.E}$. By the argument of the previous paragraph, every ground instance of $D.E'$ is redundant with respect to $\{C'\}$ for some clause $C' \in \overline{C.E}$, and therefore with respect to $\overline{C.E}$ itself. But this is precisely what it means to say that $D.E'$ is redundant with respect to $\{C.E\}$. □

We now provide an inference rule which facilitates removal of redundant clauses.

In the remainder of this chapter, let $\succ$ be a noetherian ordering on $\mathcal{A}$ which is compatible with substitutions and assume further that $\succ$ is total on the set of all ground atoms. Then the derived ordering $\succ\!\!\succ$ is also total on the set of all ground clauses. Let $O^{\succ}$ denote the inference system comprising the ordered resolution rule for $\succ$ and the ordered factorization rule for $\succ$ of the previous section, together with the following solution rule for $\succ$.

Definition 8.8.3   The *reduction rule for* $O^{\succ}$ is given by

$$\frac{S \cup \{C\}}{S}$$

provided C is redundant with respect to $S - \{C\}$ and $\succ$.

The soundness of $O^{\succ}$ is immediate. Completeness can be proved using the following lemma and theorem, and an appropriate modification of the Lifting Lemma.

Lemma 8.8.2   *If R is an ordered resolvent of the ground clauses C and D then $C \succ\!\!\succ R$ and $D \succ\!\!\succ R$.*

Proof. Let $C = \Phi \rightarrow \Psi, A$, let $D = \Phi', A \rightarrow \Psi'$, and let $R = \Phi, \Phi' \rightarrow \Psi, \Psi'$. We will show that $C \succ\!\!\succ R$; the proof that $D \succ\!\!\succ R$ is similar. If $R \succ\!\!\succ C$, then there must exist, for the atom $A \in C$, an atom $B \succ A$ in R. But this contradicts the definition of ordered resolution, since ordered resolution for ground clauses requires that A be $\succ$-maximal in $\Phi \cup \Psi \cup \{A\}$ and that A be $\succ$-maximal in $\Phi' \cup \Psi' \cup \{A\}$. Since the ordering $\succ\!\!\succ$ is total on the set of ground clauses, and since $R \neq C$, the conclusion of the lemma follows. $\square$

Theorem 8.8.1   *(Completeness of ordered resolution for ground clauses) Let S be a set of ground clauses. If S is closed under $O^{\succ}$ and if $\square \notin S$, then S is satisfiable.*

Proof. Let S be a set of ground clauses which is closed under $O^{\succ}$ and which does not contain the empty clause. As usual, we construct a model for S.

For a clause $C = \Phi \rightarrow \Psi$ let $max(C)$ be the $\succ$-maximal atom in $\Phi \cup \Psi$. Let

$$S^+ = \{C = \Phi \rightarrow \Psi \in S \mid max(C) \in \Psi\}.$$

If $S^+ = \emptyset$, then in particular the set of positive clauses of S is also empty, and so S is satisfiable. We may therefore assume that $S^+ \neq \emptyset$. Let

$X_0 = \{max(C) \mid C \in S^+\}$. By assumption, X_0 is not empty. Moreover, X_0 is certainly a model for S^+. If we have inductively constructed a model X_n for S^+ which is not minimal, we choose an arbitrary $\succ$-minimal element A_n from $\{A' \in X_n \mid X_n - \{A'\} \models S^+\}$ and define $X_{n+1} = X_n - \{A_n\}$. Let

$$\mathcal{I} = \bigcap_{n \geq 0} X_n.$$

Then clearly $\mathcal{I}$ is a model for S^+ by construction. We show that $\mathcal{I}$ further possesses the property that for every $A \in \mathcal{I}$ there exists a clause $\Phi \to \Psi, A \in S^+$ such that

1. A is $\succ$-maximal in $\Phi \cup \Psi \cup \{A\}$ and

2. $\Phi \subseteq \mathcal{I}$ and $\Psi \cap \mathcal{I} = \emptyset$

hold. This property provides the key to proving that $\mathcal{I}$ is a model of S itself.

First, given $A \in \mathcal{I}$, there must certainly exist a clause of the form $\Phi' \to \Psi', A \in S^+$ such that $\Phi' \subseteq \mathcal{I}$ and $\Psi' \cap \mathcal{I} = \emptyset$ holds, since otherwise $\mathcal{I} - \{A\}$ would be a smaller model of S^+ than $\mathcal{I}$ which is not possible. Thus 2. holds. Now let M be the set of all such clauses in S^+, and suppose that A is not $\succ$-maximal in any clause of M, i.e., assume that for every clause $\Phi' \to \Psi', A \in M$ there is some atom $B \in \Psi'$ such that $B \succ A$. Without loss of generality, B may be taken to be a $\succ$-maximal atom in Ψ' such that $B \succ A$. Then $B \in X_0$, but since $\mathcal{I}$ contains no elements of Ψ', B must be deleted from some X_k in the construction of $\mathcal{I}$. Thus $B = A_k$ for some $k \geq 0$. That is, an atom larger than A (namely, B) was removed from some X_k in the construction of $\mathcal{I}$. Let n be the smallest number such that an atom larger than A was removed from X_n. Then $X_n - \{A\}$ is also a model for S^+ (considering cases according as clauses are in M or not), and so X_{n+1} would not be $X_n - \{A_n\}$. Since this contradicts our construction, 1. must hold as well.

Finally, we show that $\mathcal{I}$ is a model of S. If there is some clause $C = \Phi' \to \Psi' \in S$ which is not satisfiable by $\mathcal{I}$, then let C be a $\succ\succ$-minimal such clause. Then certainly $C \in S - S^+$, since $\mathcal{I} \models S^+$ holds. Furthermore, we must have $\Phi' \subseteq \mathcal{I}$ and $\Psi' \cap \mathcal{I} = \emptyset$. Let A be a $\succ$-maximal element of Φ' (and hence of $\Phi' \to \Psi'$ since $C \notin S^+$). Then $A \in \mathcal{I}$, and so by the above argument, there exists a clause $D = \Phi \to \Psi, A \in S^+$ such that A is $\succ$-maximal in $\Phi \cup \Psi \cup \{A\}$, $\Phi \subseteq \mathcal{I}$, and $\Psi \cap \mathcal{I} = \emptyset$. The clause $R = \Phi, \Phi' - \{A\} \to \Psi, \Psi'$ is then an ordered resolvent of C and D for which $\mathcal{I} \not\models R$ holds. By the previous lemma we have $C \succ\succ R$. Now since S is closed under $O^{\succ}$, R must be redundant with respect to S, and so there must exist a subset S' of S such that $S' \models R$ and $R \succ\succ C'$ for all $C' \in S'$. From $\mathcal{I} \not\models R$ it follows that $\mathcal{I} \not\models S'$, and so there must exist a clause $C' \in S'$ with $\mathcal{I} \not\models C'$. But since $C \succ\succ R \succ\succ C'$, this contradicts the $\succ\succ$-minimality of C. □

9

Resolution in Sorted Logic

9.1 Introduction

With regard to improving the efficiency of automated deduction systems, the final word has not yet been spoken. In Chapter 8 we became acquainted with various techniques for pruning search spaces associated with deduction, most of which rely on restricting applications of the resolution and factorization rules. While such methods are indeed helpful in constructing more efficient resolution theorem provers, in fact some of the most promising techniques for increasing deduction efficiency have been based not on methods for restricting the application of deduction rules, but rather on modifications of the input calculi themselves. Two general tendencies in modifying calculi for efficiency are clearly discernible. The first is the development of special calculi for particular commonly occurring predicates. A classic example of this approach to improving deduction efficiency is the development of completion procedures—based on the Knuth-Bendix algorithm—for equational logic. The second tendency is that of using knowledge about special functions or predicates to arrive at more powerful unification algorithms. The fundamental idea behind this latter approach is to hand over the lion's share of the deduction work to the (deterministic) unification mechanism, and so to reduce the computational burden placed on the (nondeterministic) logical inference system.

The development of *sorted logic*,[1] which exemplifies the second tendency, was born out of two seemingly unrelated concerns. First, along with the idea of an algebraic specification came the accompanying notion of a type discipline. Strongly typed languages offer programmers an advantage over untyped ones in that many programming errors in strongly typed languages—which would first appear in untyped languages as run-time errors—can be recognized at compile time; the early debugging afforded by type-checking facilitates correct program development.[2] The second motivation for the introduction of sorts, namely, deduction efficiency, is more germane to our purposes. In this book we consider sort information primarily as a means of reducing search spaces associated with deduction in resolution theorem provers. The aim of incorporating sort information into deduction calculi is to reduce the number of possible applications of resolution and factorization rules by preventing the solution of unification problems involving terms which do not denote meaningful objects, i.e., which are not well-sorted. One can get an idea of the difference between the approaches to improving efficiency that we have seen already and the use of sort information for this purpose by observing that whereas restricting applications of resolution as in the strategies of Chapter 8 decreases the number of subterms of a given term to which a resolution rule can be applied, the use of sorted calculi actually decreases the number of terms which can be formed in the first place. Because they limit the number of terms that can be constructed, the incorporation of sorts into calculi leads to decreases in the number of terms to which resolution or factorization can be applied at all, as well as in the number of "legal" substitutions unifying terms (and, therefore, in the number of possible successful resolution steps).

The following puzzle, announced in 1978 by Lenhard Schubert, illustrates the main concepts associated with deduction in sorted logics, and has since become a famous challenge problem for automated deduction systems. Although many automated solutions to the problem appear in the literature (see [Sti86]), the most efficient solutions have been obtained using sorted formulations of it such as the one described here.

Example 9.1.1   (Schubert's Steamroller) Wolves, fish, birds, caterpillars, and snails are animals, and there is at least one of each kind of animal. Grain is a plant, and there exists at least one such plant. Every animal is an herbivore or else eats all herbivores which are much smaller than itself. Caterpillars and snails are much smaller than birds, which in turn are much smaller

---

[1]That which we are here referring to as *sorted logic* is often called *order-sorted logic* or *logic with sort hierarchy* in the literature.

[2]In many contexts, "sorts" and "types" are considered synonymous. If a distinction is made, types are usually considered to denote disjoint classes of objects, whereas the classes of objects denoted by sorts can overlap.

than fish, and fish are much smaller than wolves. Wolves eat neither fish nor grain, and birds eat caterpillars but not snails. Caterpillars and snails are herbivores. It is to be shown that there exists an animal that eats a grain-eating animal.

To represent the problem in unsorted clausal logic we use the following signature, where the predicates are intended to have the specified "meanings":

$A(x)$	x is an animal	$G(x)$	x is a grain
$B(x)$	x is a bird	$M(x,y)$	x is much smaller than y
$C(x)$	x is a caterpillar	$P(x)$	x is a plant
$E(x,y)$	x eats y	$S(x)$	x is a snail
$F(x)$	x is a fish	$W(x)$	x is a wolf

The problem can then be formulated using the clauses below. Here i and h are functions obtained by skolemization.

(1) $W(x) \rightarrow A(x)$ (2) $\rightarrow W(w)$ (3) $F(x) \rightarrow A(x)$
(4) $\rightarrow F(f)$ (5) $B(x) \rightarrow A(x)$ (6) $\rightarrow B(b)$
(7) $C(x) \rightarrow A(x)$ (8) $\rightarrow C(c)$ (9) $S(x) \rightarrow A(x)$
(10) $\rightarrow S(s)$ (11) $G(x) \rightarrow P(x)$ (12) $\rightarrow G(g)$

(14) $C(x), B(y) \rightarrow M(x,y)$ (15) $S(x), B(y) \rightarrow M(x,y)$
(16) $B(x), F(y) \rightarrow M(x,y)$ (17) $F(x), W(y) \rightarrow M(x,y)$
(18) $W(x), F(y), E(x,y) \rightarrow$ (19) $W(x), G(y), E(x,y) \rightarrow$
(20) $B(x), C(y) \rightarrow E(x,y)$ (21) $B(x), S(y), E(x,y) \rightarrow$
(22) $C(x) \rightarrow P(h(x))$ (23) $C(x) \rightarrow E(x,h(x))$
(24) $S(x) \rightarrow P(i(x))$ (25) $S(x) \rightarrow E(x,i(x))$

(13) $A(x), P(y), A(z), P(v), M(z,x), E(z,v) \rightarrow E(x,y), E(x,z)$
(26) $A(x), A(y), G(z), E(x,y), E(y,z) \rightarrow$

We will not give a resolution refutation for this set of clauses—depending on which strategy is used, the search space can range in size from a few hundred to many thousand clauses. But one reasonable idea for decreasing the search space for this problem might be to use the naturally occurring sort information to disallow certain resolution steps from the outset because they violate sort restrictions. That is, we might hope to devise a (purely syntactic) deduction calculus which more fully captures the intended semantics of the steamroller problem.

To see how we might do this, consider, for example, the resolution step

(20), (26) $\Rightarrow$ (27) $A(x), A(y), G(z), E(x,y), B(y), C(z) \rightarrow$

obtained by resolving against the atom $E(y,z)$. This step produces the new clause (27), but cannot possibly lead to a solution of the problem.

This is because the variable y in clause (20) is "of sort caterpillar," while the corresponding variable z in clause (26) is "of sort grain," and so the variable z in (27) can only be instantiated by either the constant g or the constant c. But both possibilities lead to a literal which can never be resolved away: in the instance $A(x), A(y), C(g), E(x, y), B(y), C(g) \rightarrow$ of (27) the isolated literal $C(g)$ cannot be resolved, and in the instance $A(x), A(y), G(c), E(x, y), B(y), C(c) \rightarrow$ the isolated literal $G(c)$ cannot be resolved. It is therefore impossible for (27) to lead to a derivation of the empty clause, i.e., to contribute to a solution of the Steamroller problem. (Note carefully that although (27) is obtained from (20) and (26) via the substitution $\sigma = \{x \leftarrow y, \ y \leftarrow z\}$, the fact that it contributes nothing toward a derivation of the empty clause is in no way related to the fact that σ is not idempotent.)

In a sorted version of Schubert's Steamroller, we might first introduce sorts W, F, B, C, S, and G corresponding to the taxonomic classes wolf, fox, bird, caterpillar, snail, and grain, respectively, as well as the supersorts A (animal) and P (plant). The function symbol h introduced by skolemization would then represent a function assigning to each object of sort C an object of sort P, and similarly for the function symbol i, yielding the following sorted formulation:

(1) $W \sqsubset A$	(2) $w : W$	(3) $F \sqsubset A$
(4) $f : F$	(5) $B \sqsubset A$	(6) $b : B$
(7) $C \sqsubset A$	(8) $c : C$	(9) $S \sqsubset A$
(10) $s : S$	(11) $G \sqsubset P$	(12) $g : G$
(22) $h : C \rightarrow P$	(24) $i : S \rightarrow P$	
(14) $\rightarrow M(x_C, y_B)$	(15) $\rightarrow M(x_S, y_B)$	(16) $\rightarrow M(x_B, y_F)$
(17) $\rightarrow M(x_F, y_W)$	(18) $E(x_W, y_F) \rightarrow$	(19) $E(x_W, y_G) \rightarrow$
(20) $\rightarrow E(x_B, y_C)$	(21) $E(x_B, y_S) \rightarrow$	(23) $\rightarrow E(x_C, h(x_C))$

$$(13) \ M(z_A, x_A), E(z_A, v_P) \ \rightarrow \ E(x_A, y_P), E(x_A, z_A)$$

$$(25) \ \rightarrow E(x_S, i(x_S)) \qquad (26) \ E(x_A, y_A), E(y_A, z_G) \rightarrow$$

Clause (1) codes the information that wolves are animals, clause (2) says that w is a wolf, and so on.

An agreeable side effect of this formulation is its brevity; in addition, only two nonunit clauses remain. With this formulation we have separated the static information about sort relations (clauses (1) to (12), (22), and (24)) from the formulation of the problem itself. The resolvent (27) of clauses (20) and (26) obtainable in the unsorted formulation of the problem can no longer be derived in the sorted version: intuitively, the sorted unification problem

$$\{E(x_B, y_C) \approx E(y_A, z_G)\}$$

is not solvable, since there is no object simultaneously of sort C and sort G with which both z_G and y_C can be instantiated.

9.2 Syntax and Semantics of Elementary Sorted Logic

We begin our discussion of sorted calculi with

Definition 9.2.1 An *alphabet for a sorted first-order language* consists of the following symbols:

- a countably infinite set $\mathcal{S} = \{S_1, S_2, \ldots\}$ of *sorts*,

- the *connectives* $\neg$, $\wedge$, $\vee$, $\Rightarrow$, $\Leftrightarrow$, $\forall$, and $\exists$,

- the *auxiliary symbols* "(" and ")",

- for each $S \in \mathcal{S}$, a countably infinite set $\mathcal{V}_S$ of *(sorted) variables*,

- a countably infinite set $\mathcal{F}_n$ of *function symbols of arity n* for each natural number n, and

- a countably infinite set $\mathcal{P}_n$ of *n-place predicate symbols* for each natural number n.

Sorted variables carry their sort information as subscripts, so that we write x_S for a variable x of sort S, i.e., for a variable $x \in \mathcal{V}_S$. We write $\mathcal{V}_S = \bigcup_{S \in \mathcal{S}} \mathcal{V}_S$, $\mathcal{F} = \bigcup_{n \geq 0} \mathcal{F}_n$, and $\mathcal{P} = \bigcup_{n \geq 0} \mathcal{P}_n$, and as usual we assume that the sets $\mathcal{S}$, $\mathcal{V}_S$, $\mathcal{F}_n$, and $\mathcal{P}_n$ are pairwise disjoint. We may also standardize the set of sorted variables across all alphabets having the same sort symbols, so that an alphabet for a sorted first-order language is specified by an ordered triple $\langle \mathcal{S}, \mathcal{F}, \mathcal{P} \rangle$. We write $\mathcal{V}$ rather than $\mathcal{V}_S$ when this will not lead to confusion.

Definition 9.2.2
1. A *subsort declaration* for an alphabet $\langle \mathcal{S}, \mathcal{F}, \mathcal{P} \rangle$ is an ordered pair $\langle S, T \rangle$ of distinct sorts.

2. A *function declaration* for an alphabet $\langle \mathcal{S}, \mathcal{F}, \mathcal{P} \rangle$ is a tuple $\langle f, S_1, \ldots, S_n, S \rangle$ with $f \in \mathcal{F}_n$ and $S, S_1, \ldots, S_n \in \mathcal{S}$.

3. A *signature for a sorted first-order language*, or a *sorted signature*, is an ordered quadruple $\Sigma = \langle \mathcal{S}, \mathcal{F}, \mathcal{P}, \mathcal{D} \rangle$, where $\mathcal{S}$, $\mathcal{F}$, and $\mathcal{P}$ are as in Definition 9.2.1 and $\mathcal{D}$ is a finite set of subsort and function declarations for $\langle \mathcal{S}, \mathcal{F}, \mathcal{P} \rangle$.

We write $S \sqsubseteq_\Sigma T$ rather than $\langle S, T \rangle$ for subsort declarations, and may write $S \sqsubseteq T$ when the signature Σ is clear from context. We most often write $f : S_1 \times \ldots \times S_n \to S$ for a function declaration $\langle f, S_1, \ldots, S_n, S \rangle$. When $n = 0$ we call a function declaration for f a *constant declaration*, and write $f : S$ instead of $f : \to S$. A *declaration for the sort S* is a subsort declaration of the form $T \sqsubset S$ or a function declaration of the form $f : S_1 \times \ldots \times S_n \to S$.

We use the symbol $<_\Sigma$, or simply $<$, when Σ is clear from context, to denote the transitive closure of the relation $\sqsubset_\Sigma$ determined by the set of subsort declarations of Σ; we similarly use $\leq_\Sigma$ or $\leq$ to denote its reflexive, transitive closure. In the following we always assume that the set $\mathcal{D}$ contains no cyclic sequence $S_1 \sqsubset S_2, \ldots, S_{n-1} \sqsubset S_n, S_n \sqsubset S_1$ of subsort declarations. The relation $<_\Sigma$ is therefore a partial ordering on $\mathcal{S}$, and since $\mathcal{D}$ is finite, this ordering is noetherian. If $\Psi \subseteq \mathcal{S}$, we write $min_\Sigma(\Psi)$ for the set of elements of Ψ which are $<_\Sigma$-minimal.

We build sorted terms in essentially the usual manner over the sorted variables and function symbols. We must, however, take sort information carefully into consideration.

Definition 9.2.3   Let $\Sigma = \langle \mathcal{S}, \mathcal{F}, \mathcal{P}, \mathcal{D} \rangle$ be a sorted signature and let $S \in \mathcal{S}$. A word t over $\mathcal{F} \cup \mathcal{V}_\Sigma$ is a *Σ-term of sort S* if at least one of the following holds:

- t is a variable of sort S,

- t is of the form $ft_1 \ldots t_n$ where $f \in \mathcal{F}_n$, $f : S_1 \times \ldots \times S_n \to S$ is a function declaration in $\mathcal{D}$, and t_i is a term of sort S_i for $i = 1, \ldots, n$, or

- t is a term of sort S' and $S' \sqsubset S$ is a subsort declaration in $\mathcal{D}$.

We denote the set of all Σ-terms of sort S by $\mathcal{T}_{S,\Sigma}(\mathcal{F}, \mathcal{V})$, or by $\mathcal{T}_S(\mathcal{F}, \mathcal{V})$ when there is no possibility of confusion about Σ; in this case we may refer to elements of $\mathcal{T}_S(\mathcal{F}, \mathcal{V})$ simply as *terms of sort S*. We further use the abbreviation $\mathcal{T}_\Sigma(\mathcal{F}, \mathcal{V})$, or simply $\mathcal{T}(\mathcal{F}, \mathcal{V})$, to denote

$$\bigcup_{S \in \mathcal{S}} \mathcal{T}_{S,\Sigma}(\mathcal{F}, \mathcal{V}),$$

i.e., to denote the set of all Σ-*terms*. If Σ is clear from context, we write $\mathcal{T}_S(\mathcal{F})$ for the set of ground Σ-terms of sort S, and $\mathcal{T}(\mathcal{F})$ for the set of all ground Σ-terms. Note that the third clause of Definition 9.2.3 entails that if $S \leq_\Sigma S'$ then $\mathcal{T}_S(\mathcal{F}, \mathcal{V}) \subseteq \mathcal{T}_{S'}(\mathcal{F}, \mathcal{V})$, i.e., every Σ-term of sort S is also a Σ-term of sort S' when $S \leq_\Sigma S'$. As in previous chapters, we will use parentheses in terms as desired for increased legibility.

Certain substitutions of Σ-terms for sorted variables in other Σ-terms yield words over $\mathcal{F} \cup \mathcal{V}$ which are again Σ-terms. That is, some substitutions σ preserve well-sortedness in the sense that if t is of sort S then $\sigma(t)$ is a Σ-term which is also of sort S. We single out for special consideration the class of all such substitutions.

Definition 9.2.4 Let $\Sigma = \langle \mathcal{S}, \mathcal{F}, \mathcal{P}, \mathcal{D} \rangle$ be a sorted signature. A Σ-*substitution* is a function $\sigma : \mathcal{V} \rightarrow \mathcal{T}_{\Sigma}(\mathcal{F}, \mathcal{V})$ with finite domain and having the property that $\sigma(x_S) \in \mathcal{T}_S(\mathcal{F}, \mathcal{V})$ for all $x_S \in Dom(\sigma)$. If $t \in \mathcal{T}_{\Sigma}(\mathcal{F}, \mathcal{V})$ and if σ is a Σ-substitution, then $\sigma(t)$ is said to be a Σ-*instance* of t.

Example 9.2.1 Let the sorted signature Σ comprise the sorts NAT, $EVEN$, and ODD, the function symbols 0 and s, the empty set of predicate symbols, and the following declarations:

$$
\begin{array}{ll}
EVEN \sqsubset NAT & ODD \sqsubset NAT \\
0 : EVEN & s : NAT \rightarrow NAT \\
s : ODD \rightarrow EVEN & s : EVEN \rightarrow ODD
\end{array}
$$

The term $t_0 = s(0)$ is of sort ODD (and so is also of sort NAT), the term $t_1 = s(s(x_{EVEN}))$ is of sort $EVEN$ (and so also of sort NAT). The substitution $\sigma = \{x_{EVEN} \rightarrow s(x_{EVEN})\}$ is not a Σ-substitution, since $s(x_{EVEN})$ is not of sort $EVEN$, but $\sigma' = \{x_{EVEN} \rightarrow s(s(x_{EVEN}))\}$ is a Σ-substitution.

We can also define atoms and other formulae over sorted signatures by analogy with their counterparts in unsorted logics (see Definition 3.1.3).

Definition 9.2.5 Let $\Sigma = \langle \mathcal{S}, \mathcal{F}, \mathcal{P}, \mathcal{D} \rangle$ be a sorted signature.

1. A Σ-*atom* is a word over $\mathcal{F} \cup \mathcal{P} \cup \mathcal{V}$ of the form $Pt_1 \ldots t_n$ for $P \in \mathcal{P}_n$ and $t_1, \ldots, t_n \in \mathcal{T}_{\Sigma}(\mathcal{F}, \mathcal{V})$. A *ground* Σ-*atom* is a Σ-atom in which no variables occur.

2. The set of Σ-*formulae* is the set of words over $\mathcal{F} \cup \mathcal{P} \cup \mathcal{V}$ built inductively using the following rules:

   - every Σ-atom is a Σ-formula,

   - if φ and ψ are Σ-formulae, then $\neg\varphi$, $(\varphi \wedge \psi)$, $(\varphi \vee \psi)$, $(\varphi \Rightarrow \psi)$, and $(\varphi \Leftrightarrow \psi)$ are also Σ-formulae, and

- if φ is a Σ-formula and $x_S \in \mathcal{V}$, then $\exists x_S \; \varphi$ and $\forall x_S \; \varphi$ are also Σ-formulae.

We typically represent formulae in clause form.

Definition 9.2.6   A Σ-*sequent* is an ordered pair $\langle \Phi, \Psi \rangle$ of sets of Σ-formulae, usually written in the form $\Phi \rightarrow \Psi$. A Σ-*clause* is a Σ-sequent $\Phi \rightarrow \Psi$, where Φ and Ψ are sets of Σ-atoms.

If S is a set of Σ-clauses, then we write $\overline{S}$ for the set of all ground Σ-instances of clauses in S. We write $Var(C)$ for the set of sorted variables occurring in the Σ-clause C.

As is the semantics of unsorted first-order languages, the semantics of a sorted language can be defined via interpretations in structures. The different sorts then correspond to different subsets of the carrier for the interpretation, the subsort declarations capture inclusion relations among these carrier subsets, and to every function and predicate symbol there corresponds an actual function or predicate, respectively, over the structure. In outline, we have

Definition 9.2.7   Let $\Sigma = \langle \mathcal{S}, \mathcal{F}, \mathcal{P}, \mathcal{D} \rangle$ be a sorted signature. A sorted Σ-*structure* $\mathcal{M}$ is an ordered pair $\langle M, I \rangle$ such that

1. M is a nonempty set, called the *underlying set* or *carrier* of $\mathcal{M}$.

2. I is a function on $\mathcal{F} \cup \mathcal{P} \cup \mathcal{S}$ fulfilling the following conditions:

   - $I(S) \subseteq M$ for every $S \in \mathcal{S}$,
   - $I(S) \subseteq I(T)$ for every $S \sqsubset T \in \mathcal{D}$,
   - If $f \in \mathcal{F}_n$ and $f : S_1 \times \ldots \times S_n \rightarrow S \in \mathcal{D}$, then $I(f) : I(S_1) \times \ldots \times I(S_n) \rightarrow I(S)$ is an n-ary function, and
   - If $P \in \mathcal{P}_n$, then $I(P) \subseteq M^n$ is an n-ary relation on M.

As in the unsorted case, when discussing a sorted Σ-structure $\mathcal{M}$ we will always denote its carrier by M. Then writing S^M for $I(S)$ we have

Definition 9.2.8   1. A Σ-*valuation* in a sorted Σ-structure $\mathcal{M}$ is a function $\beta : \mathcal{V} \rightarrow M$ with $\beta(x_S) \in S^M$ for all $x_S \in \mathcal{V}_S$.

2. A Σ-*interpretation* $\mathcal{I}$ is an ordered pair $\langle \mathcal{M}, \beta \rangle$ comprising a Σ-structure $\mathcal{M}$ and a Σ-valuation β in $\mathcal{M}$.

If $\mathcal{I}$ is a Σ-interpretation and t is a Σ-term, then $\mathcal{I}(t)$ is defined exactly as in Definition 4.1.3. It is easy to see that if $t \in \mathcal{T}_S(\mathcal{F}, \mathcal{V})$, then $\mathcal{I}(t) \in S^M$. If

$\mathcal{I}$ is a Σ-interpretation, the Σ-*satisfiability* relation for formulae is defined by analogy with the unsorted case (see Definition 4.1.5), with the following differences:

$$\mathcal{I} \models \forall x_S \varphi \quad \text{iff for all } a \in S^M, \mathcal{I}[x \to a] \models \varphi \text{ holds,}$$
$$\mathcal{I} \models \exists x_S \varphi \quad \text{iff for some } a \in S^M, \mathcal{I}[x \to a] \models \varphi \text{ holds.}$$

But since the semantics of the connectives is precisely as in the unsorted case, we also have a sorted analogue of Definition 5.1.4. Thus the Σ-sequent $\Phi \to \Psi$ and the Σ-formula $\bigwedge \Phi \Rightarrow \bigvee \Psi$ are semantically equivalent.

With this machinery in place, a sorted version of Herbrand's Theorem can be proved (see [SS89]). It follows that a set S of Σ-clauses is Σ-unsatisfiable iff $\overline{S}$, the set of all ground Σ-instances of clauses of S, is Σ-unsatisfiable. The Σ-satisfiability of a set of Σ-clauses can therefore be rendered in terms of the Σ-satisfiability of a corresponding set of ground Σ-clauses.

Another approach to the semantics of sorted logics is to take the parallels between Σ-satisfiability of Σ-clauses and satisfiability of unsorted clauses as a point of departure. We will show in the next section that this leads to an entirely equivalent semantics and so we actually could have defined the semantics of order-sorted logics in terms of our semantics for unsorted logics had we wished to do so. This second approach naturally draws more heavily on the semantics of unsorted clausal logic than does the self-contained one described above. It is given in terms of a transformation mapping a set of Σ-clauses describing a sorted deduction problem into a set of unsorted clauses representing an equivalent unsorted one, and yields a correspondence of problems as suggested in Section 9.1. This alternative approach therefore regards the declarations of a signature for a sorted language as restricting the ground terms and substitutions possible for use in resolution derivations in the corresponding unsorted calculus. But regardless of which of the two approaches we adopt, the crucial point is that our semantics for sorted languages must reflect our intuitions about sorts denoting subuniverses of entire universes of discourse and induced relations $\leq_\Sigma$ on sorts denoting inclusion relations on sets. This is true of both approaches to semantics for sorted logics that we have outlined here.

9.3   Relativization

Let $\Sigma = \langle \mathcal{S}, \mathcal{F}, \mathcal{P}, \mathcal{D} \rangle$ be a sorted signature with variables $\mathcal{V}_S$. Then by carefully naming the variables in $\mathcal{V}_S$, we may arrange that there is a one-to-one correspondence mapping each sorted variable $x_S \in \mathcal{V}_S$ to a unique unsorted variable $x'_S \in \mathcal{V}$. Thus if $\Sigma = \langle \mathcal{S}, \mathcal{F}, \mathcal{P}, \mathcal{D} \rangle$ is any sorted signature, then this correspondence between $\mathcal{V}_S$ and the set $\mathcal{V}$ of unsorted variables can be extended to an embedding of the set of Σ-terms into the set of unsorted terms over $\langle \mathcal{F}, \mathcal{P} \rangle$, to an embedding of the set of Σ-atoms into the set of atoms over $\langle \mathcal{F}, \mathcal{P} \rangle$, and to an embedding of the set of Σ-clauses into the set of unsorted clauses over $\langle \mathcal{F}, \mathcal{P} \rangle$ via the inductively defined injective mapping given by $(ft_1 \ldots t_n)' = ft'_1 \ldots t'_n$, $(Pt_1 \ldots t_n)' = Pt'_1 \ldots t'_n$, and $(\Phi \rightarrow \Psi)' = \Phi' \rightarrow \Psi'$. We call this mapping the *forgetful functor*, since it "forgets" the sorts of formulae. Using the forgetful functor we may also define for each Σ-substitution σ a corresponding unsorted substitution σ' by $\sigma'(x) = (\sigma(x_S))'$ for all $x \in \mathcal{V}$, where $x = (x_S)'$. Note that σ' is indeed defined for every unsorted variable x since each $x \in \mathcal{V}$ is $(x_S)'$ for some $x_S \in \mathcal{V}_S$. When it will not lead to confusion, we will refrain from distinguishing between Σ-terms, Σ-formulae, Σ-clauses, or Σ-substitutions and their unsorted counterparts, and will denote both by t, φ, C, or σ, as appropriate.

Definition 9.3.1   Let $\Sigma = \langle \mathcal{S}, \mathcal{F}, \mathcal{P}, \mathcal{D} \rangle$ be a sorted signature. We derive from Σ an unsorted signature $\Sigma^* = \langle \mathcal{F}, \mathcal{P}' \rangle$ by setting

$$\mathcal{P}' = \mathcal{P} \cup \{P_S \mid S \in \mathcal{S}\},$$

where each P_S is a new unary predicate symbol. We further define a set of clauses $S_{\mathcal{D}}$ over Σ^* by

$$
\begin{aligned}
S_{\mathcal{D}} \;=\; & \{P_S(x) \rightarrow P_T(x) \mid S \sqsubset T \in \mathcal{D}\} \\
& \cup \{P_{S_1}(x_1), \ldots, P_{S_n}(x_n) \rightarrow P_S(f(x_1, \ldots, x_n)) \mid \\
& \quad f : S_1 \times \ldots \times S_n \rightarrow S \in \mathcal{D}\}.
\end{aligned}
$$

If $C = \Phi \rightarrow \Psi$ is a Σ-clause, we define the unsorted Σ^*-clause C^* by

$$C^* = P_{S_1}(x_1), \ldots, P_{S_n}(x_n), \Phi' \rightarrow \Psi',$$

where $\{x_1, \ldots, x_n\} = Var(C)$ and $x_i \in \mathcal{V}_{S_i}$ for $i = 1, \ldots, n$. If S is a set of Σ-clauses, then we define $S^* = \{C^* \mid C \in S\}$ and $S_{rel} = S_{\mathcal{D}} \cup S^*$. S_{rel} is called the *relativization of S with respect to Σ*.

From Definition 9.3.1 it follows that the set $S_{\mathcal{D}}$ of clauses is always satisfiable, since it contains no negative clauses and so the interpretation satisfying all atoms is a model for it.

Example 9.3.1   1. Let Σ be the sorted signature of Example 9.2.1, augmented with an additional unary predicate symbol Q, and let $S = \{Q(x_{ODD}),$ $Q(s(x_{ODD})) \rightarrow Q(y_{NAT})\}$. The relativization of S with respect to Σ

is the set of clauses

$$
\begin{aligned}
S^* \;=\; \{ & P_{ODD}(x), P_{NAT}(y), Q(x), Q(s(x)) \rightarrow Q(y), \\
& P_{EVEN}(x) \rightarrow P_{NAT}(x), \\
& P_{ODD}(x) \rightarrow P_{NAT}(x), \\
& \rightarrow P_{EVEN}(0), \\
& P_{NAT}(x) \rightarrow P_{NAT}(s(x)), \\
& P_{ODD}(x) \rightarrow P_{EVEN}(s(x)), \\
& P_{EVEN}(x) \rightarrow P_{ODD}(s(x))\}.
\end{aligned}
$$

2. In Example 9.1.1, the first, unsorted formulation of Schubert's Steamroller is the relativization of the sorted formulation.

Let Σ be a sorted signature, and let $\mathcal{I} = \langle \mathcal{M}, \beta \rangle$ be an interpretation over Σ^*. Identifying an (unsorted) signature with the set of ground atoms it satisfies as discussed immediately preceding Lemma 7.4.2, we call $\mathcal{I}$ a $\mathcal{D}$-*minimal model* of $\overline{S_{\mathcal{D}}}$ if $\mathcal{I}$ is a model for $\overline{S_{\mathcal{D}}}$ such that $\mathcal{I} - \{P_S(t)\} \not\models \overline{S_{\mathcal{D}}}$ holds for all ground atoms $P_S(t) \in \mathcal{I}$. Remembering further that we have agreed to identify sorted objects (terms, clauses, etc.) and their unsorted counterparts unless doing so will lead to confusion, we show that, in every minimal model $\mathcal{I}$ of $\overline{S_{\mathcal{D}}}$, the clause sets $\overline{S}$ and $\overline{S^*}$ are satisfiability-equivalent, i.e., that $\mathcal{I} \models \overline{S}$ iff $\mathcal{I} \models \overline{S^*}$. From this fact we will be able to conclude that S is Σ-satisfiable iff S_{rel} is satisfiable (see Theorem 9.3.1). This last observation will justify our use of sorts to improve efficiency in resolution deductions: not every term over Σ^* is a Σ-term, S is typically a smaller set of axioms than is S_{rel}, and the deduction of sort information, which is performed explicitly in unsorted calculi, is built into the inference mechanism for sorted calculi. We may therefore expect that many useless resolution and factorization steps which are present in unsorted deduction can be avoided completely by passing to the sorted setting.

The next lemma guarantees that if S_{rel} is a relativization of S with respect to Σ, then $\overline{S_{\mathcal{D}}}$ captures precisely the sort information present in the declarations of Σ.

Lemma 9.3.1   *Let $\Sigma = \langle \mathcal{S}, \mathcal{F}, \mathcal{P}, \mathcal{D} \rangle$, let $S \in \mathcal{S}$, and let $t \in \mathcal{T}_\Sigma(\mathcal{F})$ be a ground Σ-term.*

1. *If $\mathcal{I}$ is a model for $\overline{S_{\mathcal{D}}}$, then $t \in \mathcal{T}_S(\mathcal{F})$ implies $P_S(t) \in \mathcal{I}$. If $\mathcal{I}$ is a $\mathcal{D}$-minimal model for $\overline{S_{\mathcal{D}}}$, then the converse holds as well.*

2. *The relation $t \in \mathcal{T}_S(\mathcal{F})$ holds iff $\overline{S_{\mathcal{D}}} \models \rightarrow P_S(t)$.*

Proof. 1. The proof is by induction on the ordering which is the lexicographic combination of the subterm ordering on $\mathcal{T}_\Sigma(\mathcal{F})$ and the induced ordering $\leq_\Sigma$ on $\mathcal{S}$. Let $\mathcal{I} \models \overline{S_{\mathcal{D}}}$ and suppose first that $t \in \mathcal{T}_S(\mathcal{F})$ be a ground Σ-term of the form $f t_1 \ldots t_n$, where $f \in \mathcal{F}_n$,

$f : S_1 \times \ldots \times S_n \to S \in \mathcal{D}$ and t_i is a ground Σ-term in $\mathcal{T}_{S_i}(\mathcal{F})$ for $i = 1, \ldots, n$ (note that $n = 0$ is possible here). Then by the induction hypothesis we may assume that $P_{S_i}(t_i) \in \mathcal{I}$ for $i = 1, \ldots, n$. Since

$$P_{S_1}(x_1), \ldots, P_{S_n}(x_n) \to P_S(f(x_1, \ldots, x_n)) \in S_{\mathcal{D}},$$

we must have that $\mathcal{I}$ satisfies the ground Σ-instance $P_{S_1}(t_1), \ldots, P_{S_n}(t_n) \to P_S(ft_1 \ldots t_n)$ in $\overline{S_{\mathcal{D}}}$. It follows immediately that $P_S(ft_1, \ldots, t_n) \in \mathcal{I}$.

If t is a ground Σ-term of sort S' with $S' \sqsubset S \in \mathcal{D}$, then by the induction hypothesis, $P_{S'}(t) \in \mathcal{I}$. Moreover, since $S_{\mathcal{D}}$ contains the clause $P_{S'}(x) \to P_S(x)$, the clause $P_{S'}(t) \to P_S(t)$ must be an element of $\overline{S_{\mathcal{D}}}$ and so $\mathcal{I} \models P_{S'}(t) \to P_S(t)$. That $P_S(t) \in \mathcal{I}$ follows.

Conversely, let $\mathcal{I}$ be a $\mathcal{D}$-minimal model of $\overline{S_{\mathcal{D}}}$ and let $P_S(t) \in \mathcal{I}$. Then by the minimality of $\mathcal{I}$ there is a clause $C \in \overline{S_{\mathcal{D}}}$ such that $\mathcal{I} - \{P_S(t)\} \not\models C$, i.e., there is a ground clause $C = \Phi \to \Psi$ such that $\Phi \subseteq \mathcal{I} - \{P_S(t)\}$ and $\Psi \cap (\mathcal{I} - \{P_S(t)\}) = \emptyset$. But then $\Phi \subseteq \mathcal{I} - \{P_S(t)\}$ implies that $P_S(t) \notin \Phi$, and thus since $\mathcal{I} \models C$ it must be the case that $P_S(t) \in \Psi$. Because of the way $S_{\mathcal{D}}$ is constructed, we must have either

$$C = P_{S_1}(t_1), \ldots, P_{S_n}(t_n) \to P_S(t)$$

with $t = ft_1 \ldots t_n$ for ground terms $t_1, \ldots, t_n$ (where $n = 0$ is possible) or

$$C = P_{S'}(t) \to P_S(t).$$

If the former holds, then there must be a declaration $f : S_1 \times \ldots \times S_n \to S$ in $\mathcal{D}$. Then since $P_{S_i}(t_i) \in \mathcal{I}$ holds for $i = 1, \ldots, n$, it follows from the induction hypothesis that $t_i \in \mathcal{T}_{S_i}(\mathcal{F})$ for $i = 1, \ldots, n$, and thus $t \in \mathcal{T}_S(\mathcal{F})$.

If, on the other hand, the latter holds, then there is a declaration $S' \sqsubset S$ in $\mathcal{D}$. In addition, $P_{S'}(t) \in \mathcal{I}$ holds, and so by the induction hypothesis it follows that $t \in \mathcal{T}_{S'}(\mathcal{F})$. Thus in this case $t \in \mathcal{T}_S(\mathcal{F})$ holds as well.

2. Follows immediately from the first part of the lemma. $\square$

Lemma 9.3.2 *Let $\Sigma = \langle \mathcal{S}, \mathcal{F}, \mathcal{P}, \mathcal{D} \rangle$ and let $\mathcal{I}$ be any model of $\overline{S_{\mathcal{D}}}$. If S is any set of Σ-clauses, then $\mathcal{I} \models \overline{S^*}$ implies $\mathcal{I} \models \overline{S}$. If $\mathcal{I}$ is a $\mathcal{D}$-minimal model of $\overline{S_{\mathcal{D}}}$, then $\mathcal{I} \models \overline{S}$ implies $\mathcal{I} \models \overline{S^*}$ is as well.*

Proof. Suppose $\mathcal{I} \models \overline{S^*}$, let $C = \Phi \to \Psi$ be any clause in S, and let $\sigma(C)$ be any ground Σ-instance of C. Consider the ground instance

$$\sigma(C^*) = P_{S_1}(\sigma(x_1)), \ldots, P_{S_n}(\sigma(x_n)), \sigma(\Phi) \to \sigma(\Psi)$$

of C^*. By hypothesis, $\mathcal{I} \models \sigma(C^*)$. Since σ is a Σ-substitution and $x_i \in \mathcal{V}_{S_i}$ for $i = 1, \ldots, n$, we have $\sigma(x_i) \in \mathcal{T}_{S_i}(\mathcal{F})$ for $i = 1, \ldots, n$. By the previous lemma, $P_{S_i}(\sigma(x_i)) \in \mathcal{I}$ must hold for $i = 1, \ldots, n$. Thus $\mathcal{I} \models \sigma(C)$. Since C and σ were arbitrary, $\mathcal{I} \models \overline{S}$.

Conversely, suppose $\mathcal{I}$ is a $\mathcal{D}$-minimal model of $\overline{S_\mathcal{D}}$ and suppose $\mathcal{I} \models \overline{S}$. Then every clause in $\overline{S^*}$ is a ground instance of a clause C^* for some clause $C \in S$. Let

$$\sigma(C^*) = P_{S_1}(\sigma(x_1)), \ldots, P_{S_n}(\sigma(x_n)), \sigma(\Phi) \to \sigma(\Psi)$$

be any clause in $\overline{S^*}$, where $C = \Phi \to \Psi \in S$. If there is some $i \in \{1, \ldots, n\}$ such that $P_{S_i}(\sigma(x_i)) \notin \mathcal{I}$, then $\mathcal{I} \models \sigma(C^*)$ trivially. If, on the other hand, $P_{S_i}(\sigma(x_i)) \in \mathcal{I}$ for $i = 1, \ldots, n$, then since $\mathcal{I}$ is a $\mathcal{D}$-minimal model of $\overline{S_\mathcal{D}}$, the previous lemma implies that $\sigma(x_i) \in \mathcal{T}_{S_i}(\mathcal{F})$ for $i = 1, \ldots, n$. This guarantees that σ is actually a Σ-substitution, and so $\sigma(C) = \sigma(\Phi) \to \sigma(\Psi)$ is a ground Σ-instance of C. By hypothesis, $\mathcal{I} \models \sigma(C)$, and so $\mathcal{I} \models \sigma(C^*)$ by construction of C^*. Since $\sigma(C^*)$ was arbitrary, $\mathcal{I} \models \overline{S^*}$. $\square$

Theorem 9.3.1 *Let $\Sigma = \langle \mathcal{S}, \mathcal{F}, \mathcal{P}, \mathcal{D} \rangle$ and let S be any set of Σ-clauses. Then S is Σ-satisfiable iff S_{rel} is.*

Proof. If $S_{rel} = S^* \cup S_\mathcal{D}$ is satisfiable, then so is S^*. By Herbrand's Theorem, $\overline{S^*}$ is satisfiable, and so by the previous lemma, $\overline{S}$ is satisfiable as well. Again by Herbrand's Theorem, S is therefore satisfiable.

Conversely, suppose S is satisfiable. Then by Herbrand's Theorem $\overline{S}$ is satisfiable. Now, every model of $\overline{S}$ can be extended to a $\mathcal{D}$-minimal model of $\overline{S_\mathcal{D}}$, since the clause sets $\overline{S}$ and $\overline{S_\mathcal{D}}$ have no ground atoms in common (the predicate symbols P_S do not appear in the signature of Σ). Suppose $\mathcal{I} \models \overline{S} \cup \overline{S_\mathcal{D}}$ for some such $\mathcal{D}$-minimal model of $\overline{S_\mathcal{D}}$. Then $\mathcal{I} \models \overline{S}$, and so by the previous lemma, $\mathcal{I} \models \overline{S^*}$. Thus $\mathcal{I} \models \overline{S^*} \cup \overline{S_\mathcal{D}}$, so that $\mathcal{I} \models \overline{S^* \cup S_\mathcal{D}}$, and therefore $\mathcal{I} \models \overline{S_{rel}}$. By Herbrand's Theorem, S_{rel} is also satisfiable. $\square$

9.4 Sorted Logic with Term Declarations

Consider Example 9.2.1 once more and suppose that we are interested only in terms of sort $EVEN$, since terms of the sort ODD do not appear in the application of this signature that we have in mind. Suppose we want to capitalize even further on the fact that a smaller signature will mean a more efficient deduction calculus, and so we want to find the sorted signature with the smallest possible number of sorts which is adequate for our purposes. It is easy to see that there exists no signature comprising only sorts $EVEN$ and NAT with the sort $EVEN$ describing precisely the same ground terms as does the signature in Example 9.2.1. Nevertheless, there is a natural way to extend the declaration part of a signature to obtain a signature minimal in this way by introducing into the signature *term declarations*, i.e., by assigning terms of certain specified syntactic shapes to have particular sorts. In self-explanatory notation, we could define a sort *EVEN* by

$$EVEN \sqsubset NAT \qquad s : NAT \rightarrow NAT$$
$$0 : EVEN \qquad s(s(x_{EVEN})) : EVEN$$

We see, then, that this sort *EVEN* in fact describes exactly the same ground terms $0, s(s(0)), s(s(s(s(0)))), \ldots$ as does its counterpart in Example 9.2.1.

To provide a uniform presentation of subsort declarations, function declarations, and term declarations, we may consider function declarations as "extended" subsort declarations, with the arguments to the function symbols taken to be terms built over the function symbols of the given signature together with its sorts, rather than over the function symbols and sorted variables. For the above example this would give

$$EVEN \sqsubset NAT \qquad s(NAT) \sqsubset NAT$$
$$0 \sqsubset EVEN \qquad s(s(EVEN)) \sqsubset EVEN$$

If we let $\mathcal{T}_\Sigma(\mathcal{F}, \mathcal{S})$ be the set of terms over function symbols and sorts (defined by analogy with Definition 3.1.2), then we may think of a term $\tau \in \mathcal{T}_\Sigma(\mathcal{F}, \mathcal{S})$ as describing a pattern or template which any given Σ-term may or may not fit. We have

Definition 9.4.1

1. A *term declaration for a sorted first-order signature* Σ is an ordered pair $\langle \tau, T \rangle$ with $\tau \neq T$, $T \in \mathcal{S}$, and $\tau \in \mathcal{T}_\Sigma(\mathcal{F}, \mathcal{S})$, written $\tau \sqsubset T$. The term τ is called a *sort term*.

2. A *signature for a sorted first-order language with term declarations*, or a *sorted signature with term declarations*, is an ordered quadruple $\Sigma = \langle \mathcal{S}, \mathcal{F}, \mathcal{P}, \mathcal{D} \rangle$ as in Definition 9.2.2, except that here $\mathcal{D}$ is a finite set of term declarations.

It is clear that the subsort declarations from Section 9.2 can be viewed as term declarations of a particular form. Identifying $f : S_1 \times \ldots \times S_n \rightarrow S$ with $f(S_1, \ldots, S_n) \sqsubset S$, as suggested above, function declarations can also be viewed as special cases of term declarations as defined here. We call a signature with term declarations *elementary* if each of its declarations is elementary, i.e., if each of its declarations is either of the form $T \sqsubset S$ or of the form $f(S_1, \ldots, S_n) \sqsubset S$, where $S_1, \ldots, S_n, S, T \in \mathcal{S}$.

The notion of a Σ-term of sort S is modified for sorted signatures with term declarations as follows:

Definition 9.4.2   Let $\Sigma = \langle \mathcal{S}, \mathcal{F}, \mathcal{P}, \mathcal{D} \rangle$ be a signature for a sorted first-order language with term declarations and let $S \in \mathcal{S}$. A word t over $\mathcal{F} \cup \mathcal{V}$ is a Σ-*term of sort* S provided either

- t is a variable of sort S, or

- t is a Σ-term of sort τ with $\tau \sqsubset S$ a subsort or function declaration in $\mathcal{D}$, where a word $t = f t_1 \ldots t_n$ over $\mathcal{F} \cup \mathcal{V}$ is a Σ-*term of sort* τ $\in \mathcal{T}_\Sigma(\mathcal{F}, \mathcal{S})$ if $\tau = f \tau_1 \ldots \tau_n$ and t_i is a Σ-term of sort τ_i for $i = 1, \ldots, n$ ($n = 0$ is possible).

Example 9.4.1   For the sorted signature Σ of Example 9.2.1 (with term declarations, rather than subsort and function declarations), 0 is a Σ-term of sort $EVEN$, and is also a Σ-term of sort NAT. The former is because 0 is a Σ-term of sort $\tau = 0$, which implies that it is of sort $EVEN$, and the latter is because $EVEN \sqsubset NAT$ is a declaration in Σ.

This definition says that a Σ-term is of sort S if it is either a variable of sort S or else is described by the pattern, or template, specified by some term declaration in $\mathcal{D}$; it goes on to prescribe what it means for the term to be described by such a pattern.

In the following we use the abbreviation $[\tau]_\Sigma$ for the set of Σ-terms of sort $\tau \in \mathcal{T}_\Sigma(\mathcal{F}, \mathcal{S})$. We also write $\| \tau \|_\Sigma$ for the set of ground Σ-terms of sort $\tau \in \mathcal{T}_\Sigma(\mathcal{F}, \mathcal{S})$. Moreover, if M_i, $i = 1, \ldots, n$, are any sets of Σ-terms, we denote by $f(M_1, \ldots, M_n)$ the set $\{ f(m_1, \ldots, m_n) \mid m_i \in M_i, i = 1, \ldots, n \}$. Then

$$[f \tau_1 \ldots \tau_n]_\Sigma = f([\tau_1]_\Sigma, \ldots, [\tau_n]_\Sigma).$$

That is, the sorts of Σ-terms are determined by the sorts of the outermost symbols of the terms. With this notation we have

$$[S]_\Sigma = \mathcal{V}_S \cup \bigcup_{\tau \sqsubset S \in \mathcal{D}} [\tau]_\Sigma$$

and we also have the identity

$$\| S \|_\Sigma = \bigcup_{\tau \sqsubset S \in \mathcal{D}} \| \tau \|_\Sigma .$$

Example 9.4.2   Consider the sorted signature $\Sigma = \langle \{A\}, \{f, g\}, \emptyset, \mathcal{D} \rangle$, where $\mathcal{D}$ comprises the declarations $a \sqsubset A$ and $f(A, g(A)) \sqsubset A$. Then $\| A \|_\Sigma$ is the set

$$\{ a, f(a, g(a)), f(f(a, g(a)), g(a)), f(a, g(f(a, g(a)))), f(f(a, g(a)), \ldots) \}.$$

It is clear that an elementary signature with term declarations can be transformed into an equivalent sorted signature without term declarations:

every declaration of the form $f(S_1, \ldots, S_n) \sqsubset S$ is transformed into the function declaration $f : S_1 \times \ldots \times S_n \to S$. In the following we will show that term declarations do not engender any essential increase in the expressiveness of a calculus. That is, it is possible to transform any signature Σ with term declarations, elementary or not, into a signature Σ' without term declarations which extends Σ in a sense to be made precise in the next definition. We see below that this transformation is *conservative* in the sense that if Σ' extends Σ and if t is a ground Σ-term of sort S, then t is also a ground Σ'-term of sort S and vice-versa; that is, the transformation leaves the set of ground Σ-terms unchanged. The idea behind this transformation is to inductively assign to each immediate subterm τ_i in a term declaration of the form $f(\tau_1, \ldots, \tau_n) \sqsubset S$ a new sort T_i and then to replace the original term declaration with $f : T_1 \times \ldots \times T_n \to S$.

Definition 9.4.3   1. Let $\Sigma = \langle \mathcal{S}, \mathcal{F}, \mathcal{P}, \mathcal{D} \rangle$ be a sorted signature with term declarations. A signature $\Sigma' = \langle \mathcal{S}', \mathcal{F}', \mathcal{P}', \mathcal{D}' \rangle$ is an *extension* of Σ provided $\mathcal{S} \subseteq \mathcal{S}'$, $\mathcal{F} \subseteq \mathcal{F}'$, $\mathcal{P} \subseteq \mathcal{P}'$, and $\mathcal{D} \subseteq \mathcal{D}'$ hold.

2. The inference system $\mathcal{F}$ for signatures comprises the following rule:

$$\frac{\langle \mathcal{S}, \mathcal{F}, \mathcal{P}, \mathcal{D} \cup \{f(\tau_1, \ldots, \tau_n) \sqsubset S\} \rangle}{\langle \mathcal{S} \cup \{T_i \mid i = 1, \ldots, n\}, \mathcal{F}, \mathcal{P}, \mathcal{D} \cup \{fT_1 \ldots T_n \sqsubset S\} \cup \mathcal{D}' \rangle}$$

where $f(\tau_1, \ldots, \tau_n) \sqsubset S$ is not elementary, $T_i = \tau_i$ if $\tau_i \in \mathcal{S}$ and T_i is a symbol not occurring in $\mathcal{S} \cup \mathcal{F} \cup \mathcal{P}$ otherwise, and $\mathcal{D}' = \{\tau_i \sqsubset T_i \mid i = 1, \ldots, n, \text{ and } \tau_i \notin \mathcal{S}\}$.

We then write $\Sigma \Rightarrow_{\mathcal{F}} \Sigma'$ if Σ goes to Σ' by an application of the above rule. The relation $\Rightarrow_{\mathcal{F}}^*$ is the transitive closure of $\Rightarrow_{\mathcal{F}}$. With the relation $\Rightarrow_{\mathcal{F}}$ on the set of signatures we have defined a transformation which "flattens" term declarations by extending signatures.

Example 9.4.3   Let $\Sigma = \langle \mathcal{S}, \mathcal{F}, \mathcal{P}, \mathcal{D} \rangle$, where $\mathcal{S} = \{EVEN, NAT\}$, $\mathcal{F} = \{0, s\}$, $\mathcal{P} = \emptyset$, and $\mathcal{D} = \{EVEN \sqsubset NAT, 0 \sqsubset EVEN, s(NAT) \sqsubset NAT, s(s(EVEN)) \sqsubset EVEN\}$, and let $\Sigma' = \langle \mathcal{S}', \mathcal{F}, \mathcal{P}, \mathcal{D}' \rangle$ where $\mathcal{S}' = \mathcal{S} \cup \{T\}$ and $\mathcal{D} = \{EVEN \sqsubset NAT, 0 \sqsubset EVEN, s(NAT) \sqsubset NAT, s(T) \sqsubset EVEN, s(EVEN) \sqsubset T\}$. Then $\Sigma \Rightarrow_{\mathcal{F}} \Sigma'$.

That the relation $\Rightarrow_{\mathcal{F}}$ is conservative follows directly from the next lemma.

Lemma 9.4.1   *Let $\Sigma = \langle \mathcal{S}, \mathcal{F}, \mathcal{P}, \mathcal{D} \rangle$ and $\Sigma' = \langle \mathcal{S}', \mathcal{F}, \mathcal{P}, \mathcal{D}' \rangle$ be sorted signatures with term declarations such that $\Sigma \Rightarrow_{\mathcal{F}} \Sigma'$. Then for all $\tau \in \mathcal{T}_\Sigma(\mathcal{F}, \mathcal{S})$, $\|\tau\|_\Sigma = \|\tau\|_{\Sigma'}$.*

Proof. We show that for all ground terms $t \in \mathcal{T}_\Sigma(\mathcal{F})$ and all $\tau \in \mathcal{T}_\Sigma(\mathcal{F}, \mathcal{S})$, $t \in \|\tau\|_\Sigma$ iff $t \in \|\tau\|_{\Sigma'}$. Define a well-founded ordering $\succ$ on pairs $\langle t, \tau \rangle$ of terms t and sort terms τ by $\langle t, \tau \rangle \succ \langle t', \tau' \rangle$ iff t' is a proper subterm of t, or else $t = t'$ and $|\tau| > |\tau'|$. The proof proceeds by induction on $\succ$.

First note that since $\Sigma \Rightarrow_{\mathcal{F}} \Sigma'$, there must exist a nonelementary declaration $f\tau_1 \ldots \tau_n \sqsubset S \in \mathcal{D}$, and so $T_i \neq \tau_i$ for at least one $i \in \{1, \ldots, n\}$, and

$$
\begin{aligned}
\mathcal{S}' &= \mathcal{S} \cup \{T_i \mid i = 1, \ldots, n\} \text{ and} \\
\mathcal{D}' &= \mathcal{D} - \{f\tau_1 \ldots \tau_n \sqsubset S\} \\
&\quad \cup \{fT_1 \ldots T_n \sqsubset S\} \\
&\quad \cup \{\tau_i \sqsubset T_i \mid i = 1, \ldots, n, \text{ and } \tau_i \notin \mathcal{S}\}.
\end{aligned}
$$

We consider cases according as $\tau \in \mathcal{S}$ or not, and in case $\tau \in \mathcal{S}$, subcases according as $\tau = S$ or not.

- Suppose $\tau \in \mathcal{S}$ but $\tau \neq S$, and suppose $t \in \| \tau \|_{\Sigma}$. Then t is not a variable, and so must be of the form $gt_1 \ldots t_k$. Then by Definition 9.4.2, $t \in \| \tau \|_{\Sigma}$ iff there exists a sort σ such that $\sigma \sqsubset \tau \in \mathcal{D}$ and t is a Σ-term of sort σ, i.e., $t \in \| \sigma \|_{\Sigma}$. But this happens iff $\sigma = g\sigma_1 \ldots \sigma_k$ where $\sigma_i \in \mathcal{T}_{\Sigma}(\mathcal{F}, \mathcal{S})$ for $i = 1, \ldots, k$ and $t_i \in \| \sigma_i \|_{\Sigma}$ for $i = 1, \ldots, k$. By the induction hypothesis, $t_i \in \| \sigma_i \|_{\Sigma'}$ for $i = 1, \ldots, k$, and so $\sigma = g\sigma_1 \ldots \sigma_k$ and $t_i = \| \sigma_i \|_{\Sigma}$ for $i = 1, \ldots, k$ iff $\sigma = g\sigma_1 \ldots \sigma_k$ and $t_i = \| \sigma_i \|_{\Sigma'}$ for $i = 1, \ldots, k$. From the construction of Σ', and since $\tau \neq S$, it follows that $\sigma \sqsubset \tau \in \mathcal{D}$ iff $\sigma \sqsubset \tau \in \mathcal{D}'$. Thus we have $t \in \| \tau \|_{\Sigma}$ iff there is a sort σ such that $\sigma \sqsubset \tau \in \mathcal{D}'$, $\sigma = g\sigma_1 \ldots \sigma_k$, and $t_i \in \| \sigma_i \|_{\Sigma'}$ for $i = 1, \ldots, k$. That is, $t \in \| \tau \|_{\Sigma}$ iff $t \in \| \tau \|_{\Sigma'}$.

- If $\tau \in \mathcal{S}$ and $\tau = S$, then $t \in \| \tau \|_{\Sigma}$ iff there exists $\sigma \sqsubset S \in \mathcal{D}$ such that $t \in \| \sigma \|_{\Sigma}$. Now if $\sigma \neq f\tau_1 \ldots \tau_n$, then the entire proof is as in the previous case. So we may assume henceforth that the only such σ is $\sigma = f\tau_1 \ldots \tau_n$. We now show that $t \in \| f\tau_1 \ldots \tau_n \|_{\Sigma}$ iff $t \in \| fT_1 \ldots T_n \|'_{\Sigma}$. This will easily prove the assertion of the lemma.

  First, we note that by the induction hypothesis, $\| \tau_i \|_{\Sigma} = \| \tau_i \|_{\Sigma'}$ for $i = 1, \ldots, n$. Second, by the definition of $\mathcal{D}'$ then for $i = 1, \ldots, n$ either $\tau_i = T_i$ or else $\tau_i \sqsubset T_i \in \mathcal{D}'$, and thus $t_i \in \| \tau_i \|_{\Sigma'}$ implies $t_i \in \| T_i \|_{\Sigma'}$. Conversely, if $t_i \in \| T_i \|_{\Sigma'}$ then $t_i \in \| \tau_i \|_{\Sigma'}$ since either $\tau_i = T_i$, or else $\tau_i \sqsubset T_i$ is the only declaration for T_i in $\mathcal{D}'$. This establishes that $\| \tau_i \|_{\Sigma'} = \| T_i \|_{\Sigma'}$ for $i = 1, \ldots, n$. We therefore have $\| f\tau_1 \ldots \tau_n \|_{\Sigma} = \| fT_1 \ldots T_n \|'_{\Sigma}$, as desired.

- Suppose $\tau \notin \mathcal{S}$. Then $\tau = g\tau_1 \ldots \tau_k$ for some $g \in \mathcal{F}_k$ and $\tau_i \in \mathcal{T}_{\Sigma}(\mathcal{F}, \mathcal{S})$. Then by Definition 9.4.2, $t \in \| \tau \|_{\Sigma}$ iff $t = gt_1 \ldots t_k$ and $t_i \in \| \tau_i \|_{\Sigma}$ for $i = 1, \ldots, k$. By the induction hypothesis, $t_i \in \| \tau_i \|_{\Sigma}$ iff $t_i \in \| \tau_i \|_{\Sigma'}$, and so it follows that $t \in \| \tau \|_{\Sigma}$ iff $t \in \| \tau \|_{\Sigma'}$. $\square$

Corollary 9.4.1   *If $\Sigma \Rightarrow_{\mathcal{F}} \Sigma'$, then $\mathcal{I}$ is a Σ-interpretation iff it is a Σ'-interpretation.*

Lemma 9.4.2   *The relation $\Rightarrow_{\mathcal{F}}$ is noetherian.*

Proof. We must show that there exist no infinite sequences of signatures of the form $\Sigma_0 \Rightarrow_{\mathcal{F}} \Sigma_1 \Rightarrow_{\mathcal{F}} \ldots$. We construct a termination function μ as follows: let $>_{mul}$ be the multiset extension of the usual greater-than ordering on the set of natural numbers. Then for each signature $\Sigma = \langle \mathcal{S}, \mathcal{F}, \mathcal{P}, \mathcal{D} \rangle$, define the multiset $\mu(\Sigma)$ of natural numbers to be

$$\mu(\Sigma) = \{|\tau| \mid \tau \sqsubset S \in \mathcal{D}, \tau \sqsubset S \text{ not elementary}\}.$$

We show that if $\Sigma \Rightarrow_{\mathcal{F}} \Sigma'$, then $\mu(\Sigma) >_{mul} \mu(\Sigma')$. Let $\Sigma' = \langle \mathcal{S}', \mathcal{F}, \mathcal{P}, \mathcal{D}' \rangle$ be as in the second part of Definition 9.4.3. Then at least one of $\tau_i \notin \mathcal{S}$ and therefore $|f\tau_1 \ldots \tau_n| > |fT_1 \ldots T_n|$. Since in addition, $|f(\tau_1, \ldots, \tau_n)| > |\tau_i|$ for $i = 1, \ldots, n$, it follows directly that $\mu(\Sigma) >_{mul} \mu(\Sigma')$. Since the ordering $>_{mul}$ is noetherian, the conclusion of the lemma is immediate. $\square$

Finally, it is clear from Part 2 of Definition 9.4.3 that a signature Σ is irreducible with respect to $\Rightarrow_{\mathcal{F}}$ precisely when it is elementary. The first part of the next theorem follows from this observation and Lemma 9.4.1; the sorted version of Herbrand's Theorem alluded to at the end of Section 9.2 guarantees that the second part of the next theorem is a consequence of the first and Corollary 9.4.1.

Theorem 9.4.1
1. *If Σ is a sorted signature with term declarations, then there is an elementary signature Σ' such that $\| \tau \|_{\Sigma} = \| \tau \|_{\Sigma'}$ holds for all $\tau \in \mathcal{T}_{\Sigma}(\mathcal{F}, \mathcal{S})$.*

2. *If S is a set of Σ-clauses, then S is Σ-satisfiable iff S is Σ'-satisfiable.*

In light of Theorem 9.4.1 we may restrict our attention to signatures without arbitrary term declarations in the following, i.e., we may restrict attention to elementary signatures. In the next section we consider resolution, and therefore unification, in such signatures. As in Chapter 8 we interpret sorted unification as a process for solving constraints.

9.5   Unification and Resolution in Sorted Signatures

From Section 9.3 we know that a sorted satisfaction problem is satisfiability-equivalent to its unsorted version, i.e., we know that a set of Σ-clauses is Σ-satisfiable iff the corresponding set of unsorted clauses comprising its unsorted formulation is satisfiable. This result suggests that unsorted satisfaction problems may be solved more efficiently by passing to sorted logics and solving corresponding satisfaction problems there. Moreover, from Section 9.4 we know that we can always restrict attention to sets of clauses built over elementary signatures when solving sorted satisfaction problems. In this section we therefore investigate resolution of sets of Σ-clauses over elementary sorted signatures Σ for sorted first-order languages, and thereby treat the more general issue of solving satisfaction problems in arbitrary signatures. Throughout the remainder of this section, Σ denotes an elementary sorted signature.

Recall from Section 8.1 that only unifiability of atoms—rather than computation of their explicit unifiers—is required to determine applicability of a resolution or factorization rule. This fact, together with the observation that constraints more liberal than just the simple equational ones imposed by the requirements of syntactic unification need to be solved in the sorted setting, forms the basis for a resolution calculus $\mathcal{R}\Sigma$ for Σ-clauses. In this section we focus on a method for solving such constraints, i.e., for performing unification in a sorted setting. We then briefly describe the calculus $\mathcal{R}\Sigma$ and indicate its completeness.

We begin with

Definition 9.5.1   Let Σ be a sorted signature. An *equational constraint over* Σ, or simply an *equation over* Σ, is an ordered pair $\langle s, t \rangle$ of Σ-terms, usually written in the form $s \approx t$. A *system of equations over* Σ, or simply a *system over* Σ, is a set of equations over Σ. The Σ-substitution σ Σ-*unifies* the equation $s \approx t$ if it unifies the Σ-terms s and t, i.e., if $\sigma(s) = \sigma(t)$. If σ Σ-*unifies* $s \approx t$ then we say that σ is a Σ-*unifier* of $s \approx t$. The substitution σ Σ-*unifies* a system E of equations over Σ if it simultaneously unifies every equation in E. We denote the set of Σ-unifiers of the system E over Σ by $u_\Sigma(E)$.

As usual, we suppress reference to Σ when this will not cause confusion.

Unification in sorted signatures is thus necessarily more restrictive than in unsorted signatures, both because the terms to be unified, as well as those with which variables can be instantiated, are required to be well-sorted. It is precisely because of these restrictions that we may expect solving sorted formulations of resolution problems to be more efficient than solving their unsorted formulations. But the introduction of sorts into deduction calculi also gives rise to some differences unrelated to efficiency concerns between sorted resolution and its unsorted counterpart. Earlier, for example, when discussing resolution in the context of unsorted signatures, we assumed the existence of at least one constant symbol in each signature in order to guarantee that the set of ground terms over that signature would be nonempty. For sorted signatures it might seem prudent to similarly require, for each sort $S \in \mathcal{S}$, the existence of a constant $a_S \in \mathcal{T}_S(\mathcal{F})$. Such a requirement is of course possible (and indeed is often made in the literature), but it is unnecessarily restrictive. In the following we will renounce such a restriction and so permit in our signatures sorts S such that $\mathcal{T}_S(\mathcal{F}) = \emptyset$. This gives rise to the following seemingly paradoxical situation:

Example 9.5.1 Let $\Sigma = \langle \mathcal{S}, \mathcal{F}, \mathcal{P}, \mathcal{D} \rangle$ with $\mathcal{S} = \{S\}$, $\mathcal{F} = \emptyset$, $\mathcal{P} = \{P\}$, and $\mathcal{D} = \emptyset$. The clause set

$$M = \{\rightarrow P(x_S), \ P(y_S) \rightarrow\}$$

is Σ-satisfiable since there are no ground Σ-terms of sort S. This situation emerges as less bizarre once we consider the relativization

$$M_{rel} = \{P_S(x) \rightarrow P(x), \ P_S(y), P(y) \rightarrow\},$$

which is clearly satisfiable.

A further difference between standard unification and sorted unification which does bear directly on the efficiency of resolution algorithms which are based on them lies in the frequent existence of more than one—and, often, infinitely many—most general unifiers for a given pair of Σ-terms.

Example 9.5.2 Let $\Sigma = \langle \mathcal{S}, \mathcal{F}, \mathcal{P}, \mathcal{D} \rangle$ with $\mathcal{S} = \{S, T\}$, $\mathcal{F} = \{a, f\}$, $\mathcal{P} = \emptyset$, and declarations $a : S$, $a : T$, $f : S \rightarrow S$, and $f : T \rightarrow T$. The system $\{x_S \approx y_T\}$ over Σ has infinitely many Σ-unifiers, namely,

$$\begin{aligned}
\sigma_0 &= \{x_S \leftarrow a, y_T \leftarrow a\}, \\
\sigma_1 &= \{x_S \leftarrow f(a), y_T \leftarrow f(a)\}, \\
\sigma_2 &= \{x_S \leftarrow f(f(a)), y_T \leftarrow f(f(a))\}, \dots
\end{aligned}$$

Moreover, each σ_i is a most general Σ-unifier of x_S and y_T. On the other hand, the simplest solution candidate, namely, $\sigma = \{x_S \leftarrow y_T\}$, is not a Σ-substitution at all.

Although the attempt to unify a system involving two variables of unrelated sorts may seem contrary to our intuition that unrelated sorts denote disjoint classes of objects, such a problem might arise, for example, in unifying the system

$$E(x_B, y_C) \approx E(x_A, z_G),$$

which can be distilled from the Steamroller problem.

The existence of infinitely many most general unifiers of a system is, of course, extremely disagreeable if one is required to produce all of them. Various classifications of signatures have been proposed with the purpose of differentiating signatures in which systems are well-behaved with respect to unification from those in which they are not. One such classification scheme makes use of so-called *regularity* of signatures (see [SS89]). On the other hand, newer approaches to deduction in sorted settings (see [CD91], [Sti86], and certain analogies in [SS89]) eschew such classifications. The difference between establishing the existence of a unifier of a system and actually producing all substitutions which unify that system becomes even more critical in the sorted setting than in unsorted calculi: fortunately, the fact that there may be infinitely many unifiers of a given system is irrelevant for our purposes, since we are not required to compute all of its possibly infinitely many unifiers, but instead need only to determine whether or not the system is unifiable.

In finding unifiers for systems of equations arising in deduction in a sorted setting, it will be convenient to have the following notions at our disposal.

Definition 9.5.2   Let $\Sigma = \langle \mathcal{S}, \mathcal{F}, \mathcal{P}, \mathcal{D} \rangle$. A *generalized sort over* Σ is a nonempty set $\Phi \subseteq \mathcal{S}$ of pairwise incomparable (with respect to $\leq_\Sigma$) sort symbols. We identify the generalized sort $\{S\}$, for $S \in \mathcal{S}$, with the sort S. If Φ and Φ' are generalized sorts over Σ, we define $\Phi \sqcap \Phi'$ to be the set of $\leq_\Sigma$-minimal elements of $\Phi \cup \Phi'$. If $\Phi = \{S_1, \ldots, S_n\}$, then we can write Φ in the form $S_1 \sqcap \ldots \sqcap S_n$.

By way of contrast with generalized sorts over Σ, in the following we will call (singleton) sorts $S \in \mathcal{S}$ the *base sorts* of Σ.

Definition 9.5.3   A *generalized signature over* $\Sigma = \langle \mathcal{S}, \mathcal{F}, \mathcal{P}, \mathcal{D} \rangle$ is a signature $\Sigma' = \langle \mathcal{S}', \mathcal{F}, \mathcal{P}, \mathcal{D}' \rangle$, where $\mathcal{D} \subseteq \mathcal{D}'$, $\mathcal{S}' = \mathcal{S} \cup \mathcal{S}''$ for some set $\mathcal{S}''$ of generalized sorts over Σ, and $\mathcal{V}_S = \emptyset$ if $S \notin \mathcal{S}$.

Technically speaking, a generalized signature is not a signature at all— according to Definition 9.2.2, signatures must contain variables of each of their sorts. But since generalized signatures behave like signatures in all other respects, we will abuse terminology and persist in referring to generalized signatures as signatures anyway.

Note that since $\mathcal{V}_S$ may be empty for some sorts $S \in \mathcal{S}'$, the set $[S]_{\Sigma'}$ may therefore also be empty for some $S \in \mathcal{S}'$. That is, $[\Phi]_{\Sigma'}$ may be empty for some generalized sorts Φ over Σ.

According to Definition 9.5.3, Σ' is a signature whose sorts happen to be (certain kinds of) sets of sorts from Σ. We will be interested in generalized signatures because they make possible finite representations of potentially infinite sets of terms satisfying certain sort conditions in their underlying signatures. If Σ is the signature of Example 9.5.2, for instance, then the set of terms t satisfying both $t \in [S]_\Sigma$ and $t \in [T]_\Sigma$—each of which, incidentally, gives rise to a unifier of the system $\{x_S \approx y_T\}$—is $\{a, f(a), f(f(a)), \ldots\}$. We will use the fact that the terms in this infinite set all have precisely sorts S and T in Σ to arrive at the finite representation $[S \sqcap T]_{\Sigma'}$ for it in Σ', provided Σ' is a generalized signature over Σ which contains the sort $S \sqcap T$. Corollary 9.5.3 below will show how this representation in turn gives rise to a finite representation for the infinitely many unifiers of $\{x_S \approx y_T\}$. Similar representations are possible in other signatures; the following observations will allow us to make this precise.

We begin by noting that if Σ and Σ' are as in Definition 9.5.3, then we might expect some relationships to hold in Σ' among sorts in S and sorts in S''. If $\mathcal{D}$ contains the declarations $S \sqsubset T$ and $S \sqsubset U$, for example, and if $T \sqcap U \in S''$, then, intuitively, we would expect $S <_{\Sigma'} T \sqcap U$ to hold. More generally, given a signature Σ for a sorted language, we can single out for special attention generalized signatures over Σ which conform to this kind of intuition. The next definition shows how to extend a signature Σ by introducing certain generalized sorts over it, as well as the relevant subsort and function declarations involving these generalized sorts.

Definition 9.5.4   Let $\Sigma = \langle \mathcal{S}, \mathcal{F}, \mathcal{P}, \mathcal{D} \rangle$ be a signature.

1. The $\sqsubset$-*extension rule* and the $\rightarrow$-*extension rule* for term declarations in Σ are given by:

   - $\sqsubset$-*extension*
     $$\frac{S \sqsubset S'}{S \sqcap T \sqsubset S' \sqcap T}$$
     where $S, S', T \in \mathcal{S}$.

   - $\rightarrow$-*extension*
     $$\frac{f : S_1 \times \ldots \times S_n \rightarrow S \qquad f : T_1 \times \ldots \times T_n \rightarrow T}{f : S_1 \sqcap T_1 \times \ldots \times S_n \sqcap T_n \rightarrow S \sqcap T}$$
     where S_i, T_i, S, and T, $i = 1, \ldots, n$, are in $\mathcal{S}$.

2. The inference system $\mathcal{D}\Sigma$ is applicable to generalized signatures and comprises the following rules (the names of the rules have deliberately been reused to suggest a correspondence):

   - $\sqsubset$-*extension*
     $$\frac{\langle \mathcal{S}, \mathcal{F}, \mathcal{P}, \mathcal{D} \rangle}{\langle \Sigma \cup \{T\}, \mathcal{F}, \mathcal{P}, \mathcal{D} \cup \{S \sqsubset T\} \rangle}$$
     if $S \in \mathcal{S}$, and $S \sqsubset T$ is the conclusion of an application of the $\sqsubset$-extension rule for term declarations.

- $\rightarrow$-*extension*

$$\frac{\langle \mathcal{S}, \mathcal{F}, \mathcal{P}, \mathcal{D} \rangle}{\langle \Sigma \cup \{S\}, \mathcal{F}, \mathcal{P}, \mathcal{D} \cup \{f : S_1 \times \ldots \times S_n \rightarrow S\} \rangle}$$

if $S_i \in \mathcal{S}$ for $i = 1, \ldots, n$, and $f : S_1 \times \ldots \times S_n \rightarrow S$ is the conclusion of an application of the $\rightarrow$-extension rule for term declarations.

If Σ' is obtained from Σ by $\sqsubset$-extension ($\rightarrow$-extension) then Σ' is called a $\sqsubset$-*extension* (resp., $\rightarrow$-*extension*) of Σ. We write $\Sigma \Rightarrow \Sigma'$ if $\Sigma \neq \Sigma'$ and Σ' is a $\sqsubset$-extension or a $\rightarrow$-extension of Σ. We write $\Sigma \Rightarrow^* \Sigma'$ if there exist signatures $\Sigma_1, \ldots, \Sigma_n$ such that $\Sigma \Rightarrow \Sigma_1 \Rightarrow \ldots \Rightarrow \Sigma_n \Rightarrow \Sigma'$. In this case we say that Σ' is an *extension* of Σ. Note that if $\Sigma \Rightarrow^* \Sigma'$, then Σ' is a generalized signature over Σ and is therefore an extension of Σ in the sense of Definition 9.4.3. A generalized signature Σ is *complete* if every extension of Σ is again Σ. If Σ' is a complete extension of Σ, then Σ' is called a *completion* of Σ.

Note that if $\Sigma = \langle \mathcal{S}, \mathcal{F}, \mathcal{P}, \mathcal{D} \rangle$, $\Sigma' = \langle \mathcal{S}', \mathcal{F}, \mathcal{P}, \mathcal{D}' \rangle$, and $\Sigma \Rightarrow^* \Sigma'$, then every sort in $\mathcal{S}'$ is either in $\mathcal{S}$ or is a generalized sort over Σ, and $\mathcal{D} \subseteq \mathcal{D}'$. Thus Σ' must in fact be a generalized signature over Σ.

Example 9.5.3 Let Σ be the signature of Example 9.5.2. Since Σ contains no subsort declarations, only $\rightarrow$-extensions are possible. One possible completion of Σ is the generalized signature $\Sigma' = \langle \mathcal{S}', \mathcal{F}, \mathcal{P}, \mathcal{D}' \rangle$, where $\mathcal{S}' = \{S, T, S \sqcap T\}$ and $\mathcal{D}'$ comprises the declarations

$$
\begin{array}{ll}
a : S & f : S \rightarrow S \\
a : T & f : T \rightarrow T \\
a : S \sqcap T & f : S \sqcap T \rightarrow S \sqcap T.
\end{array}
$$

Note that $[S]_\Sigma = [S]_{\Sigma'}$, $[T]_\Sigma = [T]_{\Sigma'}$, and

$$[S \sqcap T]_{\Sigma'} = \{a, f(a), f(f(a)), \ldots\} = [S]_{\Sigma'} \cap [T]_{\Sigma'}$$

hold.

As illustrated by the above example, if Σ' is an extension of any signature $\Sigma = \langle \mathcal{S}, \mathcal{F}, \mathcal{P}, \mathcal{D} \rangle$, then by construction $[S]_\Sigma = [S]_{\Sigma'}$ for all $S \in \mathcal{S}$. The next lemma establishes that if Σ' is complete, then $[S \sqcap T]_{\Sigma'} = [S]_{\Sigma'} \cap [T]_{\Sigma'}$ holds for all $S, T, \in \mathcal{S}$, as well. That is, if Σ' is a complete extension of Σ, then the sorts in Σ' indeed serve as finite representations of potentially infinite sets of terms over Σ—and therefore of potentially infinite sets of Σ-unifiers—in precisely the intended manner.

Lemma 9.5.1 *Let $\Sigma = \langle \mathcal{S}, \mathcal{F}, \mathcal{P}, \mathcal{D} \rangle$ and $\Sigma' = \langle \mathcal{S}', \mathcal{F}, \mathcal{P}, \mathcal{D}' \rangle$, and suppose that $\Sigma \Rightarrow \Sigma'$. Then for any sorts S and T of $\mathcal{S}$, we have $[S \sqcap T]_{\Sigma'} \subseteq [S]_{\Sigma'} \cap [T]_{\Sigma'}$. If Σ' is complete, then in fact $[S \sqcap T]_{\Sigma'} = [S]_{\Sigma'} \cap [T]_{\Sigma'}$ holds.*

Proof. We first show that $t \in [S \sqcap T]_{\Sigma'}$ implies $t \in [S]_{\Sigma'} \cap [T]_{\Sigma'}$ for all $S, T \in \mathcal{S}$. We define a well-founded ordering $\succ$ on pairs of the form $\langle t, S \sqcap T \rangle \in \mathcal{T}_{\Sigma'}(\mathcal{F}, \mathcal{V}) \times \mathcal{S}'$ by $\langle t, S \sqcap T \rangle \succ \langle t', S' \sqcap T' \rangle$ iff either t' is a proper subterm of t, or $t = t'$ and either $S' <_{\Sigma'} S$ or $S' = S$ and $T' <_{\Sigma'} T$. The proof proceeds by induction on the ordering $\succ$.

Let $t \in [S \sqcap T]_{\Sigma'}$. If $S \sqcap T \in \mathcal{S}$, then the conclusion of the lemma is immediate by the construction of Σ'. So we may suppose that $S \sqcap T \notin \mathcal{S}$. The induction hypothesis guarantees that for all proper subterms t' of t, and for all $S', T' \in \mathcal{S}$, $t' \in [S' \sqcap T']_{\Sigma'}$ implies $t' \in [S']_{\Sigma'} \cap [T']_{\Sigma'}$. It also entails that for all $S' \in \mathcal{S}$ such that $S' <_{\Sigma'} S$ and for all $T' \in \mathcal{S}$, $t \in [S' \sqcap T']_{\Sigma'}$ implies $t \in [S']_{\Sigma'} \cap [T']_{\Sigma'}$. Since there are no variables of sort $S \sqcap T$ in Σ', either $\mathcal{D}'$ contains a function declaration of the form $f : T_1 \times \ldots \times T_n \to S \sqcap T$ such that $t = f t_1 \ldots t_n$ with $t_i \in [T_i]_{\Sigma'}$ for $i = 1, \ldots, n$, or $\mathcal{D}'$ contains a subsort declaration of the form $U \sqsubset S \sqcap T$ such that $t \in [U]_{\Sigma'}$.

- Suppose $\mathcal{D}'$ contains a function declaration of the form $f : T_1 \times \ldots \times T_n \to S \sqcap T$, and $t = f t_1 \ldots t_n$ with $t_i \in [T_i]_{\Sigma'}$ for $i = 1, \ldots, n$. Then by the construction of generalized signatures, the declaration $f : T_1 \times \ldots \times T_n \to S \sqcap T$ is obtained by $\to$-extension, and so each T_i must be of the form $U_i \sqcap V_i$. Moreover, $\mathcal{D}$ must contain the declarations $f : U_1 \times \ldots \times U_n \to S$ and $f : V_1 \times \ldots \times V_n \to T$, and so $U_1, \ldots, U_n, V_1, \ldots, V_n \in \mathcal{S}$. Let $i \in \{1, \ldots, n\}$. Since $\langle t, S \sqcap T \rangle \succ \langle t_i, U_i \sqcap V_i \rangle$ for $i = 1, \ldots, n$, we can apply the induction hypothesis, and so from $t_i \in [U_i \sqcap V_i]_{\Sigma'}$ follows $t_i \in [U_i]_{\Sigma'} \cap [V_i]_{\Sigma'}$. Therefore $t \in [S]_{\Sigma'} \cap [T]_{\Sigma'}$.

- Suppose $\mathcal{D}'$ contains a declaration of the form $U \sqsubset S \sqcap T$ with $t \in [U]_{\Sigma'}$. By the construction of generalized signatures, this declaration is obtained by $\sqsubset$-extension, and so U is of the form $S' \sqcap T$. Then $\mathcal{D}$ must contain the subsort declaration $S' \sqsubset S$, which implies $S' <_{\Sigma'} S$ and $S' \in \mathcal{S}$. Hence $\langle t, S \sqcap T \rangle \succ \langle t, S' \sqcap T \rangle$, and we can apply the induction hypothesis. This yields that $t \in [S']_{\Sigma'} \cap [T]_{\Sigma'}$ since $t \in [S' \sqcap T]_{\Sigma'}$. Finally, from $S' <_{\Sigma'} S$ follows $[S']_{\Sigma'} \subseteq [S]_{\Sigma'}$, and therefore $t \in [S]_{\Sigma'} \cap [T]_{\Sigma'}$.

We now show that $[S]_{\Sigma'} \cap [T]_{\Sigma'} \subseteq [S \sqcap T]_{\Sigma'}$ holds if Σ' is complete. Let $t \in [S]_{\Sigma'} \cap [T]_{\Sigma'}$. We prove by induction on $\succ$ that $t \in [S]_{\Sigma'} \cap [T]_{\Sigma'}$ implies $t \in [S \sqcap T]_{\Sigma'}$ for all terms $t \in \mathcal{T}_{\Sigma'}(\mathcal{F}, \mathcal{V})$ and all $S, T \in \mathcal{S}$. If $S \sqcap T$ is in $\mathcal{S}$, the conclusion of the lemma is immediate. So suppose that $S \sqcap T$ is not in $\mathcal{S}$. Then there can be no variable which is of sort $S \sqcap T$ in Σ', and so t

cannot be a variable. Since $S, T \in \mathcal{S}$, we have $t \in [S]_{\Sigma'} \cap [T]_{\Sigma'} = [S]_{\Sigma} \cap [T]_{\Sigma}$, and therefore by Definition 9.2.3 (at least) one of the following three cases obtains.

- Suppose there exists a subsort declaration $S' \sqsubset S$ in $\mathcal{D}$ such that $t \in [S']_{\Sigma}$. Since $S' <_{\Sigma} S$, we have $\langle t, S \sqcap T \rangle \succ \langle t, S' \sqcap T \rangle$, so that by the induction hypothesis, $[S']_{\Sigma'} \cap [T]_{\Sigma'} = [S' \sqcap T]_{\Sigma'}$. Then $t \in [S']_{\Sigma} \cap [T]_{\Sigma} = [S']_{\Sigma'} \cap [T]_{\Sigma'} = [S' \sqcap T]_{\Sigma'}$. But since Σ' is complete, the declaration $S' \sqcap T \sqsubset S \sqcap T$ must be in $\mathcal{D}'$. Thus $t \in [S \sqcap T]_{\Sigma'}$.

- If there exists a subsort declaration $T' \sqsubset T$ in $\mathcal{D}$ such that $t \in [T']_{\Sigma}$, then the proof proceeds similarly.

- Suppose $t = f t_1 \ldots t_n$ and $\mathcal{D}$ contains declarations $f : S_1 \times \ldots \times S_n \to S$ and $f : T_1 \times \ldots \times T_n \to T$ such that $t_i \in [S_i]_{\Sigma} \cap [T_i]_{\Sigma}$ for $i = 1, \ldots, n$. Then since $S_1, \ldots, S_n, T_1, \ldots, T_n \in \mathcal{S}$, we can conclude that $t_i \in [S_i]_{\Sigma'} \cap [T_i]_{\Sigma'}$ for $i = 1, \ldots, n$ as well. Since for each i, $\langle t, S \sqcap T \rangle \succ \langle t_i, S_i \sqcap T_i \rangle$, the induction hypothesis applies to give $t_i \in [S_i \sqcap T_i]_{\Sigma'}$ for $i = 1, \ldots, n$. But since Σ' is complete, the declaration $f : S_1 \sqcap T_1 \times \ldots \times S_n \sqcap T_n \to S \sqcap T$ must be in $\mathcal{D}'$. Thus $t \in [S \sqcap T]_{\Sigma'}$.
  □

The hypothesis that Σ' is complete is necessary for the conclusion $[S \sqcap T]_{\Sigma'} = [S]_{\Sigma'} \cap [T]_{\Sigma'}$ to hold. Indeed, if Σ is the signature of Example 9.5.2, then the signature $\Sigma' = \langle \mathcal{S} \cup \{S \sqcap T\}, \mathcal{F}, \mathcal{P}, \mathcal{D} \cup \{a : S \sqcap T\} \rangle$ is a $\to$-extension of Σ. Note that Σ' is not complete, since it does not contain the declaration $f : S \sqcap T \to S \sqcap T$. Moreover, $[S \sqcap T]_{\Sigma'} = \{a\}$ whereas $[S]_{\Sigma'} \cap [T]_{\Sigma'} = \{a, f(a), f(f(a)), \ldots\}$.

Corollary 9.5.1 *If Σ' is a complete extension of $\Sigma = \langle \mathcal{S}, \mathcal{F}, \mathcal{P}, \mathcal{D} \rangle$, then $[S \sqcap T]_{\Sigma'} = [S]_{\Sigma} \cap [T]_{\Sigma}$ for all $S, T \in \mathcal{S}$.*

Proof. This is a direct consequence of the previous lemma and the observation that $[S]_{\Sigma} = [S]_{\Sigma'}$ for all $S \in \mathcal{S}$.

Corollary 9.5.2 *If $\Sigma = \langle \mathcal{S}, \mathcal{F}, \mathcal{P}, \mathcal{D} \rangle$ is a complete extended signature, then $[S \sqcap T]_{\Sigma} = [S]_{\Sigma} \cap [T]_{\Sigma}$ for all $S, T \in \mathcal{S}$.*

Proof. Follows from the fact that Σ is a complete extension of Σ. □

As promised, we can use the notions of generalized sorts and generalized signatures to solve sorted unification problems. If Σ' is a complete extension of Σ, then Corollary 9.5.1 implies that for every generalized sort

$\Phi = S_1 \sqcap \ldots \sqcap S_n$ over Σ, $[\Phi]_{\Sigma'} = [S_1]_\Sigma \cap \ldots \cap [S_n]_\Sigma$ holds. Although Φ is not, in general, a sort in Σ itself, if $\Phi = S_1 \sqcap \ldots \sqcap S_n$ for $S_i \in \mathcal{S}$, we may nevertheless abuse notation and write $[\Phi]_\Sigma$ to abbreviate $[S_1]_\Sigma \cap \ldots \cap [S_n]_\Sigma$. This notation will prove convenient in the remainder of the section.

Definition 9.5.5

1. Let $\Sigma = \langle \mathcal{S}, \mathcal{F}, \mathcal{P}, \mathcal{D} \rangle$. A *sort constraint* (or simply a *constraint*) c over Σ is a set of ordered pairs of the form $\langle t, \Phi \rangle$, where t is a Σ-term and Φ is a generalized sort over Σ. We usually write $t : \Phi$ in place of $\langle t, \Phi \rangle$.

2. The Σ-substitution σ Σ-*unifies* the sort constraint c over Σ provided $\sigma(t) \in [\Phi]_\Sigma$ holds for all $t : \Phi \in c$. By $u_\Sigma(c)$ we denote the set of all Σ-unifiers of c. The constraint c is said to be *more general than* c' (with respect to Σ) if $u_\Sigma(c') \subseteq u_\Sigma(c)$. In this case, we write $c \leq_\Sigma c'$, or $c \leq c'$ if Σ is clear from context.

3. A constraint $c = \{x_1 : \Phi_1, \ldots, x_n : \Phi_n\}$ over Σ is in Σ-*solved form* if $x_i \neq x_j$ for $i \neq j$ and $i, j = 1, \ldots, n$. The constraint c is a Σ-*solution* for c' if c is in Σ-solved form and $c' \leq_\Sigma c$. The constraint c is a *most general* Σ-*solution* for c' if c is a Σ-solution for c' and if $c \leq c''$ for all Σ-solutions c'' of c'.

4. The set $\mathcal{L} = \{c_1, c_2, \ldots\}$ of constraints in Σ-solved form is a *general* Σ-*solution* for the constraint c if

$$u_\Sigma(c) = \bigcup_{k \geq 0} u_\Sigma(c_k).$$

It is clear that the set $\mathcal{L}_0$ of all Σ-solutions for a constraint c represents a general Σ-solution of c.

The following relationship between sorted and unsorted unification holds.

Lemma 9.5.2 *Let $\Sigma = \langle \mathcal{S}, \mathcal{F}, \mathcal{P}, \mathcal{D} \rangle$ be a signature, let $E = \{s_1 \approx t_1, \ldots, s_n \approx t_n\}$ and let $\{x_1, \ldots, x_m\} = Var(E)$, where for each $i = 1, \ldots, m$, $x_i \in \mathcal{V}_{S_i}$, $S_i \in \mathcal{S}$. Then $u_\Sigma(E) = u(E) \cap u_\Sigma(c)$, where $c = \{x_1 : S_1, \ldots, x_m : S_m\}$.*

Proof. For each Σ-substitution σ,

$$\sigma \in u(E) \cap u_\Sigma(c) \quad \text{iff} \quad \sigma \in u(E) \text{ and } \sigma \in u_\Sigma(c),$$

and this holds iff

$$\sigma \in u(E) \quad \text{and } \sigma \text{ is a } \Sigma\text{-substitution,}$$

i.e., iff $\sigma \in u_\Sigma(E)$. $\square$

We say that the constraint c in Lemma 9.5.2 is *associated with* E. Lemma 9.5.2 reduces the process of unifying systems of sorted terms to that of finding substitutions which simultaneously unify their unsorted counterparts and solve their associated constraints. The next lemma provides a practical means of finding such substitutions. If c is a constraint and σ is a Σ-substitution, write $\sigma(c)$ for the constraint $\{\sigma(t) : \Phi \mid t : \Phi \in c\}$.

Lemma 9.5.3 *Let E be an equational system in solved form, let σ_E be the substitution represented by E, and let c be a constraint over Σ. Then*

$$u(E) \cap u_\Sigma(c) = u(E) \cap u_\Sigma(\sigma_E(c)).$$

Proof. Let $t : \Phi \in c$ and let $\sigma \in u(E)$. That $\sigma\sigma_E = \sigma$ clearly holds. From this it follows that $\sigma(\sigma_E(t)) = \sigma(t)$ and thus $\sigma(\sigma_E(t)) \in [\Phi]_\Sigma$ iff $\sigma(t) \in [\Phi]_\Sigma$. Thus $\sigma \in u_\Sigma(c)$ iff $\sigma \in u_\Sigma(\sigma_E(c))$, and the conclusion of the lemma follows. $\square$

Corollary 9.5.3 *Let E be an equational system and let c be its associated constraint. If E' is a most general solution for E and $\mathcal{L} = \{c_1, c_2, \ldots\}$ is a general Σ-solution of $\sigma_{E'}(c)$, then*

$$u_\Sigma(E) = u(E') \cap \bigcup_{k \geq 0} u_\Sigma(c_k).$$

Proof. We calculate

$$
\begin{aligned}
u_\Sigma(E) &= u(E) \cap u_\Sigma(c) \\
&= u(E') \cap u_\Sigma(c) \\
&= u(E') \cap u_\Sigma(\sigma_{E'}(c)) \\
&= u(E') \cap \bigcup_{k \geq 0} u_\Sigma(c_k),
\end{aligned}
$$

since $\mathcal{L}$ is a general solution of $\sigma_{E'}(c)$. $\square$

This corollary illustrates the expected benefits of sorted solutions of an equational system E: we may consider each such system E together with its associated constraint, and then try to solve the (more restrictive) resulting problem. For example, we might first search with the help of the inference system in Section 7.2 for an unsorted solution E' for the system E, and then construct the constraint c associated with E and search for a general Σ-solution for the constraint $\sigma_{E'}(c)$. If E, E', and $\mathcal{L}$ are as in Corollary 9.5.3, then we call the ordered pair $E'.\mathcal{L}$ a *general sorted solution for* E.

With the concept of a general sorted solution for a system we can provide finite representations of potentially infinite sets of unifiers for systems of sorted terms, by providing finite representations of the sort constraints they embody. It is easy to verify that the pair

$$\{x_S \approx y_T\}.\{y_T : S \sqcap T\}$$

represents a general sorted solution for the system $\{x_S \approx y_T\}$ of Example 9.5.2, for instance, because $S \sqcap T$ represents the sort constraint on y_T, and hence on x_S, that it embodies. Here

$$[S \sqcap T]_\Sigma = \{a, f(a), f(f(a)), \dots\},$$

and the essential feature of the formalism describing this solution is that the (finite) generalized sort $S \sqcap T$ represents the infinite set $[S \sqcap T]_\Sigma$ of terms.

Although the general solution for the constraint $\{x : S, y : T\}$ associated with the system $\{x_S \approx y_T\}$ happens to comprise the single constraint $\{y : S \sqcap T\}$, the following example shows that generalized solutions for constraints need not always be singletons.

Example 9.5.4   Let $\Sigma = \langle \{S, T, W\}, \{a, b, g\}, \emptyset, \mathcal{D} \rangle$, where $\mathcal{D}$ comprises the declarations

$$
\begin{array}{ll}
S \sqsubseteq W & T \sqsubseteq W \\
a : S & b : T \\
g : S \rightarrow S & g : T \rightarrow S
\end{array}
$$

Further, let c be the constraint $\{g(x_W) : S\}$. Clearly the two constraints

$$c_1 = \{x_W : S\} \quad \text{and} \quad c_2 = \{x_W : T\}$$

are both Σ-solutions of c. If $\sigma = \{x_W \leftarrow t\} \in u_\Sigma(c)$, then $g(t) \in [S]_\Sigma$ holds. Thus we must have either $t \in [S]_\Sigma$ or $t \in [T]_\Sigma$. In the first case $\sigma \in u_\Sigma(c_1)$, and in the second case $\sigma \in u_\Sigma(c_2)$. Thus $u_\Sigma(c) = u_\Sigma(c_1) \cup u_\Sigma(c_2)$, i.e., $\{c_1, c_2\}$ is a general Σ-solution for c. Finally it is clear that there can be no general Σ-solution for c consisting of a single constraint.

We are at last in a position to introduce an inference system which calculates a most general Σ-solution for any sort constraint which has a Σ-solution, and which returns the information that the constraint possesses no Σ-solution otherwise. Given a signature Σ, let Σ' be any complete extension of Σ, and let $c = \{t_1 : \Phi_1, \dots, t_n : \Phi_n\}$ be a sort constraint over Σ. Then $\Phi_1, \dots, \Phi_n$ are all generalized sorts over Σ, and so $\Phi_i = S_{i1} \sqcap \dots \sqcap S_{in_i}$ for some sorts $S_{ij} \in \mathcal{S}$. Now $u_\Sigma(c)$ is the set of all Σ-substitutions σ such that $\sigma(t_i) \in [\Phi_i]_\Sigma$ for $i = 1, \dots, n$. But $[\Phi_i]_\Sigma = [S_{i1}]_\Sigma \cap \dots \cap [S_{in_i}]_\Sigma$ by definition, and this is precisely the same set of terms as $[S_{i1}]_{\Sigma'} \cap \dots \cap [S_{in_i}]_{\Sigma'}$ since each S_{ij} is a sort in Σ for all i and j. Moreover, it follows from Lemma 9.5.1 that $[S_{i1}]_{\Sigma'} \cap \dots \cap [S_{in_i}]_{\Sigma'} = [\Phi_i]_{\Sigma'}$. Thus $t_i \in [\Phi_i]_\Sigma$ iff $t_i \in [\Phi_i]_{\Sigma'}$, and so we have that $u_\Sigma(c)$ is precisely the same as $u_{\Sigma'}(c)$. We may therefore solve any sort constraint over a signature Σ by passing to a complete extension Σ' of Σ and solving the sort constraint over Σ' instead, and so, without loss of generality, we define our inference system for complete signatures only. Note that in a complete signature $\Sigma = \langle \mathcal{S}, \mathcal{F}, \mathcal{P}, \mathcal{D} \rangle$, constraints are of the form $\{t_1 : S_1, \ldots, t_n : S_n\}$ where $S_i \in \mathcal{S}$ for $i = 1, \ldots, n$.

Definition 9.5.6 Let $\Sigma = \langle \mathcal{S}, \mathcal{F}, \mathcal{P}, \mathcal{D} \rangle$ be a complete signature. The inference system $\mathcal{U}\Sigma$ for solution of sort constraints over Σ is given by the following inference rules:

- *Decomposition*

$$\frac{c \cup \{ft_1 \ldots t_n : S\}}{c \cup \{t_1 : S_1, \ldots, t_n : S_n\}}$$

  if $f : S_1 \times \ldots \times S_n \to S \in \mathcal{D}$.

- *Subsort*

$$\frac{c \cup \{t : S\}}{c \cup \{t : S'\}}$$

  if $S' \sqsubset S \in \mathcal{D}$ and $t \notin \mathcal{V}$.

- *Intersection*

$$\frac{c \cup \{x : S_1, x : S_2\}}{c \cup \{x : S_1 \sqcap S_2\}}$$

- *Clash*

$$\frac{c \cup \{ft_1 \ldots t_n : S\}}{\bot}$$

  if $\mathcal{D}$ contains no declarations for S.

- *Empty Sort*

$$\frac{c \cup \{x : S\}}{\bot}$$

  if S is empty.

Here the symbol $\bot$ stands for any unsolvable constraint. The last two failure rules are not actually necessary; they serve only to break off useless computation in a timely manner.

We write $c \Rightarrow_{\mathcal{U}\Sigma} c'$ in case $c' \neq c$ and c' is obtained from c by an application of a rule from $\mathcal{U}\Sigma$. A $\Rightarrow_{\mathcal{U}\Sigma}$-*derivation* out of S_0 is a sequence $S_0, S_1, S_2, \ldots$ of constraints such that, for each natural number n, $S_n \Rightarrow_{\mathcal{U}\Sigma} S_{n+1}$ holds. A constraint c is said to be $\mathcal{U}\Sigma$-*irreducible* if no rule in $\mathcal{U}\Sigma$ applies to c. It is clear that a constraint which is $\mathcal{U}\Sigma$-irreducible and distinct from $\perp$ is in Σ-solved form.

Lemma 9.5.4   *The inference system $\mathcal{U}\Sigma$ is terminating. i.e., there exists no infinite $\mathcal{U}\Sigma$-derivation $c_0 \Rightarrow_{\mathcal{U}\Sigma} c_1 \Rightarrow_{\mathcal{U}\Sigma} c_2 \ldots$.*

Proof. It suffices to restrict attention to the subsystem of $\mathcal{U}\Sigma$ comprising the first three rules. Let c be a sort constraint. We associate with each constraint c the multiset

$$\mu_1(c) = \{|t| \mid t : S \in c\},$$

as well as the multiset

$$\mu_2(c) = \{S \mid t : S \in c\},$$

and we use these to construct the termination function μ defined by $\mu(c) = \langle \mu_1(c), \mu_2(c) \rangle$. If $\succ$ is the lexicographical combination $(>_{mul}, (>_\Sigma)_{mul})$, where $>$ is the usual ordering on the natural numbers, then $\succ$ is clearly a noetherian ordering.

We show that if $c \Rightarrow_{\mathcal{U}\Sigma} c'$, then $\mu(c) \succ \mu(c')$, and from this the conclusion of the lemma directly follows. An application of the rule *Decomposition* reduces μ_1, an application of the rule *Subsort* reduces μ_2 and leaves μ_1 unchanged, and the rule *Intersection* decreases μ_1. $\square$

While every $\mathcal{U}\Sigma$-step need not preserve unifiers, Lemma 9.5.5 guarantees that there is always at least one unifier-preserving computation step.

Lemma 9.5.5   *Let $\Sigma = \langle \mathcal{S}, \mathcal{F}, \mathcal{P}, \mathcal{D} \rangle$ be a complete extended signature. Let c be a constraint and let $\{c_1, \ldots, c_n\}$ be the set of constraints obtainable from c via respect to $\Rightarrow_{\mathcal{U}\Sigma}$. Then $u_\Sigma(c) = u_\Sigma(c_1) \cup \ldots \cup u_\Sigma(c_n)$.*

Proof. Let $c = \{t_1 : S_1, \ldots, t_k : S_k\}$ be a constraint. It suffices to see that if $\{c_1, \ldots, c_n\}$ is the set of constraints obtainable from c by applications of rules of $\mathcal{U}\Sigma$ to a single element $t_i : S_i$ of c, then $u_\Sigma(c) = u_\Sigma(c_1) \cup \ldots \cup u_\Sigma(c_n)$, i.e., if $\{c_1, \ldots, c_k\}$ is the set of constraints obtainable for c by single applications of rules in $\mathcal{U}\Sigma$ to $t_i : S_i$, then $\sigma \in u_\Sigma(c)$ iff there exists a $j \in \{1, \ldots, n\}$ such that $\sigma \in u_\Sigma(c_j)$.

- If $t_i : S_i$ is of the form $x : S$ for an empty generalized sort S, then $\perp$ is the only constraint obtainable from c, and indeed $u_\Sigma(c) = \emptyset = u_\Sigma(\perp)$.

- If $t_i : S_i$ is of the form $x : S$ and there exists a $j \in \{1, \ldots, k\}, j \neq i$ such that $t_j : S_j$ is of the form $x : S'$, then $c - \{x : S, x : S'\} \cup \{x : S \sqcap S'\}$ is the only constraint obtainable from c, and

$$
\begin{array}{ll}
\sigma \in u_\Sigma(\{x : S \sqcap S'\}) & \text{iff} \\
\sigma(x) \in [S \sqcap S']_\Sigma & \text{iff} \\
\sigma(x) \in [S]_\Sigma \cap [S']_\Sigma & \text{iff} \\
\sigma(x) \in [S]_\Sigma \text{ and } \sigma(x) \in [S']_\Sigma & \text{iff} \\
\sigma \in u_\Sigma(\{x : S, x : S'\}). &
\end{array}
$$

Thus $\sigma \in u_\Sigma(c)$ iff $\sigma \in u_\Sigma(c - \{x : S, x : S'\} \cup \{x : S \sqcap S'\})$.

- If $t_i : S_i$ is of the form $f z_1 \ldots z_m : S$ and there is in $\mathcal{D}$ no declaration for S, then $\bot$ is the only constraint obtainable from c, and $u_\Sigma(\bot) \subseteq u_\Sigma(c)$ clearly holds. If, on the other hand, $\sigma \in u_\Sigma(c)$, then $\sigma(f z_1 \ldots z_m) \in [S]_\Sigma$, which is not possible by Definition 9.2.3, and so indeed $u_\Sigma(c) = u_\Sigma(\bot)$.

- If $t_i : S_i$ is of the form $f z_1 \ldots z_m : S$ and there is in $\mathcal{D}$ a declaration $f : T_1 \times \ldots \times T_m \to S_i$ or a subsort declaration $S' \sqsubset S_i$, then we first show that if $c \Rightarrow_{\mathcal{U}\Sigma} c_k$ by a transformation in $\mathcal{U}\Sigma$ applied to $\{t_i : S_i\}$, then $u_\Sigma(c_k) \subseteq u_\Sigma(c)$. Note that if there exist such declarations in $\mathcal{D}$ then the only possibility is that $c \Rightarrow_{\mathcal{U}\Sigma} c_k$ by either the rule *Decomposition* or the rule *Subsort*.

  - If $c \Rightarrow_{\mathcal{U}\Sigma} c_k$ by the rule *Subsort*, then c_k is of the form $c - \{t_i : S_i\} \cup \{t_i : S'\}$ for $S' \sqsubset S_i \in \mathcal{D}$. Then if $\sigma \in u_\Sigma(c_k)$ then $\sigma(t_i) \in [S']_\Sigma \subseteq [S_i]_\Sigma$.

  - If $c \Rightarrow_{\mathcal{U}\Sigma} c_k$ by the rule *Decomposition*, then c_k is of the form $c - \{f z_1 \ldots z_m : S_i\} \cup \{z_1 : T_1, \ldots, z_m : T_m\}$ with $f : T_1 \times \ldots \times T_m \to S_i \in \mathcal{D}$. Then if $\sigma \in u_\Sigma(c_k)$, we have $\sigma_j \in [T_j]_\Sigma, j = 1, \ldots, m$, so that $\sigma(f z_1 \ldots z_m) \in [S_i]_\Sigma$, and therefore $\sigma \in u_\Sigma(\{t_i : S_i\})$. Thus if $\sigma \in u_\Sigma(c_k)$ then $\sigma \in u_\Sigma(c)$.

We now show that if $\sigma \in u_\Sigma(c)$ then there must exist some $j \in \{1, \ldots, n\}$ with $\sigma \in u_\Sigma(c_j)$. Let $\sigma \in u_\Sigma(c)$, so that, in particular, $f(\sigma(z_1)) \ldots (\sigma(z_m)) = \sigma(f z_1 \ldots z_m) \in [S_i]_\Sigma$. Then by Definition 9.2.3 there either exists a subsort declaration $S' \sqsubset S_i \in \mathcal{D}$ such that $\sigma(f z_1 \ldots z_m) \in [S']_\Sigma$, or there exists a function declaration $f : T_1 \times \ldots \times T_m \to S$ such that $\sigma(z_k) \in [T_k]_\Sigma$ for all $k = 1, \ldots, m$.

If there is a subsort declaration $S' \sqsubset S_i$ with $\sigma(f z_1 \ldots z_m) \in [S']_\Sigma$, then there is some $j \in \{1, \ldots, n\}$ such that $c_j = c - \{f z_1 \ldots z_m : S\} \cup \{f z_1 \ldots z_m : S'\}$. In this case $c \Rightarrow_{\mathcal{U}\Sigma} c_j$ and $\sigma \in u_\Sigma(c_j)$ as above. If, on the other hand, there is a function declaration $f : T_1 \times \ldots \times T_m \to S_i$ with $\sigma(z_k) \in [T_k]_\Sigma$ for $k = 1, \ldots, m$, then there is a $j \in \{1, \ldots, n\}$ with $c_j = c - \{(f z_1 \ldots z_m) : S_i\} \cup \{z_k : T_k \mid k = 1, \ldots, m\}$. In this case, the above implies that $\sigma \in u_\Sigma(c_j)$ as well. $\square$

Corollary 9.5.4   *The set of $\mathcal{U}\Sigma$-irreducible constraints resulting from derivations out of c comprises a general Σ-solution of c.*

The transformations for sorted unification presented here provide the basis for a sorted resolution calculus $\mathcal{R}\Sigma$; sorted versions of the resolution and factorization rules are defined precisely as are their unsorted counterparts for clause closures (see Definitions 8.1.2 and 8.1.3). We need only observe that the condition "provided ... is solvable" now refers to Σ-solvability. Restrictions of sorted resolution corresponding to those of Chapter 8 for clause closures can also be defined by analogy with restrictions for unsorted resolution. The completeness proof for the resolution calculus carries over unchanged, and so we have the following result.

Theorem 9.5.1   *(Completeness of $\mathcal{R}\Sigma$ for sorted clauses) If S is an unsatisfiable set of Σ-clauses, and if $S_0, S_1, \ldots$ is a fair $\mathcal{R}\Sigma$-derivation such that $S_0 = S$, then there exists an $n \geq 0$ such that S_n contains the empty clause.*

Moreover, in the sorted setting there exists, in addition to the usual redundancy criteria for unsorted clauses, a fourth notion of redundancy. Note that if $x_S \in Var(C)$ with $\mathcal{T}_S(\mathcal{F}) = \emptyset$, then C is clearly redundant according to Definition 8.1.1 since the set $\overline{C}$ of ground instances of C is empty.

To conclude this chapter, we revisit the example of Schubert's Steamroller (Example 9.1.1) and the signature

$$\Sigma = \langle \{A, B, C, F, G, P, S, W\}, \{b, g, f, h, i, s, w\}, \emptyset, \mathcal{D} \rangle,$$

where $\mathcal{D}$ comprises the following declarations:

$W \sqsubset A$	$w : W$	$F \sqsubset A$
$f : F$	$B \sqsubset A$	$b : B$
$C \sqsubset A$	$c : C$	$S \sqsubset A$
$s : S$	$G \sqsubset P$	$g : G$
$h : C \to P$	$i : S \to P$	

Completion of this signature gives no new clauses, i.e., Σ is already complete. The sorted clause set representing the Steamroller problem comprises the following clauses from before:

(1) $M(z_A, x_A), E(z_A, v_P) \;\to\; E(x_A, y_P), E(x_A, z_A)$

(2) $\to M(x_C, y_B)$	(3) $\to M(x_S, y_B)$	(4) $\to M(x_B, y_F)$
(5) $\to M(x_F, y_W)$	(6) $E(x_W, y_F) \to$	(7) $E(x_W, y_G) \to$
(8) $\to E(x_B, y_C)$	(9) $E(x_B, y_S) \to$	(10) $\to E(x_C, h(x_C))$
(11) $\to E(x_S, i(x_S))$	(12) $E(x_A, y_A), E(y_A, z_G) \to$	

With the sorted hyperresolution calculus $\mathcal{H}\Sigma$ we obtain the following contradiction from the above set of clauses:

$(1),(3),(11) \Rightarrow (13) \quad \rightarrow E(y_B, y_P), E(y_B, x_S).\{x_S : A, \ y_B : A, \ i(x_S) : P\}$

$(9),(13) \Rightarrow (14) \quad \rightarrow E(y_B, y_P)$

$(1),(14),(4) \Rightarrow (15) \quad \rightarrow E(y_F, y_P), E(y_F, x_B).\{y_F : A, \ x_B : A\}$

$(1),(15),(5) \Rightarrow (16) \quad \rightarrow E(y_W, y_P), E(y_W, x_F), E(y_F, x_B).\{x_F : A, \ y_F : A,$
$\qquad\qquad\qquad\qquad\qquad y_W : A, \ x_B : P\}$

$(16),(7) \Rightarrow (17) \quad \rightarrow E(y_W, x_F), E(y_F, x_B).\{y_P : G\}$

$(17),(6) \Rightarrow (18) \quad \rightarrow E(y_F, x_B)$

$(12),(14),(18) \quad \Box.\{x_F : A, \ x_B : A, \ y_P : G\}$

Only the new associated sort constraints are noted here. The equality constraints are always Σ-solved and are rendered here as most general Σ-unifiers. Each sort constraint here can be shown to be Σ-solvable.

9.6   Complexity of Sorted Unification

In the preceding section we investigated the solution of sort constraints—and thus of unification problems—in elementary signatures. In this section we will turn our attention to determining the complexity of the sorted unification problem. We will show through a reduction of the unification problem to the satisfiability problem for propositional formula (SAT) that the sorted unification problem is NP-complete. The proof is as in [SS89]. For the basic definitions of complexity theory, see [GJ79].

Theorem 9.6.1 *The following problem, called* unification in a sorted signature, *is NP-complete:*

Given an (elementary) signature Σ and two Σ-terms s and t, does there exist a sorted unifier of s and t?

Proof. We must establish two facts, namely, that unification in a sorted signature is in the class of problems NP and that every problem also in NP can be reduced to the problem of unification in a sorted signature.

First, it is not hard to see that a Σ-substitution σ can be chosen and it can be verified whether or not $\sigma(s) = \sigma(t)$ holds, all in polynomial time. Thus unification in a sorted signature is in the class of problems NP.

In the remainder of the proof we establish the NP-completeness of unification in a sorted signature by reducing the NP-complete problem SAT to it. SAT is the problem of deciding whether or not a set of clauses is satisfiable.

Let the set $S = \{C_1, \ldots, C_m\}$ of clauses over the set $P = \{P_1, \ldots, P_n\}$ of propositional symbols be given. We first define a signature Σ with sorts T, F, and $BOOL$, as well as the declarations

$$T \sqsubset BOOL \qquad F \sqsubset BOOL$$
$$t : T \qquad\qquad f : F$$

$$and : BOOL \times BOOL \rightarrow BOOL$$
$$or : BOOL \times BOOL \rightarrow BOOL$$

$and : T \times T \rightarrow T$	$or : T \times T \rightarrow T$
$and : T \times F \rightarrow F$	$or : T \times F \rightarrow T$
$and : F \times T \rightarrow F$	$or : F \times T \rightarrow T$
$and : F \times F \rightarrow F$	$or : F \times F \rightarrow F$
$not : BOOL \rightarrow BOOL$	$not : F \rightarrow T$
$not : T \rightarrow F$	

Then for some fixed set $\{x_1, \ldots, x_n\} \subseteq \mathcal{V}_{BOOL}$, we define a transformation θ which assigns to each set of clauses over P a Σ-term as follows:

$$
\begin{aligned}
\theta(P_i) &= x_i \text{ for } i = 1, \ldots, n \\
\theta(A_1, \ldots, A_n \rightarrow \Psi) &= or(\theta(A_1), \theta(A_2, \ldots, A_n \rightarrow \Psi)) \\
\theta(\rightarrow B_1, \ldots, B_m) &= or(not(\theta(B_1)), \theta(\rightarrow B_2, \ldots, B_m)) \\
\theta(\square) &= f
\end{aligned}
$$

Now let $s_i = \theta(C_i)$ for $i = 1, \ldots, m$. We show that the set S is satisfiable exactly when the constraint $\{s_1 : T, \ldots, s_m : T\}$ is Σ-solvable. If S is empty, then there is nothing to prove, so we may suppose that S is nonempty. If S is satisfiable, then there is an interpretation $\mathcal{I} \subseteq P$ such that for every clause $\Phi \rightarrow \Psi$ in S either $\Phi \not\subseteq \mathcal{I}$ or else $\Psi \cap \mathcal{I} \neq \emptyset$ holds. Let σ be the Σ-substitution defined by

$$
\sigma(x_i) = \begin{cases} t & \text{if } P_i \in \mathcal{I} \\ f & \text{otherwise} \end{cases}
$$

It is now easy to check that $\sigma(s_i) \in [T]_\Sigma$, $i = 1, \ldots, m$, holds and so the constraint $\{s_1 : T, \ldots, s_m : T\}$ has a Σ-solution.

Conversely, let σ be a Σ-substitution such that $\sigma(s_i) \in [T]_\Sigma$, $i = 1, \ldots, m$. If $C \in S$, then $\sigma(\theta(C)) \in [T]_\Sigma$, and, in particular, if $\sigma(\theta(C)) \neq f$ then $C \neq \square$. Let $C = \Phi \rightarrow \Psi$. By the specification of the binary connective "or," if $\sigma(\theta(C)) \in [T]_\Sigma$ then there exists either a $P_i \in \Phi$ with $\sigma(\theta(P_i)) = \sigma(x_i) \in [F]_\Sigma$ or a $P_j \in \Psi$ with $\sigma(\theta(P_j)) = \sigma(x_j) \in [T]_\Sigma$. We define the interpretation $\mathcal{I}$ by

$$\mathcal{I} = \{P_i \mid \sigma(\theta(P_i)) \in [T]_\Sigma, i = 1, \ldots, n\}.$$

Then clearly either $\Phi \not\subseteq \mathcal{I}$ or $\Psi \cap \mathcal{I} \neq \emptyset$, i.e., $\mathcal{I}$ satisfies C. Since C was arbitrary, $\mathcal{I}$ satisfies S. $\square$

References

[AHU74] Aho, A., Hopcroft, J., and Ullman, J. 1974. *The Design and Analysis of Computer Algorithms*. Reading, MA: Addison-Wesley.

[Bez90] Bezem, M. 1990. Completeness of resolution revisited. *Journal of the ACM* 74: 227–237.

[BG90] Bachmair, L. and Ganzinger, H. 1990. Completion of first-order clauses with equality by strict superposition. In *Proceedings of the Tenth International Conference on Automated Deduction*, LNCS 449, pp. 427–441. New York: Springer-Verlag.

[BM76] Bondy, J.A. and Murty, U.S.R. 1976. *Graph Theory with Applications*. New York: Macmillan Press.

[CB83] Corbin, J. and Bidoit, M. 1983. A rehabilitation of Robinson's unification algorithm. *Information Processing* 83: 909–914.

[CD91] Comon, H. and Delor, C. 1991. Equational Formulae with Membership Constraints. Université de Paris-Sud, Centre d'Orsay, Rapports de Recherche no. 649.

[Chu36] Church, A. 1936. A note on the entscheidundsproblem. *Journal of Symbolic Logic* 1: 101–102. Reprinted in: M. Davis, ed., *The Undecidable*, pp. 110-115. Hewlett, NY: Raven Press, 1965.

[CL73] Chang, C.C. and Lee, R.C. 1973. *Symbolic Logic and Mechanical Theorem Proving*. San Diego, CA: Academic Press.

[Com90] Comon, H. 1990. Solving inequations in term algebras. In *Proceedings of the Fifth IEEE Symposium on Logic in Computer Science*, pp. 62–69. Los Alamitos, CA: IEEE Computer Society Press.

[Dav83] Davis, M. 1983. The prehistory and early history of automated deduction. In, Siekmann and Wrightson, eds., *Automation of Reasoning I*. New York: Springer-Verlag.

[Der87] Dershowitz, N. 1987. Termination of rewriting. In *Rewriting Techniques and Applications*, pp. 69–116. San Diego, CA: Academic Press.

[Duf91] Duffy, D. 1991. *Principles of Automated Theorem Proving*. New York: Wiley.

[Fit90] Fitting, M. 1996. *First-Order Logic and Automated Theorem Proving, Second Edition.* New York: Springer-Verlag.

[Gal86] Gallier, J.H. 1986. *Logic for Computer Science.* New York: Harper & Row.

[Gib85] Gibbons, A. 1985. *Algorithmic Graph Theory.* New York: Cambridge University Press.

[GJ79]   Garey, M.R. and Johnson, D.S. 1979. *Computers and Intractability: A Guide to the Theory of NP-Completeness.* New York: Freeman.

[Hal60] Halmos, P.R. 1960, *Naive Set Theory.* New York: Springer-Verlag.

[JS94]   Johann, P. and Socher-Ambrosius, R. 1994. Solving simplification orderings constraints. In *Proceedings of the First International Conference on Constraints in Computational Logic*, LNCS 845, pp. 352–367. New York: Springer-Verlag.

[KB70]   Knuth, D.E. and Bendix, P.B. 1970. Simple word problems in universal algebra. In *Computational Problems in Universal Algebra.* Tarrytown, NY: Pergamon Press.

[KK71]   Kowalski, R. and Kuehner, D. 1971. Linear resolution with selection function. *Artificial Intelligence* 2: 227–260.

[KN86]   Kapur, D. and Narendran, P. 1986. NP-Completeness of the set unification and matching problems. In *Proceedings of the Eighth International Conference on Automated Deduction*, LNCS 230, pp. 489–495. New York: Springer-Verlag.

[Lov70] Loveland, D.W. 1970. A linear format for resolution. In *Proceedings of the IRIA Symposium on Automatic Demonstration*, LNM 125, pp. 147–162. New York: Springer-Verlag.

[Lov78] Loveland, D.W. 1978. *Automated Theorem Proving: A Logical Basis.* New York: North-Holland.

[Men79] Mendelson, E. 1979. *Introduction to Mathematical Logic.* New York: Van Nostrand.

[MM82]   Martelli, A. and Montanari, U. 1982. An efficient unification algorithm. *Transactions on Programming Languages and Systems* 4: 258–282.

[Pla93] Plaisted, D. 1993. A polynomial time constraint satisfaction test. In *Proceedings of the Fifth International Conference on Rewriting Techniques and Applications*, LNCS 690, pp. 405–420. New York: Springer-Verlag.

[PW78]   Patterson, M.S. and Wegman, M.N. 1978. Linear unification. *Journal of Computer and System Sciences* 16: 158–167.

[Rob65] Robinson, J.A. 1965. Automated deduction with hyper-resolution. *International Journal of Computational Mathematics* 1: 227–234.

[SS89]   Schmidt-Schauss, M. 1989. *Computational Aspects of an Order-Sorted Logic with Terms Declarations*, LNAI 395. New York: Springer-Verlag.

[Sti86] Stickel, M. 1986. Schubert's steamroller problem: Formulations and solutions. *Journal of Automated Reasoning* 2: 89–101.

[Uri91] Uribe, T. E. 1991. Sorted Unification and the Solution of Semilinear Membership Constraints. University of Illinois, Urbana, IL Technical Report, no.UIUCDCS-R-91-1720.

[WCR65] Wos, L., Carson, D., and Robinson, G.R. 1965. Efficiency and completeness of the set of support strategy in theorem proving. *Journal of the ACM* 12: 698–709.

Index